1-F

£5 =

# FEMINISM AND DISABILITY

# FEMINISM AND DISABILITY

by Barbara Hillyer

University of Oklahoma Press : Norman and London

This book is published with the generous assistance of the Wallace C. Thompson Endowment Fund.

Portions of chapters 2, 4, 5, and 6 were published elsewhere under the name Barbara Hillyer Davis and are reprinted here with permission: "Women, Disability and Feminism: Notes Toward a New Theory," *Frontiers* 8, no. 1 (1984): 1–5; "Time, Productivity and Disability," *Midwest Feminist Papers V,* Midwest Sociologists for Women in Society (1985): 30–34; "Disability, Productivity and Pace," *Free Inquiry in Creative Sociology* 13, no. 1 (May 1985): 51–56; "Disability and Mother-Blaming," *Sojourner: The Women's Forum* 11, no. 12 (Aug. 1986): 18–19; "Disability and Grief," *Social Casework* 68, no. 6 (June 1987): 352–57. Chapter 1 was first printed in two periodicals that are no longer in print: "Feminism and the Handicapped," *Sister Advocate* 5, no. 9 (Sept. 1979): 6–7; *Women, A Journal of Liberation* 7, no. 2 (1980): 34–36.

**Library of Congress Cataloging-in-Publication Data**

Hillyer, Barbara, 1934–
    Feminism and disability / by Barbara Hillyer.
      p.  cm.
    Includes index.
    ISBN 0-8061-2500-4
    1. Handicapped women—United States—Psychology.  2. Feminist theory.  3. Parents of handicapped children—United States.  I. Title.
HV1569.3.W65H55     1993
362.4'082—dc20                                92-50714
                                                    CIP

To Jennifer and Freda

# CONTENTS

# PREFACE

The women's liberation movement taught me to look for, to listen to, each woman's experience in all its particularity, its detail, and to try to tell my own story honestly, thoughtfully, without denial or distortion. What I have tried to do in this book is to present my own experience for women to think about. It is my contribution to feminist thought because I am, before anything else, a feminist thinker.

The disability rights movement taught me to struggle with the experience of human limitation, to hear each person's story in distinctive detail, as I tried to understand where the boundary may lie between ability and disability, between physical and social, between the personal and the political. Here I learned anew the other movement's first lesson, that the personal is political.

I am an eclectic and omnivorous reader. Everything I have

read during the past ten years influenced the writing of this book. Although I have read much more deeply in the literature of the several disciplines mentioned here than the specific citations may show, my purpose has not been a complete review of the literature. For me, the interesting ideas come, always, from the juxtaposition of two or several different texts. The substance of feminist thought lies in the space between them, where an idea from one causes a re-vision, a re-membering of a concept from the other. Often for me the writing that encourages such interdisciplinary spinning comes from an auto-biography or a nonacademic work in popular psychology. Feminist thinking is a collective endeavor that may be sparked by any writing or talk that provides a glimpse of a woman's life. This book is written in the spaces between, the interactions among, many disciplines, many genres, and several levels of discourse. Especially, it is written in the margins and between the lines of two bodies of personal experience literature, female and disabled. It is written in my own voice.

The "objective" scholar, the feminist teacher, the grieving parent, the advocate for disability rights and for women's rights, the mother of a woman with a severe organic brain dysfunction, and the limited, embodied crone are all here in this book. They are not separable because they are not separated in my life. Sometimes they have been. I was certainly taught to separate them by my formal education and by more general acculturation. Such separations are one of the subjects explored in the book. In particular, the questions of how to read and write and talk about disability are addressed in chapter 3.

I wrote this book because of the dissonance between the ideas of the feminist and disability movements and between professional and personal literature and experience. As that dissonance is the subject of the book, it is of course reflected in my writing. If readers find it uncomfortable not to know which voice they are hearing at any given point in the book, their discomfort reflects my experience.

My own experience is one among many primary sources for this writing. Except in chapters 1 and 13, it is not the principal focus, but it is integral to the discussion, along with many other primary sources (women's personal narratives) and secondary ones (professional, scholarly, and theoretical literature).

The process of thinking through the subjects of these chapters and situating those thoughts in both movements is grounded in my life, including its limitations. I state at several points in the book that I have met my own physical and emotional limitations during my daughter Jennifer's lifetime. I am also very much aware that wide reading and conscientious acknowledgment of difference does not alleviate the limitations of my white, middle-class, and academic perspective. Other books and writings will surely follow this one, addressing those issues of race and class and culture that are outside my present reach. Disability is joining the steadily increasing body of feminist literature about difference. No single woman's perspective can touch on all differences, but as each joins the stream, our thinking deepens. This is one woman's contribution to the collective process of feminist thought.

BARBARA HILLYER

*Norman, Oklahoma*

# ACKNOWLEDGMENTS

This book grew out of two movements: the women's liberation movement and the disability rights movement. It was inspired by a commitment to both.

Many people shared in the making of the book over the ten years of my writing and the twenty-seven years of Jennifer's life so far. Susan Koppelman and Elizabeth Curry first encouraged me to think of the project as a book. Susan's personal and professional support and her willingness to challenge my ideas and test them against her experience of disability have been essential to the process of my thinking and writing.

Yvonne Duffy, Helen Kutz, and Susan Contratto provided valuable criticism of or contributions to early drafts of the chapter on mother-blaming. Nan Bruckner and Kathi George helped me revise "Notes Toward a New Theory." Emily Abel provided a thorough review of the chapter on caregivers. Although in the end I disagreed with some of them, I found their careful reading enormously helpful.

Elaine Barton, Teresa Long, and Jane Rickman typed and then talked through the early drafts of several chapters, contributing to the research for years afterward. Ronnie Bordo did a heroic, efficient, and patient job of typing the final drafts. Many student employees of the Women's Studies and Human Relations departments at the University of Oklahoma typed notes and found references for me. Leesa Young, Deborah Jackson, Dreama Moon, and Pam Kirby did so for the final draft.

I discussed parts of the manuscript with many women who live with disabilities, and many more influenced my ability to think about these matters. Among them are Joanna Russ, Nancy Mairs, JoAnn Koepke, Lillian Holcomb, Annette Kolodny, Nancy Osborne, Carol Gendron Hoffenkamp, and Helen Kutz. No one who lives in Norman, Oklahoma, and cares about disability can fail to be influenced by Gail Dunsky and Steve Brown. I thank them all, along with the many National Women's Studies Association (NWSA) women who attended and contributed to disability sessions. For several years I attended disability studies sessions at the Western Social Sciences Association conferences as a mostly silent listener, where I was influenced by many of the presenters including, of course, Irving Zola and Adrienne Asch.

Several groups have been essential to the development of my thoughts about disability issues: the Child Study Center parent support group, the Pauls Valley State School Parent-Guardian Association, my Tuesday and Wednesday women's groups, the friends of Bill W. and Lois W., the NWSA disability caucus, and students in my feminist theory seminars.

Many of my most valuable insights came from Jennifer's social workers, teachers, attendants, and house parents. I am grateful to them for expanding my thinking as well as for their care for Jennifer. Ellidee Thomas, M.D., by her example, gave me hope for truly reciprocal care between doctors and mentally disabled people. Freda Jones and Ellen Donaldson helped me learn to care for myself without denying Jennifer's centrality in my life.

I am grateful to three institutions for helping me do this work: the Cradle Society arranged Jennifer's adoption by our family;

the Child Study Center helped us to care for Jennifer in three of her most critical life crises and later afforded me an opportunity to cofacilitate a parent support group for five years; the University of Oklahoma provided two sabbatical leaves for work on the manuscript.

George Henderson, the chair of my department, has been unfailingly supportive. Although he himself writes a book a year, he has been patient with the ten years I spent on this manuscript and has provided the support services and research assistance I needed to finish it. He has been a helpful, respectful colleague and friend.

At the University of Oklahoma Press, two editors, Tom Radko and Kimberly Wiar, encouraged me to finish the book and to make it better. Four readers provided helpful suggestions for improving the manuscript and encouraged me to finish it. I thank Barbara Siegemund-Broka for her thoughtful, insightful copy-editing. She made the process mechanically easy and intellectually challenging.

Above all, I am grateful to my personal friends and family for their continuous support. Besides those mentioned above, Emily Toth taught me to lighten up, and to speak up. Kristen Watts-Penny and Constance Lindemann listened and discussed and participated in an ongoing way in my whole, diverse life. Bob Davis, Jennifer's dad, showed me that there are other good ways of parenting besides my own. My mother, Wanda Hillyer, and children, Megan Davis and John Davis, have taught me most of what I know about love and loyalty and the difficulties of growing up with a disabled child in the family. My partner, Jo Soske, made the writing possible, listening as I developed ideas, reminding me to write when I didn't want to, and appreciating the results when I did. She and her son, my friend, Jon Soske, were supportive and loving as I wrote the book and lived (and sometimes "acted out") the feelings that went with it.

Especially, I am grateful to Jennifer.

# FEMINISM AND DISABILITY

# THINKING ABOUT JENNIFER, 1979

Teaching about women, I clearly see how individual lives may be illuminated by the discovery that the personal is political. Studying women's experience, I see how mothers' self-concepts sometimes diminish their daughters. Analyzing women's roles, I compare them with other minorities, including people with disabilities.

When I do any of these things, I think about my daughter Jennifer, and I wonder when I will be able to articulate the political importance of her relationship to me, whether my view of myself as one who handles hardship with grace diminishes her, and if I can present intelligibly, even to myself, what I have learned about womankind from her struggle as a disabled girl.

Jennifer is fourteen and she is afraid to grow up. Her fear is realistic. It is frightening for a girl to become a woman and even more frightening for a woman to be an adult in our society. But for Jennifer, growing up is more frightening than for most girls because she has to learn that the feminist promise—a girl can be anything she dares try to be—is meaningless. Jennifer is disabled, physically and mentally, and most of the things a man or woman might learn to be are beyond her ability, but not beyond her hope. She is frustrated and angry and afraid.

As her mother, I am frustrated and angry and afraid, too. And as a feminist intellectual I am troubled by my inability to define my relationship to Jennifer in a way that makes as much sense as the rest of my developing analysis.

Until she was ten, Jenny fit very well into my understanding of what it means for mothers and daughters to become sisters. She is just a year younger than her sister, and although her development was slower and her body couldn't perform as competently as Megan's, they were plainly on the same track, girls who were learning their capacities, developing individuality, growing through childhood into an expanded, challenging world. We all knew that someday they would be women like me and that my feminist work would make their womanhood better. Supporting their personhood was as rewarding as nurturing them in infancy had been. I was sorry that they had to grow in a sexist society but sure of my ability to give them confidence and pride in being women.

When she was ten, Jenny changed her name to Jennifer, an assertion in which I rejoiced as one who knows the power of naming. She said that since she was growing up, she needed a more grown up name. It was the last gesture she made that fit comfortably into my feminist theory. At the same time, she was beginning to understand and to struggle against accepting the fact that she could not learn the things other children learn, that she was not going, even with difficulty, to become a woman like me or like most other women she knew. My own realization came slower; Jennifer taught me the limits of her life.

At ten, she was angry at the boys in her class who said girls couldn't be football players. Girls, she said, can be anything. Jennifer planned to be a bullfighter. Last year, at thirteen, she planned to be a gymnast. But her body betrays her. She can't walk upstairs with assurance. She is terrified of escalators. The terror is realistic, and the dreams of bullfighting and balance beams are not.

How am I to assimilate these facts into my motherhood without depriving her of dreams? How into my feminism without a biological determinism that will undermine my own belief in womankind?

What Jennifer was trying to figure out (and what I still want to know) is what it means to be a whole person when your mind or body is incomplete. Her body is not reliable; this is a situation that many women have experienced. We have too easily assumed in recent years that it is a condition all of us should be able to overcome with exercise or willpower. This neo-puritan ethic is frustrating to Jennifer; she can jog, but that won't help her write or play tennis or tie her shoes. When someone gave her a booklet that said growing up would be fun if she learned about diet and exercise and make-up, she threw the book out the window. I empathize with that gesture.

One of the strengths of women's culture, I believe, is the high value we have placed on empathy and on meeting the emotional needs of others. That part of my mothering of Jenny has given us both great satisfaction. She has difficulty articulating her feelings, and I have learned to speak them for her. I can sometimes explain to her the meanings of experiences that are very confusing to her. This also is the great strength of her daughtering. I am cerebral and usually repress my emotions. Jenny functions almost entirely on an emotional level; she provides for my deficiency as I do for hers. We love each other deeply, but we don't know how to do the next, hard thing: to enable Jennifer to grow up.

Our interdependency was too much like a traditional marriage, so deeply based on dichotomies: intellectual/emotional, dependent/reliable, weak/strong, passive/aggressive. Of course she must break free, and of course we both broke open as she pulled away.

It is possible for me, with the help of a therapist, a lot of close friends, and a fine library, to regain my emotional self, to become whole. Because some of those friends are sister-daughters I can—or hope I can—achieve some better definition of what it means to mother, to daughter. But here is where my theory stumbles: Jennifer, losing me as her cognitive half, cannot gain that part of her self in any way I can understand. Her mind really does not work very well; its neural connections are as erratic as those that control her muscles.

And I, helplessly watching Jennifer's inability to grow up and her equally frustrating inability to stay a child, realize that my own hope for and patience with other women comes out of the optimistic belief that they are capable of growing up, that they can learn, that each has a consciousness that can be raised.

I like to exchange ideas with traditional women. Because they value women's experience and don't wish to "think like men," I believe they can examine their lives and learn to understand them. But what am I to think of women like Jennifer, whose life can only be examined from outside her self, by someone else?

Some women are genuinely, permanently weak. Much feminist hope is based on the love of women for their potential strength. It is much more difficult to be woman-identified if a woman cannot be defined as potentially aware. If we can love the seriously limited woman for who she *is* and not who she may become, how does that love differ from the old way of loving girls as vulnerable objects of protection or as pets? The question has implications for our relationship to children, as well. If belief in children's rights is based on their ability to become aware, we may patronize their awareness or discriminate between them on the basis of growth potential.

It is much too easy to sentimentalize Jennifer's role as my disabled daughter and my own as her mother, to make my nurturing and her childlike nature a permanent, admirable stasis. But she is angry and so am I. Madonna-mothering requires a younger and more passive child. And my rejection of passivity and dependency for myself precludes my wanting it for another woman.

When she was younger, I could present myself as one who copes gracefully with the medical and educational problems of a beautiful "handicapped" little girl. This role-playing had its rewards for both of us; I was admired for my strength and she for her sweetness. But it didn't help either of us to mature. Now we must find ways for her to care for herself and resources to help her do so.

Even the better answers our society offers for disabled people trouble me as a feminist who is also Jennifer's mother. She thinks of herself as homeless, someone who belongs nowhere, and that assessment, like her fear of escalators, is realistic.

Our society has two principal models for homes for dependent people, both based on the traditional nuclear family. The first and most "natural" (i.e., less institutional) of these is marriage, and it is tempting, even to one who mistrusts marriage as an institution, to hope that a woman like Jennifer will marry a nice man who will take care of her. But the wife in such a marriage would be unable either to relate to her partner as a peer or to leave the marriage if it proved unhappy (or even abusive). We have come to understand that a woman's ability to support herself is crucial to the maintenance of options for her, but some disabled people are unable to support themselves.

Indeed, even in sheltered workshops there is an assumption that retarded people will be able to do work involving some physical dexterity (such as cafeteria serving or factory assembly work) and that physically disabled people will be able to rely on mental or verbal competence (as in telephone sales or office work). Where both disabilities occur, a common solution is parental care more appropriate to a younger child. In the best institutions this pattern has recently changed. Efforts are made to acknowledge the emotional and even sometimes the sexual needs of the clients and to treat them less as children. The best case workers avoid the stereotyping inherent in disability "labeling" and try to understand the individuality of the people they help. Some agencies have encouraged marriage between retarded people, for example. Although this is certainly progress over the treatment of dependent adults as if they were children, such marriages are subject to all the deficiencies of marriage as an institution, especially for dependent wives. Where the partners are people whose mental and emotional capacities are, like Jennifer's, especially vulnerable to the influence of television, the traditional sex roles will probably be reinforced by marriage. An agency that avoids labeling by handicap may willingly label by sex role.

Moreover, many of the best resources for handicapped people are sponsored by religious denominations whose doctrines are heavily invested in preserving traditional sex roles and in suppressing sexuality, as well. These organizations may be enlightened in their treatment of their clients as whole, individual people, but they affirm this "normality" by reinforcing conventional social roles.

Of course I will be relieved if there are places where Jennifer can be protected and nurtured, perhaps loved and even married. And of course I want her to be accepted as she is, not punished or patronized for her inability to be as intelligent or well coordinated as others. But after the most hopeful and most realistic of planning, I return to those questions whose answers matter most to me and that I cannot answer. Because I believe in the value of an examined life, how can I relate to a woman who cannot examine her life? Since I know the difficulty for women of growing up, how shall I understand a woman who can't grow up entirely? Because I understand mothering to be nurturing independence, how can I mother this dependent woman? As our society's responses to disability range from neglect through sentimentality, how can I object to sex-role stereotyping if it is done with respect? Above all, how can I teach a girl I love that she can't be what she wants to be?

I don't know the answers to any of these questions, but I consider them basic questions for feminism. If conventional femininity is handicapping, an understanding of the double-bind of disabled women is essential to our efforts toward social change. To the extent that feminist theory relies on women's ability to understand their situation, it fails to touch the situation of the woman with mental disabilities. When we argue against female dependency in marriage or elsewhere, we should not ignore the existence of individual women who may be unable to avoid dependency. As our institutions respond to the rights of people with disabilities to live as "normally" as possible, we must remember that "normal" women's lives are often oppressive—inadequate models for the dignity of disabled women.

Knowing Jennifer is much more complicated—more painful, more joyful—than these questions suggest. Of course she is a complex, dynamic individual, and of course no other disabled person is exactly like her. But as she struggles to become a woman, I struggle with these questions. Without some tentative answers, I cannot know what it means to say the personal is political or what it means to be a feminist mother. When I consider what it is to be a woman, I have to think about Jennifer.

# NOTES TOWARD A
# NEW THEORY

Discussions of the impact of disability on women almost always reveal troubled relationships between disabled people and the women who care for them, whether the caregivers are intimates or professionals. Often there are similarly troubled relationships among caregiving women themselves. These problems are intricately connected to other difficulties with sisterhood that have been more directly addressed in feminist theory.

My own experience as the mother of a young woman with both physical and mental disabilities is not reflected at all in feminist literature, even though mother-daughter relationships are often discussed there.[1] Likewise in literature about disabilities, the feminist implications of our situation are seldom addressed. As Jennifer became an adult and she and I had to work to understand what that means to someone who is mentally retarded and "dependent," I looked for ways of integrating my feminist philosophy with our struggle for survival. What I have learned has important implications for feminist theory, partly because the experience of women with disabilities and of those who care for them is so deeply felt. The emotional depth that resonates in the best feminist theory is intrinsic to our lives.

Relationships among women in the care and treatment of disabled people are greatly complicated by social expectations about disabled people, about women (especially mothers and daughters), and about professional caregivers. All of these expectations, often deeply internalized, are closely related to stereotypes of femininity and are quite handicapping for both the woman with disabilities and the woman who cares. However, women's traditional values and morality provide a potential for great strength in these relationships and for an important expansion of feminist theory.

## INDEPENDENCE, PRODUCTIVITY, AND HANDICAP

Basic to working out relationships among women in connection with disability are social expectations about dependence and independence. Both professional and popular literature define dependence as a problem. For the disabled person, the problem is how to cope with being dependent. For caregivers, the problem is frustration and fatigue from caring for the dependent other. This reasoning is based on the dichotomy between masculine independence and feminine dependence as if only the polarized extremes were possible or desirable. The dichotomy is strongly reinforced by the cult of the body that at least implies that adequate adults will be strong and "fit," especially in physical but also almost incidentally in emotional terms. The notion that the possessor of one trait cannot participate in its opposite leads to excesses at both extremes by people with disabilities and by their caregivers as well.

Of course, a disabled woman may merely subside into pleasant, feminine passivity, accepting her inability, say, to jog as representing a more generalized inability to be responsible for her life; but she may just as disastrously refuse to develop any realistic understanding of her own body. For example, a few years ago when I facilitated a discussion of disability and dependence at a feminist meeting, several participants expressed great admiration for a paraplegic woman they had heard about who insisted on building her own house without the aid of a contractor or other able-bodied help. No one questioned the possibly inappropriate or excessive quality of her "independence."

Audre Lorde presents the external pressure toward both of these extremes in her own experience after a mastectomy, when the hospital's bland reinforcement of her passivity made her feel like "totally inert, emotionally vacant, psychic mush," and the people designated to help her "adjust" insisted that she should deny the reality of her changed body by wearing a prosthesis and behaving as if she were unchanged.[2]

For the female caregiver, the dichotomized expectations are self-contradictory. Caring requires that exceptional physical and emotional strength be exercised in traditionally feminine occupations that require subordinate behavior (housewife, nurse). The female caregiver is expected to be available, dependable, and constant—to give structure to a potentially chaotic world. At the same time, these behaviors may be seen as threatening or emasculating, especially, but not exclusively, if the disabled person is a male. Moreover, she may be discouraged from expressing the qualities normally acceptable in women, such as emotional responsiveness.[3]

Closely related to the emphasis on independence is our strong social ethic of productivity, which has very serious implications for disabled people and accounts in part for stress in relationships among women who care for them. When disabilities limit the productivity of one person, there is a corresponding pressure on others to make up for the loss. Parents and teachers are encouraged to work at giving the illusion that the disabled person is independent or productive, and they may therefore strive to shift this burden to each other or to other professionals. A teacher of children with disabilities may, for example, be judged successful if she transfers an increasing share of instruction to the mother to be done at home.[4] Infant stimulation programs sometimes require ten or more hours a day of intensive work with a child at home.

Mothers of disabled children are held more accountable than others to an externally defined concept of adequate mothering because of their increased contact with social agencies, medical institutions, and special education. Yet their experience is actually more chaotic and less manageable than most.[5] For example, staff members in institutions for emotionally disturbed children and for retarded children have criticized mothers for being unable to handle at home children whom they themselves have great difficulty handling in the institutional setting.[6]

For the intimate caregiver, care for herself may run counter to an important personal (and feminine) value: care for others. Therapists or counselors may encourage a caregiver's "self-actualization" as if there were no institutional barriers to relief from full-time responsibility for that other person. Both intimate and professional caregivers frequently suffer from burnout. Both may make substantial personal investments in a severely disabled person without being rewarded by improvement.

Relationships between disabled women and women caregivers are often especially troubled. If the disabled woman does not play out the feminine role, she may threaten the caregiver's own feminine self-concept and, at the same time, her "masculine," strong, and dominant role as the independent opposite of the disabled woman's dependent stance. Our society's excessive emphasis on independence undermines the disabled woman's relationship with her female caregiver by increasing the resentment of proffered help, whether or not it is needed. Resentment of help may increase the caregiver's burden; the social legitimacy of such resentment may inhibit the articulation of the caregiver's own needs.[7]

However, disabled people are sometimes made more dependent than they need be by the caregiver's need to be needed. Thus the caregiver may be required to be more than adequately competent and productive, filling her own quota for these qualities and at the same time providing services that will enhance or replace such qualities in the disabled person. At the same time, the disabled woman may be required to be less than adequately competent and productive in order to enhance the caregiver's self-concept as one who is needed, thus ensuring continuation of her services.

It is interesting to look at the concept of "handicap" in this connection. A physical attribute is a handicap only when it is seen as a significant barrier or when it has an adverse effect on relationships. In this definition the physical disability may be a handicap to both the disabled person and the caregiver. Indeed, if the caregiver (a mother, daughter, or partner of the disabled person) is perceived as inseparable from the one she cares for, her physical, mental, or emotional fitness may itself be a handicap. For example, I know of two women who added the work loads of their mothers to their own career and child-rearing responsibilities when the mothers were disabled with Alzheimer's disease. Although they recognized that their mothers were no longer able to perform or even understand the work they had done before, the daughters were expected, and expected themselves, to maintain such traditions as providing meals for the harvesters and the church group simply because the mother, who was still alive and physically present, had always done so. The daughters were able to do the work; they adopted the mothers' commitments, which were inappropriate to their own life-styles, as if they were their own—and in addition to their own. In these cases, the caregiving daughter is handicapped because her ability to do the work of two places a heavy burden of productivity on her and because such super-human responsibilities increase the stress in her relationship with the disabled mother and with others.

Where the disabled-caregiving pair are mother and daughter, an exaggeration of "normal" separation needs is combined with exceptional intimacy, often an empathic or "symbiotic" connection. My adolescent daughter needed to separate from me as much as her able-bodied and -minded sister did, but she had none of Megan's survival skills. Jennifer needs around-the-clock adult supervision for her own safety. As she cannot articulate her emotions, she relies for protection on her caregiver's ability to interpret them and to prevent her expressing them in self-destructive ways (for example, by running into traffic or jumping out of a moving car). Our relationship during her early adolescence was symbiotic in that I could empathically understand her distress and she provided an almost purely emotional balance to my tendency to intellectualize. Her need to separate from me, the one who interprets her world to her and to others, was in a sense self-destructive, as separation would leave her unprotected and uninterpreted.

When a psychologist described this relationship to me as symbiotic, I had difficulty with the concept, not because I denied our exceptional intimacy but because the dependence was so unbalanced. She needed me for survival; my need for her was less basic, more complex. The concept of symbiosis is commonly used in developmental psychology to describe the relationship of infants to their mothers. Benedek and Balint have observed that male psychologists fail to acknowledge the asymmetry in this relationship[8]—the same asymmetry that I experienced with Jennifer. Transferral of the concept of infant symbiosis and individuation to disabled people outside of infancy increases the probability of such distortions.

Against the social and personal pressures epitomized in the issues of independence and productivity, both disabled women and women caregivers need a clear understanding of their situation *as women* to enable them to develop a reciprocal relationship, an understanding that meeting needs need not be so one-sided.

## FEMINIST THEORY

To bring together women's experience of disability with feminist theory requires a thorough reexamination of both. All feminist issues are encompassed; all knowledge about disability must be reevaluated. The suggestions I sketch out in this chapter and elaborate in the rest of the book are derived from my process of moving back and forth between the ideas of the disability and women's movements. They are grounded in my life and Jennifer's and elaborated when our lives conflict with what I read in feminist theory or when our lives give a surprising or different twist to my understanding of that theory.

The concept of "boundary living"[9] has particular relevance to disabled women and intimates who care for them because both have more than average contact with patriarchal institutions and less than average choice about the ones with which they interact. These typically include medicine in many of its subinstitutions; government, including law, welfare, and other social service departments; education; and religion. Often these institutions overlap, as in treatment facilities operated by churches that also offer public school special education classes under their auspices. Women seeking access to treatment must accept the whole "package" in such situations. Regardless of the women's preferences, they are dependent on the institution for services. Outright resistance to the institution's philosophy or to its usual way of doing things may cause partial or even total withdrawal of those services. Mothers of hospitalized children report strongly negative reactions from staff members if the mothers declare their own needs, especially if the child is "hard to handle." Mary Daly, who acknowledges that women cannot live entirely outside of patriarchal institutions, urges us to choose to live on their boundaries, where each woman can be self-centering instead of being absorbed into the male-centered thinking of the institution itself. Daly's suggestion that feminists must decide which institutions' boundaries they will inhabit may seem cruelly ironic when life itself is at stake. Whether the boundary is freely chosen or not, however, an intensive exploration of how to maintain the stability of one's center on the boundary while conserving the energy needed for survival is crucial, and the choice must be exercised despite the centripetal force of the institution and the temptations of becoming entirely passive or even a collaborator in the institution's values.[10]

Recent feminist discussions of women and nature emphasize the closeness of women to life and death and to the individual quality of human development, positing that women are more experienced than men with change, both positive and negative.[11] Recognizing the complexity of individuals and of their interrelationships, women are more likely than men (and thus more likely than male-designed institutions) to recognize that all people need help in development at all stages. Experiences of disability that may enrich the development of feminist theory on this point include the recognition that death is not always the worst thing that can happen to a person; that senility and degenerative diseases undermine belief in life as a growth process; that full, internalized acknowledgment of the body's "real" condition permits the elimination of phony or excessive heroism; that human beings are limited; that some losses cannot be repaired; and, above all, that female strength and weakness must be integrated.

For both the disabled woman and the caregiver, achieving these insights involves an intensive, integrated, emotional, intellectual, and physical process of self-centering that includes recognition of the reality of the problem and the experience of grief. At least since Mary Daly's *Beyond God the Father* was published in 1973, a basic tenet of most feminist philosophy has been that "transcendence" comes not from denying one's self but from coming to live from within the self. For all of us the difficult work of finding this self includes the body, but people who live with disability in a society that glorifies fitness and physical conformity are forced to understand more fully what bodily integrity means. As Adrienne Rich observed of childbirth, avoidance of pain and ignorance of our own bodies leaves us out of touch with ourselves, our own limits, our transience.[12]

To be in touch with one's limitations, as people with disabilities are forced to be, makes one feel less safe.[13] To examine the meaning of this lack of safety is to explore the nature of one's own "real" condition—not idealized or misinterpreted by the culture. Women, Jean Baker Miller says, can develop a different understanding of weakness and the paths out of it if we learn to work with our feelings of vulnerability.[14] For women with disabilities, the greater temptation may be to be swamped by these feelings; for caregivers, to deny them entirely. But because both experience both temptations, they have at least the potential for working together on getting through the vulnerability to the underlying central identity of each individual. In a culture like ours that values optimism and a cheery willingness to minimize difficulties, it is very difficult to see oneself as a person with a serious problem. Yet that is exactly what is required of anyone who must live with a disability, whether the cause is physical or social or both.[15] Recognition that she is a person with a serious difficulty defined from within forces a woman to find significance in her life as it is. If both the woman with disability and the caring woman acknowledge their vulnerability and the seriousness of their separate but related problems, they can collaborate in working on the paths out of weakness. Such collaboration, including creative conflict, may help us change the definition of dependence.

Excessive insistence on one's own independence is an understandable reaction to being defined as dependent or incompetent. The reaction is common in the women's movement and accounts for the feminist ideal that emphasizes physical fitness and mechanical competence, a model that is especially difficult for a woman with disabilities to adopt.[16] She may therefore have more incentive than people who can approximate that image to define herself as an individual whose identity comes from within and not from any social ideal, not even a supposedly feminist one. As she does so, she may well encourage her caregiver to undertake a comparable reevaluation of her own superwoman routine.

Feminist theory has given considerable attention to the necessity of confronting existential questions—the void, the deep center of the self—and of recognizing the complex emotions surrounding female subordination. A related confrontation that has received very little attention in feminist theory and that is of crucial importance to people who live intimately with disability is grief. The fact of unusual empathic intimacy between the caregiver and the person whose disability occasions grief for both may, if it is not blocked by the decorum of the illness,[17] enable them to compare their experience of grief and see how it is shaped by their differences and the different external pressures on them. Recognition of the chronicity of grief and its place in one's central values counters romanticized versions of nobility and suffering and false expectations either of permanent mourning or of the normality of grief "stages" derived from observations of bereavement.

Beatrice Wright has suggested that we impose mourning on disabled people as a defense of our own values.[18] For example, if a woman cannot use her legs but refuses to mourn for the loss, we may be forced to ask questions about why we place such a high value on walking around. If a woman with a chronic illness adapts her pace to her illness and does not grieve over the loss of a conventionally rapid pace, we may have to question the high value we place on rushing around. Margaret Voysey, though, reports that parents of disabled children need social legitimation of their suffering because the pressure to behave as if their situation is "normal" overwhelms their trust in their own feeling that it is out of control.[19] The process of understanding one's grief involves an understanding of these external pressures as well as a willingness to experience one's own pain. Acceptance of oneself as accessible to suffering is surely part of that existential courage that Daly says women are called to bear.[20]

One reason for the great difficulty most of us have in working out ways of changing dependent-caregiver relationships is our logical reliance on the concept of equality—that people should be treated the same—an ideal that is especially difficult to attain when one person can walk or see or hear or reason and the other cannot. Carol Gilligan points out that this premise is basic to the ethic of justice that characterizes the highest value in masculine morality, but women's morality places a higher value on an ethic of care, whose premise is that no one should be hurt. Gilligan argues that both perspectives converge in maturity for both sexes.[21] If we examine the disabled-caregiving pair in the light of Gilligan's analysis, we can see that reciprocity would require understanding of the caregiver's needs for equality as well as the disabled woman's need for care, and vice versa.

Disabled people force us to face the problem of reciprocity, the investment in a relationship by both participants. Reciprocity involves the difficulty of recognizing each other's needs, relying on the other, asking and receiving help, delegating responsibility, giving and receiving empathy, and respecting boundaries. It also involves, as Eleanor Roosevelt pointed out, the ability to accept what we are unable to give and what others are unable to give,[22] a much harder doctrine. Feminists who live with disabilities tell me that they are especially frustrated at others' unwillingness to believe them when they describe very accurately what they cannot do. Yet when, in the same feminist groups, women with visible disabilities say clearly what they can do, their offers are frequently ignored or minimized. For caregivers these problems are compounded. As the disability that limits them "belongs" to someone else, it may be interpreted not as a limitation but as an excuse. Moreover, because women are taught to place a high value on giving and to avoid even the appearance of selfishness, it is hard for us to receive help or ask that someone else meet our needs. And it is correspondingly easy to judge a woman who says she is unable to give but needs care from others. My point is not merely that we should change these patterns, but that the reciprocity worked out between a woman with disabilities and a caring woman can serve as a model for the rest of us only if we attend thoughtfully to what they have learned and believe them when they tell us about it.

Romanticization of the recipient of help and of such notions as strength through adversity is not reciprocal. It holds the other to a higher standard of ability to suffer than oneself. One painful aspect of mothering a seriously disabled child is living with the frequent well-meant comments on how admirably strong one is for coping with such a difficult problem when, in fact, the situation seems out of control and one is just barely coping. Another is receiving unrealistic praise of the child's "progress" or "normal" qualities when the mother knows that the child is not progressing or normal. I am almost undone when people single out Jennifer's beauty for comment, as it is not only irrelevant to the difficult problems posed by her disabilities but is also an ironic commentary on the social value we give to physical appearance. Far from making her life easier, her prettiness is a disadvantage when it enables people to overlook her real needs. Saying that I am wonderfully strong because I can bear a tragedy that the speaker could not bear does not merely deny my reality; it also measures me against a standard (one who suffers bravely) different from that by which the speaker measures herself. Saying that the child is progressing when she is deteriorating and urging me to agree denies my reality and requires of me an irrational optimism that makes me responsible for the other person's comfort.

I suggest that women with disabilities and those who care for them can work out a model of reciprocity for others, but of course this is not easy. A serious problem, especially when the disabled person is a child or is mentally or emotionally handicapped, is that the person needing help lacks a realistic sense of the caregiver's needs. If the caregiver can see articulating her own needs as training in reciprocity, the imbalance in this situation may be partially redressed while at the same time the woman's ethic of responsibility for the dependent other is honored. Miller points out that subordinates usually lack a realistic evaluation of their own capacities and problems;[23] training in reciprocity may, therefore, be a significant strategy for modifying the dominant-subordinate relationship between disabled people and caregivers.

One premise of feminist therapy—that a primary goal is equality in the client-therapist relationship—is an important key to restructuring asymmetrical relationships among women in other situations. As Martha Thompson observes, building on Rich's theory, when relationships between women are primary and reciprocal, including an exchange of both tangible and intangible resources, we will be able to make a profound commitment to not draining each other of our resources.[24]

This above all is what both disabled women and those who care for them ask of each other; together they ask it of the feminist community. These women often lack, even in feminist groups, that community of like-minded women[25] that is necessary for women's health and sometimes even survival. As Miller observes, growth requires engagement with difference and with people embodying the difference.[26] A diverse, experienced, frequently invisible group embodying a wide range of difference, these disabled and caregiving women are a valuable resource for feminist growth and change.

CHAPTER

3

# LANGUAGE AND BIOGRAPHY

To speak of the connections between feminism and disability is instantly to encounter a complex problem of language. How are we to find a vocabulary that is simultaneously accurate, acceptable to both political movements, and sensitive to the feelings of the people involved? And, having chosen a vocabulary, however inadequate, how can we speak of women's experience with disability in a way that respects individual voices, while applying to their experience an analysis that will almost certainly differ from some of the beliefs about women or about disability held by individual feminists, disability activists, or people with various illnesses and disabilities, or by groups representing these individuals? People in feminist organizations may adopt a particular term, such as "differently abled," based on the preference of one disability group and then find that the term is completely unacceptable to another. The politics of both movements (feminist and disability) are such that the implications of each term are constantly reexamined and criticized. The word "disabled" itself was once considered less acceptable than "handicapped," then more acceptable, then acceptable in its noun but not in adjective form (as: "a person with a disability," not "a disabled person"). Language is controversial and political acceptability changes.

Furthermore, "disability" and "chronic illness and disability" are such global terms, encompassing so many physical, mental, and psychological conditions, that experiences of people with one disability may differ enormously from those with another; and even within groups, individual experience as well as consciousness vary considerably. Shared social experiences of stigma, medical "management," and social clumsiness only partly override these differences. A decision to tell the truth about one's own experience is invariably affected by the desire to be understood or accepted by listeners who may include people of various political and psychological persuasions and varying degrees of denial. There are multiple specialized vocabularies for any one disability, and these may contradict each other linguistically, medically, or both.

Personal narratives are probably the best source of information about women's disability experience, but these are rarely feminist, usually authored by articulate middle-class individuals, and necessarily limited to disabilities that permit reading, writing, and thinking or at least the ability to be interviewed. Personal accounts of degenerative or "terminal" illnesses are often edited and completed by other people who have their own agendas from outside the disability experience. An enormous body of popular and professional literature supplements personal narratives, and it too is seldom feminist, often only superficially "objective," and susceptible to the varying biases of writers and publishers.

Nevertheless, a reasonably adequate disability language can be identified, and a deliberate mix of personal narratives with popular and professional literature makes feminist disability analysis possible.

## POLITICALLY CHARGED LANGUAGE

When I first spoke and wrote about feminism and disability, I spoke of "the handicapped" with some assurance. I was careful to define the term and to make clear that it encompassed social discrimination, in contrast to "disabled," which described a physical problem that makes an individual unable or less able to do certain things. By the time that first essay was published, in 1979, its subtitle, "Feminism and the Handicapped," was embarrassing—not because I had abandoned my handicapped/disabled distinctions, but because I had encountered people in the disability community who were passionately opposed to using the word "handicapped" at all, unless it was part of an attack on insensitive able-bodied people who used the word. And saying "*the* handicapped" was beyond the pale, suggesting as it does that the person, rather than the society, carries the label, and with it the responsibility for her socially induced problem.

As a lifelong respecter of language and a politically active feminist, I knew that attending to the words we use and think is a profoundly political act. I determined to find out which words people with disabilities condemned and which they preferred. Of course I also intended to be sure that the words I used were approved as well by thoughtful feminists. Thus I encountered for the first time the thicket of conflicting interpretations and voices through which a woman must walk who wants to speak "correctly" in two word-conscious, political communities at once.

At the time, few feminists were conscious of disability issues, and those few were angry about lack of accessibility and generalized ignorance about disability issues. Women's music was beginning to be signed, but we were far from the sophisticated debates of the late eighties over whether concert-signing as an art form was so artistic that it undermined communication with deaf people and whether it achieved or falsified the consciousness of those without hearing impairments. To write a paragraph like this one was to be seriously tangled in the thicket. Each word pertaining to disability was—and still is—a potential trap. Language that offends either feminists or women with disabilities interferes with communication. Listeners will discount what is said by someone who appears to be insensitive to the personal/political issues involved.

During the eighties, a consensus that still holds today emerged on many disability words, mostly because many feminists agreed to respect the decisions about language of political disability groups. For example, most agree that such frankly derogatory terms as "idiot," "cripple," and "gimp" are not acceptable because they are insulting. Obviously incorrect when used by a TAB (temporarily able-bodied) person, they are nevertheless frequently used by individuals with disabilities, who often call each other "crip" or "gimp" in a playful tone with political undertones in much the same way that black people sometimes call each other "nigger." "Supercrip" carries much of the same mix of admiration and cultural criticism that "superwoman" does for feminists. When the subject is a woman, both political analyses are implied. The joke is very serious: supercrip women risk their lives denying or proving that they can overcome their human limitations.

The etiquette that surrounds the use of these words is elaborate. The speaker or writer must establish her credentials as a person with a disability who knows disability language and can choose whether or not she uses it because she is either disabled enough or politically active enough in the right organizations. Still, it can be dangerous for a person with the wrong disability to use the in-group language of another group—for example, for a blind person to use "crip" in a group of wheelchair users who do not know her well enough to evaluate her political credentials.

Nancy Mairs calls herself a cripple because "I want to see me as a tough customer . . . who can face the brutal truth of her existence squarely," but she won't call another person a cripple: "It is the word I use to name only myself." In other contexts, she uses "disabled" or "handicapped" because "if they are vague, at least they hint at the truth."[1] Mairs's suggestion that cripple implies heroism rather than the social devaluation assumed by most who reject the term expresses a dynamic that motivates much of the discussion of disability language, the dialectic between admiration for courage against the odds and acceptance of limitations as a normal human condition. To say that a woman is "confined to a wheelchair," for example, is generally considered an unacceptable usage because it stresses limitation; the phrase "uses a wheelchair" is preferred as it describes the woman's ability as a user of a tool.[2] But a woman who wants to emphasize the ways in which she is limited by the absence of public transportation with wheelchair lifts may appropriately emphasize her confinement.

Generally the word "victim" is considered unacceptable since it insinuates passivity and helplessness. In the women's movement, women who have been battered are called "survivors," not victims, to emphasize their strength. People with cancer are described as fighters, not victims.[3] Nancy Frick rejects the label "polio victim" because it narrows the person's life to the encounter with a virus instead of seeing it as one fact among many about that person's life.[4] But Anne Finger, whose credentials as a disability speaker are impeccable, challenges her own political correctness when she writes about Huntington's disease that it kills its victims. She says that "the political voice in my head says, don't say victims, think of some neutral way of saying that, say 'before it kills those who carry its gene' and then I think no, victim is the right word."[5] Its victims lose control of their bodily functions, their speech, their minds.

Like "victim," the passive voice is suspect to people with disabilities as it is to feminists, as it often implies victimization and dependency, that things "happen" to us.[6] "When we stoop to honor such language, to treat it as meaningful, we deny our agency in the world."[7] Julia Penelope, who made this statement, is careful to distinguish between denying our own agency and refusing to name the real agent, both of which are involved in uses of the agentless passive.[8] When I say that "my friend has been paralyzed since 1984," I present her as a victim of paralysis without making it clear that the paralysis was caused by a doctor's mistake. When an oppressed group describes its situation without naming the oppressor, its passivity becomes the whole message and the fact of oppression is obscured.

One outcome of the use of the passive voice and of such words as "victim" is that nondisabled people are reinforced in their ableism. "One of the bases of ableism is the assumption that as lesbians with disabilities we would want to be cured. . . . I neither seek a cure nor would ever want to be able-bodied because I not only enjoy my life as a blind lesbian, but feel that it is a positive part of me and a part of which I am intensely proud. I celebrate my culture in all its non-visual ways."[9] The ableist assumption that the lack of a particular ability is personal to the individual (read: victim) implies that it is of no concern to "normal," nondisabled people. It therefore, as Kirsten Hearn suggests, depoliticizes the exclusion of those with disabilities from other political groups.[10]

Most people agree in principle, with individual exceptions such as Mairs's use of "cripple" and Finger's of "victim," that these words of social devaluation or subordination are unacceptable, but almost every other word that is commonly used of people with disabilities is controversial. As I have suggested, a consensus has gradually developed about "disability" and "handicapped." "Handicapped" is taken to describe limitations from societal causes and must be used accurately to indicate those causes. One is handicapped, for example, because there is no elevator in the two-story building, not because one's disability makes it impossible to use stairs. A disability is a physical condition or sometimes a mental or emotional condition. But even these terms are controversial. The World Health Organization, for example, defines "handicap" as "a disability that constitutes a disadvantage for a given individual in that it limits or prevents the fulfillment of a role that is normal for that person" depending on "age, sex, social and cultural factors. A disability becomes a handicap when it interferes with doing what is expected."[11] The United States government defines "handicapped individual" as "any person whose physical or mental impairment limits one or more of the person's major life activities,"[12] and this includes in the word "handicapped" the definition that disability groups prefer to call disability. Further, both definitions confuse health status with social role performance.[13] Some people with disabilities choose not to receive government benefits because of their political disagreements with these definitions. For many more, the necessity of accepting them in order to receive benefits serves to confuse the clarity of other, arguably preferable, definitions.

Apart from such official distinctions, women's informal reactions to what the words sound like in ordinary usage affect our willingness to adopt preferred usage uncritically. Some object to "people with disabilities" for the same reasons that caused others to reject "handicapped." A member of the Union of Physically Impaired Against Segregation, for example, points out that it "makes our lack of abilities sound like an inevitable result of our physical condition, whereas it is usually the result of society failing to provide us with the necessary aids." This group then chooses "impairment" for the physical condition and "disablement" for the social one,[14] echoing the World Health Organization, which defines "impairment" in the same way.[15] No matter how carefully one defines each of these words, it is not helpful to use any one of them "to mean something quite different from what everyone else means unless you say so each time."[16] As recently as 1980, Gliedman and Roth found reversed definitions of handicap and disability so widespread that they looked to such other words as "allomorph" to denote the biological aspects of disability.[17] Even those who use "disability" as the preferred word to mark those whose physical conditions limit their ability to perform certain tasks in our society argue that "there is no reason to assume that medical conditions are disabilities,"[18] but rather that "disability is largely a social construct."[19] Mainstream, Inc., an organization that assists people with disabilities in finding mainstream employment, uses both "disability" and "handicap," arguing "that people have a right to be called whatever they wish"[20]—surely an uncommonly accepting position on the use of politically charged language. Many disability rights activists use "handicapism" to describe institutional oppression and stereotyping.[21]

Like Marj Schneider, I use "disability" as "that has been the term that the movement itself has chosen, by and large,"[22] with carrying the awareness that what is excluded from "by and large" may trip me if I forget to watch my step. Writers are most likely to deviate from such carefully chosen terminology in two places: where preferred usage seems clumsy in its repetitions and where part of the purpose is to convey feelings. After multiple uses of "women with disabilities," an occasional "disabled woman" seems not too serious a slip. Although I do this more than occasionally, I try to be conscious when I do, and willing to be challenged. As for conveying feelings, I respect most those women who make it plain that that is what they are doing. Joyce Davies, for example, says that "when I use 'crippled' I am stressing the hardness and purely *physical* fact of paralysis. The word, in its dark intensity, blots out the power and the hope of the spirit."[23] Davies also likes the word "lame" because "it is gentle and informal. . . . If 'lame' should seem a vague term like 'thin' or 'fat' or 'pretty,' so much the better. Most of us would like nothing more than to melt in with the crowd—unlabeled, almost unnoticed."[24] Such usage confirms the limitation, refusing to cover its personal meaning with politically motivated denial.

Sara Atatimur, a politically active feminist who is blind, suggests that "attempts to eradicate words such as 'disability' and 'handicap' represent wishes to deny that such a problem exists and thus to avoid dealing with it."[25] This awareness is one side of the dialectic that keeps us arguing about such words, the other side being the desire to achieve social change by raising awareness of language.

Linda Henley, a journalist struggling with both sides of that dialectic, says, "When 'good words' suddenly become 'bad words' with relative frequency—say, more often than once every 20 years—it makes me wonder whether it's the word that's bothering people or the concept itself."[26] Of course the politically wise response to that question is that it is both the word and the concept.

## DIFFERENCE AND CHALLENGE

Recognizing that the debate over these mainstream words, valuable though it may be, hardly challenges the underlying patriarchal dualism between handicapped and normal, disabled and able, several feminist groups have suggested alternatives: "differently abled," "physically different," "physically challenged." These terms have the advantage of implying that disabilities are ordinary differences like many others, not negative opposites to a positive norm.

Yvonne Duffy advocates the term "differently abled" because it says that women with disabilities are able to do the same things as the nondisabled but in different ways.[27] In discussions with mixed disabled-nondisabled groups, I have seen the term raise the consciousness of supposedly nondisabled women about their own ways of using their strengths to work around areas in which they are less able. Where the phrase is deliberately used as a consciousness-raiser and not just the latest politically fashionable term, it can educate and enlighten. Similarly, Mary Ambo argues that "physically challenged" is an accurate descriptor for her, as she is challenged by each new activity and meets it as a physical adventure.[28] Used to raise consciousness, the term can increase respect for the resourcefulness and courage of the challenged one and make the nondisabled woman see how "normal" it is to be so challenged, as she herself faces comparable adventures when she tries new activities.

But there are problems with these words, which seem to be more enthusiastically embraced by feminists with mixed abilities than by disability groups. They are too inclusive, they minimize real problems, and they imply that the truth is shameful. "Differently abled" is problematic precisely because it is intended to include everyone, to make the woman with a disability just like everyone else: able to do some things and not others. As Nancy Mairs suggests, this is "semantic hopefulness," like that which "transformed countries from undeveloped to developed, then to less developed and finally to developing nations. People have continued to starve in those countries during the shift." Adopting a term such as "differently abled," she says, is "to pretend that the only differences between you and me are the various ordinary ones that distinguish any one person from another," when in fact, she has a "calamitous disease."[29] Merry Cross observes the same thing about the phrase "physically different," that it minimizes or denies "the fact that these differences do make at least some aspects of our lives hard or impossible."[30] Although ordinary differences may be suggested by the phrase, it may also imply a norm from which the "physically different" one deviates. The reinforcement of this socially constructed norm is another problem with the usage. Black people do not describe themselves as having "differently colored skin," nor do lesbians affirm themselves as "differently sexual."[31] Such identification of oneself as basically like everyone else blocks the probability of a nonassimilationist political analysis: Black is Beautiful. Further, it prevents acknowledgment of the individual's feelings, her sense of loss, frustration, and anger.[32]

Furthermore, the "different" phrases let able-bodied people off the hook, as they imply that everyone is able and therefore can devise a way to get where she wants to be without help.[33] Sexism, ableism, ageism, racism, and heterosexism interact to disable people; euphemisms do not change that.[34] Using them implies that there is something that needs to be covered up, that it is shameful to be limited,[35] that it is rude to point out that one is disabled.[36]

## EUPHEMISM AND LIMITED LANGUAGE

The strength of the "different" phrases is that they challenge devaluation; their weakness is that they are euphemisms that can be used to deny services or to minimize real problems. "Exceptional children" are still retarded, and their "special needs" involve more than benevolent acceptance. The "special" child is a euphemized child.[37] "Physically challenged" people may need more than strong muscles to help them climb mountains; indeed their muscles may be untrainable and their challenges may be mental and emotional as well as physical.[38]

Moreover, indirect ways of describing disabilities disguise agency. Julia Penelope points out that the phrase "hidden disabilities" suggests that the individual with the disability is hiding it when in reality other people are unable to perceive it because of the assumption that everyone is able-bodied unless they announce that they are not.[39]

The use of visual words poses a particularly difficult problem. Ours is a highly visual culture, so many of our metaphors are visual. Some people advocating sensitivity to the experience of visual impairment have argued that we should avoid visual metaphors associating blindness with lack of insight, insight with the ability to see, seeing with knowing, and so on.[40] Indeed some feminists have argued that conceptualizing people in terms of pictures is a male distancing technique that objectifies women and children.[41] By extension, saying, "I see what you mean" or "he is blind to the implications of what he is saying" not only hurts or offends blind people[42] but participates in a male "view" of the world. Instead, women are urged to use nonvisual alternatives: not "blind," "myopic," "shortsighted," but "unaware of," "insensitive to," "unconcerned about."[43] The editorial collective of the *Lesbian Insider/Insighter/Inciter* removed "insight" from their title when they were told that the term is insensitive to people with visual impairment.[44] The problem here is not that some visually impaired people may be offended by the term, but that the notion of insight, visual though it may be, is thus eliminated not merely from the wordplay of the title, but also from its political statement: that politics and theory and separation are linked. Likewise, deleting words from our vocabularies because they are patriarchal, we lose concepts that are important. Once when I presented a paper, I read a quotation from a woman who described her experiences with grief over her child's disability as a time of darkness. After my talk, I was challenged by audience members for the racism of that statement, equating darkness (thus blackness) with a negative experience. As I try to be careful about language and also to quote women accurately, I struggled with this issue for some time. It was a struggle not because I could not see the point, but because the concept of the "dark night of the soul" seems to me really, profoundly, to be a metaphor about the natural world, where moonless nights are not necessarily associated with skin color.

I agree with Julia Penelope that "thinking about what we say commits us to changing how we think,"[45] and I am therefore willing to reconsider such phrases as "I was paralyzed by fear," "She is blind to her own oppression," or "That's a lame excuse." Usually, today, I do not use them, but thinking about what I say does not always mean that I will not say something. I may say it deliberately, knowing what it implies. Linda Henley points out that "a racist, sexist church might as well have a racist, sexist hymnal. Even the best words can only go so far in healing a wound if the cause of that wound is still doing its damage."[46] The dark night may be scary because one cannot see in it, where seeing is a high cultural value, even if it has nothing to do with skin color. If I choose to describe a spiritual experience as a dark night, I want to be conscious of how reliant I am on seeing, how limiting that is, how dissimilar it may be to someone else's experience. Then if I choose to use the term, I have thought about it; I may even tell my reader or listener what I think. To refuse to say it, after such thought, is to embrace an unnecessary conceptual limitation.

JoAnn Giudicessi says that she wants to talk about her blindness, an impossibility if people eliminate the word and all its associations from their vocabulary. "Blind people have to feel respect and comfort about themselves, and using the word 'blind' is very important in making that transfer. . . . You can refer to me as blind, because I'm not ashamed of it."[47] Giudicessi is objecting to words like "sightless," "visually impaired," and "hard of seeing"; the objection can (carefully) be extended to visual metaphors. To avoid all visual imagery in deference to the blind may discriminate against the deaf for whom visual experience is central, as well as against any sighted person for whom visual ability is very important to her self-concept. To use a visual metaphor thoughtfully may not be insensitive.

Positive names meant to disguise unpleasant realities permeate the disability experience: "Hope Workshop, where there is no hope; New Opportunities Center, where people are one step away from the institution; Garden of Optimism; Home of the Angels; Guiding Hands Home; Rescue Mission; Convalescent Hospital; . . . Spastic Children's Foundations where adults are served. . . . Even the label group home is a sign of deviancy."[48] Jennifer lives in an institution called the Center for Family Love, designed for people who cannot live with their families. Such euphemisms do not, in fact, reduce the stigma associated with disability; they metaphorically intensify it. If we see such a name, we know it labels a concentration of stigmatized people, though we may not know which specific disability is being euphemized.

More difficult for the uninitiated to decipher are the inappropriate (to nonprofessionals) comparisons embodied in professional language. For example, "moderate" mental retardation is a significant disability to family members who are comparing it to "normal" intelligence, while it is not so bad to the initiated person who knows it means moderate in comparison to profound retardation. Jeff Lyon cites a research study that described a group of premature infants, 30 percent of whom had neurological or intellectual disabilities (spasticity in all four limbs, severe degeneration of brain tissue, developmental delay) as having "a *relatively low incidence* of neurologic and intellectual morbidity." Of course 30 percent is low relative to the 100 percent of such infants who would probably die without technological intervention, but their families are hardly "encouraged" (the researchers' descriptor of the appropriate response to their findings) by these relatively positive conditions.[49] "Independent for most activities of daily living" is a common descriptor for people with substantial disabilities. Bryan Jennett reports frequent encounters with people who have made "remarkable recoveries" from brain injuries, but are "hemiplegic, dysphasic, and dependent." The recovery is remarkable in comparison to the initial coma but not in comparison to the person's former self, before the injury.[50] Intended to give some precision to medical diagnostic categories, these words are euphemisms from the layperson's perspective, and are cruelly misleading in terms of ordinary family life.

Still more serious negative effects occur when such linguistic misunderstandings extend into public policy. "Mildly" retarded people are often assumed to be capable of "independent" living because a few IQ points remove them from the category of "moderately" retarded. Compared to profoundly retarded people, those with moderate retardation function so well that they may be bureaucratically pressed toward a supervised independence that would be more appropriate for their mildly retarded cohorts, and so on. I use the word "bureaucratic" deliberately, because inappropriate placements are far more likely to be a result of pressure from agency personnel who read the individual's file than of practical evaluation by those who know the individual personally. Concerning acquired immune deficiency syndrome (AIDS), Randy Shilts's analysis of "AIDSpeak" shows the impact of political language on public health policy. Beginning with the transformation of "AIDS victims" into "people with AIDS" (PWAs), "as if contracting this uniquely brutal disease was not a victimizing experience," he traces a series of similar changes: "promiscuous" became "sexually active," "blood and semen" became "bodily fluids," and so on. "The new vernacular," Shilts says, "allowed virtually everyone to avoid challenging the encroaching epidemic in medical terms."[51] The language derived from everyone's good intentions—to protect the feelings of those who had the virus, educate the public, demedicalize human courage and suffering, medicalize a discourse that was heterosexist and racist. But AIDSpeak is a language of euphemism and its inaccuracies can be life threatening. To say that a person who has human immunodeficiency virus (HIV) antibodies has been "exposed" misrepresents the truth that the individual is infected.[52] People who are not initiated into the hidden realities behind the euphemisms behave in ways that risk their lives, believing that "scientists don't really know" means that scientists cannot prove that AIDS is spread by sexual contact or that they cannot prove it is not caused by casual contagion.[53] And public health policy based on euphemism cannot directly treat the epidemic in the ways that other epidemics have been treated.

AIDSpeak is a political form of euphemism, designed to advance the probably altruistic agendas of various cultural groups. The users protect PWAs from a language that has become charged with homophobic or racist implications and protect themselves from acknowledging certain epidemiological facts. Another variety of euphemism, designed to protect the user from awareness of disturbing social issues, is what Kenneth Clark calls sociological euphemisms, "detached, legal, political, socioeconomic, or psychological terms," "the kind of conceptual apparatus that once adopted, requires us to ignore such intense human experiences as pain, suffering, humiliation."[54] Thus "maturity" comes to mean "learning to accept one's social oppression."[55] "Disengagement" means that "well adjusted old people just fade out into death, automatically relinquishing their roles and involvement."[56] Sociological euphemism is a form of academic discourse, of scholarly "objectivity," of mythological masculine discourse that has been repeatedly challenged by feminist scholars.[57] "Scholarship which has been presented to us as 'objective,' 'rational,' 'analytical,' 'dispassionate,' 'disinterested,' and *'true'* is in fact rooted in an irrational and distorted androcentric vision . . . its implicit passion and interest is the preservation of patriarchy, of elite male power."[58] Scholarly objectivity (behind which white male able-minded and -bodied privilege stands unchallenged) and medical objectivity converge when they address disability, not merely to deny the person's pain, but also to objectify her or him as the object of detached seeing and to distort that image further by rendering "scientific" the biases of disability history. For example, the study of congenital defects is called "teratology," from the Greek word *teratos* (monster).[59] Ordinary people do not recognize such derivatives; at the same time, medical practitioners are often unwilling to attend to their patients' vernaculars.[60] The resulting miscommunication reinforces the patient's status as an object, incapable of fully understanding her or his treatment or the superior dialect of the doctor. Unacknowledged because it is usually unconscious is the pejorative treatment of the one who is formally designated, in Greek, a monster.

Innumerable parents have objected to the description of mother-infant relations as "object" relations only to be convinced by long explanations that the word "object" is appropriate because the child's internalized mother is not the mother herself. But the language reinforces cultural objectification of women, and insistence on using the word "object" translates a social judgment into a psychiatric "truth" that each of our mothers can be only an object to us on the deepest psychological level. Carol Gilligan suggests that we replace object language with "internal mother."[61] The importance of this challenge to "received" scholarly language to people who are multiply objectified by disability, gender, class, and patient status is enormous. Where "object relations" are assumed to be distorted by the child's or the parent's disability, the "objective" language of the object relations theorist underscores the "monster's" separation and discounts that person's sense of connection, affection, or suffering.

The notion that scholarship should be objective is used to discount any "expert" who becomes an advocate for "subjects." When the subject is disabled, one's values may come from the facts the scholar has studied, but only if those facts include the affective components of the subject's experience. Wolf Wolfensberger, who has been criticized for his lack of traditional scholarly objectivity in that he advocates for people with mental retardation, responds, "Look at what the retarded suffer. There is bodily damage, functional loss, rejection by parents and society, segregation, status degradation, involuntary poverty, impoverishment of experience, loss of autonomy, of control, and of their own freedom." Further, he says, they know they cause anguish to those who love them.[62] To acknowledge these effects of the disability breaks the denial encoded in scholarly objectivity.

My own approach to the language of disability has been influenced by my training in the humanities, which encourage an interpretive relativism. My reading of the texts of disability studies crosses the artificial boundaries among disciplines, so I have tended to treat each of them as a humanities scholar's text, where "objectivity" requires not an abstract and supposedly value-free system of labels or observations but a close reading of the values embedded in the background or context of that system. I agree with Nancy Chodorow, who, working on the boundary between psychoanalysis and humanism, chooses to "privilege both empirical 'reality' and theory [to] draw upon a variety of interpretive and explanatory strategies."[63] The scholarly language of "empirical reality" is seductive precisely because it is divested of emotion, it protects the speaker and reader from identifying with the human dimensions of disability experience, of thinking that I, like my "subject," may bleed, become exhausted, lose my health or my reason, learn to do without those things I think I need. "The words we are comfortable with, the words that sound acceptable, rational, scientific, and intellectually sound, are comfortable precisely because they are the language of estrangement."[64]

## BIOGRAPHY

That women should tell our own stories and that we should listen to many such stories before analysis becomes possible is an article of faith among feminists. I therefore began my work on women and disability with the idea that I would find as many women's personal stories as I could and, since the personal is political, this would lead me to a political analysis. Overall, this idea has proved true or at least possible, but along the way I have encountered problems very similar to those involved in finding an adequate, politically acceptable, but sensitive language. Women's stories about disability are available in several forms: autobiographies, personal essays, biographies by someone else (often a family member), interviews in periodicals or anthologies, anecdotes in scholarly or popular books, and reports by researchers on interviews with their subjects. Since I began this work, several collections of essays and stories by and about women with disabilities have been edited by feminists. These are the best source for stories told with some woman-centered consciousness, but by far the majority demonstrate no such awareness. To honor the woman's own words while reporting what she reveals that she may not know becomes a challenge rather like that of explaining that the child's mother really does see her experience as a dark night of the soul, that her words cannot be changed without falsifying her experience.

Autobiography is a selective retelling of one's story, reordered, retrospective, and biased by both the requirements of form and changes in the writer's understanding of the meaning of what she remembers. The act of writing about disturbing events encourages the writer to rethink them, with such significant, physically measurable results as improved immune function.[65] Diaries, usually seen as immediate records of events or feelings as they happen, actually reshape them, redefining the situation and one's reactions. The writing is "an act of controlling, delimiting, and shaping one's emotional expression"[66] and a structure in which the writer distances herself from her emotions by composing the form of their presentation. When the record is intended for publication, it is further shaped by the message the writer and the publisher intend to communicate. Among disability narrators, these messages may include religious beliefs, the idea of heroic struggle against the odds, or whatever the individual believes the meaning of suffering may be. A classic illustration of how this works is Marie Killilea's books, written in the late 1940s and 1950s about her daughter, Karen, who had cerebral palsy. The family's dedication to making Karen as normal as possible and Karen's heroic optimism as she struggles to walk are the focal point of the story, which is singularly lacking in any negative emotion. Everyone, especially Karen, is portrayed as relentlessly optimistic.[67] A reader who wants to discover the stresses Karen's disability causes her family must search the background of the narrative until, apparently quite unexpectedly, Karen as a young adult decides to use a wheelchair despite her fear that her family will be angry at this disruption of their twenty-year commitment to her walking. Knowing that Karen finds walking a limitation on her independence, one can reread the heroic narrative and find traces of compulsion and denial that are masked for the superficial or uninitiated reader.

Marie Killilea's books tell Karen's story and only incidentally her own, which is shaped by her belief in the ideal forties family, which copes beautifully with adversity. The fashion in parental narratives was different in the 1980s. In these works, anger with the medical establishment or with social policies often structures the narrative, as does willingness to acknowledge family stress. Peggy and Robert Stinson's *The Long Dying of Baby Andrew,* for example, documents the frustrations and anger of Andrew's parents with the inhumanity of technological medicine, using excerpts from the parents' diaries to show the human costs.[68] Two recent biographies of people with amyotrophic lateral sclerosis (ALS, or Lou Gehrig's disease) illustrate the way the writers' agendas shape the narratives. Both use the diaries of highly articulate subjects. Roni Rabin's book is a celebration of her father David's life and his ability to accomplish in spite of the disease.[69] Andrew Malcolm's book about a woman referred to by the pseudonym Emily Bauer focuses on her struggle to be permitted to die.[70] The stories are remarkably similar, even to the ability of the two highly educated writers[71] to use computers in order to communicate when they were completely paralyzed, yet the biographies read differently because one celebrates life while the other honors death.

Some biographies seek not to present emotional realities but to disguise them. The Killilea family seems to have experienced hard times merely as an opportunity for optimism and courage. Jill Sager says that she used repeated retellings of her stories to protect herself from her emotions, keeping the stories vague so that she could be distant enough from the feelings to survive. And yet, with each retelling she creates an opportunity to remember the feelings, when she has distance enough and support.[72] In her extraordinary analysis of two German novelists, Christa Wolf and Ruth Rehmann, Marie-Luise Gaettens tracks their ideas on the uses of memory to *avoid* understanding the past, to falsify it. Both authors, she says, see "the habit of remembering in anecdotes" as a way of avoiding confrontation with "the ambiguities and the disturbing aspects of the past." Wolf and Rehmann are remembering their childhood in Nazi Germany. The effort of their writing is to remember the background, the suppressed information behind the anecdotes, in order to reconstruct memories that are not censored and encapsulated: to break silence. By cooperating with "the social production of memory as a legitimizing ideology for a social order based on forgetting," women in particular "internalize this system of amnesia upheld by the society in which they grew up."[73] To remember what society has insisted we forget is both an affirmation of self and an assertion of political competence—based on the insights we did not want to have, because knowing produces grief and requires action. In the case of disability literature, sentimentalized or valorized memoirs encapsulate the disability experience in private, intrapsychic life so that social issues are rendered invisible. What of the ALS victim who cannot afford a computer or command an audience respectful of her Ph.D.? Irving Zola, summarizing research on autobiographies of people with disabilities, points out that what is missing may be more "instructive" than what is included. In particular, he notes the frequent omission of any detailed description of the physical disability itself, especially in its chronic aspects.[74] The omission may reflect cultural devaluation of less-than-able embodiment, or denial, or encapsulated memory, where the religious truth or the person's valor, or even the doctors' care or lack of care, override the individual's awareness of her own experience. Marilynn Phillips reminds us that publishers' preferences may have as much to do with the prevalence of such denial as the authors' own participation in the cultural silencing of their embodied disability.[75]

Autobiography, diaries, and letters have been described as women's forms, reflecting the multiplicity of roles and the fragmentation of consciousness that characterize women's lives.[76] Estelle Jelinek defines autobiography as the work a woman writes "with the intention of its being her life story,"[77] thus distinguishing it from the male notion of an "embracing singleness of life line."[78] Jelinek finds in her study of women's autobiographies a sense of "alienation from the male world" along with "the positive delineation of a female culture." To convey this double message, women choose "disjunctive narratives and discontinuous forms."[79] Writing of disability biographies almost twenty years earlier, Erving Goffman observed that the single plot-line of biographers is very different from the "multiplicity of selves" that one sees when observing the individual from the perspective of social roles because one may sustain several social roles simultaneously.[80] Jelinek suggests that women writing their own biographies recapitulate those several social roles as well as a non-chronological awareness of the multiplicity of their lives. A similar phenomenon characterizes the oral personal experience narrative on which Marilynn Phillips bases her research on disabled women's experience.[81] Phillips works in the tradition of folklore, but Emily Hancock, a developmental psychologist, uses a similar method. She conducts a series of interviews with each woman in her study in order to get past the woman's "narrative capsule," her practiced way of telling her story, to the complexity of the "less easily explained aspects" of her life. To analyze these more complex stories, Hancock focuses on their narrative structures, their organization, patterns, and omissions.[82] The issue is not so much what happens in a woman's life as how she makes sense of it.

Plainly, the societal context of the autobiography has a significant influence on the sense a woman can make of her life. Marie Killilea in the late 1940s conceptualized her experience as a matter of private effort expended in the nuclear family. Anne Finger,[83] writing in the late 1980s, interpreted her experience in the context of two political movements (disability and feminist) that consider private experience to be shaped and distorted by public policy. Nellie McKay, tracing the history of black women's autobiographies, observes that in the nineteenth century the writer's task was to convince white readers that black people were human and capable of telling their own stories, including triumph over cruel masters and mistresses, while in the twentieth century, the narratives are success stories, demonstrating ambition, hard work, and achievement.[84] In the latter case, vulnerability, weakness, and fear are excluded, much as they are in disability success stories. A collection of success stories will reveal mainly the achievement and only indirectly, if at all, the disappointments of the disability experience. Furthermore, the personal accounts that are collected and analyzed are usually those of highly educated and articulate people and may not be representative in terms of resources and class.[85]

The most sophisticated discussion I have encountered of the politics of disability storytelling is in the discussions of AIDS. In addition to Randy Shilts's analysis of AIDSpeak, discussed above, Cindy Patton describes the constraints on storytellers to speak within their own separate spheres in the AIDS discourse: the "experts" in scientific terms about treatment, the PWAs about suffering (or about living with the virus), and "volunteers" about courage. "AIDS knowledge formations tended to silence people speaking out of character."[86] Yet many PWAs exercised medical competence, volunteers experienced despair, doctors observed courage, and so on. Patton describes the way in which "scientific" discourse, because it is privileged, tends to override the other perspectives, especially silencing or distorting the speech of "minority communities."[87] In the case of AIDS, because members of the scientific community participated in the minority communities (gay, drug-using, and disability) and minority people (especially gay) learned and used scientific language, the rigidity of the boundaries between the two modes of discourse was exposed, and individuals' stories reflected that discovery.

Storytellers, even when their intentions are to reinforce a particular interpretation (religious or antireligious, technological or antitechnological, for examples), provide evidence of other realities, those that are missing or hidden within the dominant paradigm. Feminists have tried to decode women's real experience from the male language in which our stories are told. Apart from the esoteric analyses of feminist deconstructive literary critics, there are many simpler, more accessible evidences of these efforts. Bettina Aptheker turns to the stories told by artists and writers for "evidence of other realities, the experiences that have been erased from individual and collective memories by the internal corrosion of colonization."[88] Elizabeth Minnick focuses on the relationship between the woman biographer and her woman subject, positing that genuine reciprocity in that relationship (even if the subject is dead) precludes "a falsely abstracted nonrelational objectivity" on the part of the writer and, significantly, the reader. The relationship of the three women (subject, writer, and reader) connects women across time and cultures precisely because each is a conscious participant in the relationship that, then, is not entirely subsumed under the rules of male-defined discourse. The demands of the relationship "become invitations to a more complex and more truthful understanding."[89] bell hooks, reviewing Frigga Haug's anthology *Female Sexualization: A Collective Work of Memory,* suggests the importance of telling stories with the deliberate intention of linking the several individual experiences to a collective reality, enabling the woman writer and reader "to see ourselves as part of history." Such a process "makes us live our lives more consciously."[90]

The conscious reader of disability biography must simultaneously respect the woman's own words, recognize the biographer's or editor's relationship to those words, and honor herself as reader. In doing so, the boundaries of correctness, both academic and political, are likely to be transgressed.

## ACADEMIC AND POLITICAL CORRECTNESS

Biographies—especially autobiographies—are suspect as sources of academic research. The biases of writer and reader are assumed to contradict the ethic of scholarly objectivity. That such objectivity is a delusion is well known but commonly ignored, or, even more commonly, acknowledged and *then* ignored. Except in the case of literary analyses like Jelinek's, when biographies are used in academic writing, they are generally analyzed on some scale of measurement, whether quantitative or "qualitative,"[91] or as anecdotal historical evidence. To mix autobiography with social science research and theory as I have done, considering it neither anecdotal nor less significant, is deliberately to violate the boundaries between academic disciplines, to treat research data and the literature of rehabilitation as only texts among many other kinds of texts.[92]

Feminist theory, of course, supports such a use of women's personal experience narratives but tends to segregate them along disciplinary lines, analyzing them for developmental information if the writer is a psychologist, for social information if she is a sociologist, to illustrate the development of ideas if she is an historian or a philosopher, and so on. My assumption that autobiographers' statements are *facts* to be used alongside other kinds of facts is eclectic, unscientific, and academically incorrect. What it enables me to do is to think about what is known or can be known about disability as women experience it in its complex, multiform, disorganized dailiness. Although each biographer shapes and censors her experience in the retelling, together they provide a collage with medical and social scientific knowledge that I believe can yield an insight less academically correct, less formal, closer to the messiness of disability experience itself.

The use of texts, like the use of words, can be suspect where our narratives, like our language, are male formed. The issue for feminist theory, in both cases, is how to find a language that is simultaneously accurate, academically correct, politically acceptable, and sensitive to individuals' experience. When women began to resist the use of masculine generic pronouns, we came up against the barriers of standard English grammar. Mixing singular and plural pronouns by substituting "their" for "his" violated a grammatical rule, while not doing so violated a political rule. It took a while for women to find ways to obey both rules or to become comfortable with the violation of one of them. Similarly, a decade of experimentation was necessary before most users of disability language were fully comfortable with avoiding the word "handicapped," and even the most fluent speakers of politically sensitive language occasionally say "disabled woman" instead of "woman with disabilities." Although activists like Anne Finger struggle with the usage, sometimes they find words like "victim" accurate and necessary. The experience of disability hurts, and as each woman tells her story, some part of that story is about being hurt. "Did I think because I stand up on platforms and make speeches about disability rights, did I think because I know so much that I was exempt from feelings of self-hatred? Did I think because I can talk about it with big words, 'internalized oppression,' 'human diversity and interdependence,' did I think that because I understand so much that I was exempt from the hurt?" "I have thoughts," Finger says, "that would not be approved by *Disability Rag*."[93]

In a valuable analysis of the political pressures in the lesbian community, Sarah Hoagland points out that when analysis gives way to rules, people who follow the rules (even if they lack understanding) are privileged over those whose reservations may come either from analysis or from a different life experience. This overreliance on rules leaves the community as a whole "unable to evaluate many responses";[94] thus not only individual words but whole narratives are unheard or angrily resented because they ignore or break the rules. When Elizabeth Bouvia was struggling for the right to die, critics in the disability community were angry at her betrayal of their goal of presenting a positive image of disability to the world. Bouvia's hope-lessness violated that important political goal. Their rule (always appear competent and able) discounts her reality. "Mrs. Bouvia does not stand for all disabled people, neither is she an isolated example of unhappiness."[95] Bouvia's despair may come in part from internal-ized oppression, but it probably includes biochemical depression, physical pain, and suffering outside the experience of the rule mak-ers. To suggest that she deny her experience (or that the media refuse to report it) is to emphasize the importance of symbolic unity to the exclusion of an accurate understanding of one common part of dis-ability experience. Ann Ferguson suggests that intolerance of value disagreement is more common among women concerned with build-ing a culture than among those building a political movement be-cause movement builders "will tend to recognize the need for strate-gic and tactical thinking, which inevitably involves disagreements, experimentation and changes in political positions."[96] The distinction between political activists and culture builders is not clear in the dis-ability movement (nor was it in the early days of lesbian feminism). Scrupulosity about language is a form of consciousness-raising use-ful to political change; it also strengthens the cultural bonds among like-minded language users. Bouvia's critics were political activists whose agenda was assimilation. To urge assimilation across disabili-ties is to deny difference of the most profound and basic kind. Bouvia attempted assimilation in a variety of ways before she changed her views on the value of life.

Political pressure on family members to disguise their own real suffering as a result of someone else's disability can distort their narratives as it increases their pain. Maggie Strong describes a com-mon dilemma of wives of chronically ill men, the pressure never to complain or express anger because "sick is sacred." "Anger is en-demic to chronic illness. You just aren't allowed to express it. You can call a WASP a WASP, but can you call a crip a crip? You've got to call a crip 'differently abled' or 'someone who lives with illness.' "[97] As an advocate for Jennifer, I am adept at disability talk, never slip-ping in conversation (though I sometimes do, deliberately, in this book) into calling her "a retarded person" rather than "a woman with mental retardation," but the truth is that adherence to the rules of correct disability language obscures my experience. Her retardation is in my experience the formative basis of her personality, ahead of any of her other personal qualities. She is retarded more than she is sweet or angry, and I never call her "a person with sweetness" or "a person with anger." Although the professionals in her life consistently call her a "client," their relationship to her is in reality more custodial than collegial. May Sarton says that she is honest about "the horror of senility" because she wants to be *present* to the pain of others who experience it as she has and "not to deny the physical facts which make transcendence difficult if not impossible. I have thought of those who share my pain, rather than of Judy who does not care, does not know, and is not in pain."[98] To disguise the pain denies the human connection, whether the disguise is meant to satisfy the demands of scholarly objectivity or those of political activism.

Outsiders to the disability movement, caregivers like Strong and Sarton constitute a kind of women's auxiliary, expected to support the movement and perhaps to facilitate its communication with the women's movement[99] and the professional community, but discredited for focusing on themselves instead of more exclusively on the disabled person. Although the mother of a severely disabled child knows intimately what it means to live with that disability, she does not know it from within and thus, to be politically accepted within the movement, she must defer to those who are themselves disabled, even with disabilities radically different from those of her child. Such women are useful advocates, so their "help" is valued; but they are outsiders who frequently articulate the negative side of disability experience and its burden on themselves, so they are suspect. There are some things that they had best not say too publicly, things that are best said by those with disabilities: "We are not easy to deal with. We are expensive, frequently not beautiful, and often violate strongly-held norms of socially appropriate behavior and appearance. To integrate us into society will take substantial effort, time, thought, and planning."[100] Privileging the stories of disabled women is thus a form of political correctness. As I have chosen to treat equally the disability stories of nondisabled women, I cross over yet another boundary of correct behavior.

There are many other barriers that determine insider/outsider status, including those between women whose disabilities coincide with old age and the younger spokeswomen for the movement,[101] between people with physical impairments and those with mental disabilities,[102] between deaf and blind people,[103] between mobility-impaired and hearing-impaired people,[104] between birth-disabled and newly disabled people.[105] The disability movement has its assimilationists and its separatists, as do the other civil rights movements; but because accessibility has been an overriding initial goal, assimilationists predominate. Indeed, the goal of accessibility made it possible for the movement to overcome the barriers between disability subgroups so that wheelchair access, sign language interpreters, tape recordings for those with visual impairment, and some other social accommodations were advocated by people with other disabilities and then by other fair-minded citizens.[106] As accessibility improves and assimilation increases, language barriers between disabled and nondisabled people weaken. At the same time, insistence on politically sensitive language use may become more rigid. When one is mainstreamed, one learns the mainstream language, is more likely to be exposed to overt prejudice, and in reaction becomes more insistent on correct usage and more ready to take offense. Statements about disability, even from advocates, become more suspect if the speaker's disabilities are not obvious or if the speaker is self-identified as nondisabled. As in any political movement, "some of my best friends are . . ." is a forbidden statement.

As I have negotiated my way through these difficult passages, I have found that no amount of explanation, no flourishing of credentials (whether personal or academic), alleviates mistrust or accusations of insensitivity. What finally enables one to be heard across the boundaries—sometimes—is not simply "correct" language (which changes too often to be reliable), but words and stories that are multiple, diverse, and accurate.

## MULTIPLE LANGUAGES, DIFFERENT STORIES

An accurate and nonlabeling language, based on identity, not stereotypes, is the desirable goal behind campaigns to change disability words. Although euphemisms abound, they are a form of excess; behind them is a desire for accuracy. Rejecting insults ("imbecile") and labels ("the mentally disabled"), most people with disabilities prefer more specific, accurate words ("bipolar disease," "Down's syndrome").[107] Of course the boundary between accurate words and labels, especially diagnostic labels, is often uncertain. Feminists are cautious about diagnostic terminology, which has often been used to blame the victim of societal or personal oppression, but insurance reimbursement and government services require its use and on occasion it has been valuable to women. For example, the label "post-traumatic stress disorder" has facilitated our understanding of the psychological impact of violence against women.[108] Some women with disabilities reject all labels to the extent of denying their obvious need for services,[109] while others prefer them.[110] The point in both cases is that people want to be seen as individuals, not merely labels, and yet the struggle for an adequate disability language requires naming one's experience. As Gwyneth Matthews suggests, labels are a problem not because of the actual words, but because they set the labeled person apart. Thus positive labels may also be harmful if one is labeled "courageous" or "an inspiration."[111] To insist on the widespread use of one's own chosen label in preference to all others is to treat a single person's perspective as if it were the whole Truth, a practice of which women have often been victims. Merrill Mushroom suggests, instead, that we name the condition, state our own opinion of it, and distinguish this from other possible opinions, and that we name individuals, not groups.[112] Even the woman who has a particular disability (say, cerebral palsy or post-polio syndrome) can appropriately speak for herself, not for all others with that disability. Anyone who has been uncomfortable with another woman's use of "we" for all feminists or all lesbians understands how being included in a group can in fact make one feel excluded or marginalized.[113]

To avoid pejorative or even positive labels is not, unless it is done thoughtlessly, to avoid coherent, organized thinking. Indeed, the value of recognizing a label and naming one's opinion of it is precisely that it makes us self-conscious; it signals willingness to change. "I remain convinced that becoming self-conscious about our linguistic choices gives us immediate access to our thought processes and that continued monitoring of what we are about to say will gradually enable us to unlearn patriarchal ways of thinking and create new conceptual patterns in their place."[114] Thoughtless rejection of politically incorrect words—or, indeed, of scientifically correct words—promotes ignorance. Far from encouraging self-consciousness, it merely accepts another person's judgment without evaluating it.[115]

What I deduce from all this is the value of a rich, complex language. Instead of creating dichotomies between good and bad words, we can use accurate, individual descriptors. Instead of taking for granted the meanings assigned by one or another political group, we can struggle with distinguishing our own definitions from theirs. The process is awkward; it slows down talk; it is uncomfortable.[116] It slows down thought and increases its complexity. "We need complex language . . . to understand and affect complex phenomena."[117] As Julia Penelope reminds us, "There are worse consequences than being wordy. We'll do far less damage to ourselves and others if we take the time to construct sentences that describe, as accurately as possible, what we perceive and feel."[118]

The same willingness to be complex, to speak and read and write in many, diverse voices, can characterize our use of women's biographies, the narratives of our many individual experiences. Bonnie Zimmerman has suggested that we attend to "the connecting exchange of language" instead of the politics of identity.[119] This, I think is where the complexity of our scrupulously individual statements can begin to form women's movement. To repeat each woman's story is essential, of course, but the next and crucial task is to attend to the "connecting exchange" between them. Thereby we weave a more complex, colorful, significant web, composed of many women's stories, of many women's words.

CHAPTER

# PRODUCTIVITY AND PACE

Time management is one of the ways cultural values are transmitted and enforced. For this reason, minority groups, by their deviance from cultural assumptions about time, make clearer what these assumptions are. Minority activist groups often symbolize their philosophy of integration or separatism by teaching their members to adopt the pace of the dominant culture or to reject it in order to affirm their cultural autonomy. People with disabilities, because biological factors strongly affect their adaptation to society's usual pace, provide special insight into the nature of time in our society and its relationship to the very high value we give productivity.

Literature about time distinguishes between "self" and "occupational" time,[1] between "organic" and "linear" time,[2] between "polychronic" and "monochronic" time.[3] These distinctions have in common a concept of time as imposed from inside the individual or from outside by social institutions. Parents of children who are multihandicapped, people with chronic, degenerative, or terminal illness and those who care for them, and some others with disabilities characteristically make decisions about time that run counter to significant values and expectations in our society.

The impact of disability on pace is usually sufficiently dramatic and continuous to force attention to pace and to the cultural values that make "deviant" pace a problem. Pace is an issue for people with disabilities, not only in society at large but also in feminist communities. Although some theoretical feminist statements advocate our getting in touch with organic or "natural" ways of being, in practice most feminist groups have been demanding about time management and productivity.

People with disabilities and those who care for them are often—usually—handicapped by the expectations of others and even of themselves in these areas, but their situation as people who must live in an ongoing relationship with their disabilities forces an integrated, internalized awareness of the body's (and of the mind's or the spirit's) real condition, which can serve as a model of self-centering for women who are not so personally pressed in this particular way. Feminist theory is full of important statements about women's ability to know ourselves, our transience, our lack of safety, our feelings of vulnerability. These are, to be sure, characteristics or potential characteristics of the female condition, but they are experienced in a particularly acute, deep form by women with disabilities and women who care for disabled people.

To conserve the energy needed for survival and also maintain a stable center of oneself, to avoid draining other women of their resources, to accept what we are *not* able to give, to understand realistically what we *are* able to give, to take the time for experiencing pain, to make oneself accessible to grief—these are all crucial tasks for women's becoming in which feminists with disabilities often are more experienced and thus more able than others among us. All of these tasks and many others integral to the daily lives of disabled people involve a deliberate, thoughtful series of compromises with conventional standards of time and productivity. The ability to know one's own pace and to accept and cooperate with each other person's pace is at the heart of this experience.

When I first proposed to speak and then to write about feminism, disability, and pace, I had in mind the fact that several of my friends who have chronic, "hidden" disabilities (lupus, ulcerative colitis, diabetes) have learned to recognize subtle signals from their bodies that enable them to accomplish whatever tasks have top priority for them by managing the pace of their lives, matching pace to their abilities and their limits in a way that most of us do not. I thought we could learn something from them, probably about slowing down and setting priorities, and I wanted to think about the implications of their discoveries about pace for feminist discussion of women's closeness to nature. When I set out systematically to learn more about this skill I found the subject much more complicated than I had foreseen.

The first and most obvious complication is, of course, that the range of disabilities is enormous and of course individuals' responses to them vary. Many people with what I will call "classic" physical disabilities (blindness, deafness, amputated or paralyzed limbs) are superwomen or -men, determined to work harder and accomplish more than anyone else; having been labeled less competent than the able-bodied white male "norm," they try to be more competent. Some individuals, however, respond to illness or injury by collapsing: refusing to do anything if they cannot do it all. Individuals who have terminal and/or degenerative diseases (cancer, multiple sclerosis [MS], muscular dystrophy) and the parents or other intimate caregivers of people with such diseases often attend much more consciously and deliberately to pace. And those who care for people with dementing diseases (Alzheimer's, Huntington's), with mental retardation, and with mental illnesses are especially aware of the effect of one person's pace on others.

A further complication in my exploration of the subject is that adaptations to changed pace are often barely conscious, especially after long experience, and sometimes they are closeted or simply not discussed because of the social stigma on deviant pace or because it is just too much trouble to explain the deviant behavior to people who have other interpretations of it.

An episode in my feminist community made this clear to me as I was writing an early draft of this chapter. One Sunday in Oklahoma City, there was a very important pro-choice rally that I did not attend. What I did instead was to drive forty miles in the other direction to take my nineteen-year-old daughter to lunch at Hardee's restaurant. My absence from the rally was noted, and it complicated my relationship with some of the women who expect me to be a role model and who have their own reasons to suspect that I am not feminist enough. Choosing fast food over a rally would seem at best a cynical choice.

My decision was based on the rhythm of my relationship with Jennifer. Five years before, despite the fact that one psychologist called our relationship "symbiotic," I would not have made the same decision. Instead, I would have reorganized my life so I could do both activities. Although I would have been "feminist enough" for those two hours, Jennifer would have been "out of sync" with my earlier or later visit, and there would have been emotional/physical reverberations for both of us for days.

What made the decision effortless (it just "felt right") was a discovery I made about time, including pace or rhythm—a discovery that runs counter to significant values and expectations in our society. It is a characteristic discovery for people like Jennifer and me. To reach it, I had to know as much about my own limitations as about hers, and as much about her abilities as about mine. Furthermore, I did not know at the time which sisters were keeping score on my nonappearances, and I had to be willing to let the misunderstandings happen, without explanations and excuses. That is, I had to let go of my own preference for the societal expectations of fast pace and superwoman performance, and for political acceptability as well.

## LIMITATION, FATIGUE, AND THE SUPERPERSON

Disabilities place limits on individuals. That is a controversial statement only because our society has tended to generalize from the specific, often narrow limit to the whole person. Some limits are so subtle, or invisible, as to make no impact on pace or life-style, but usually even minor disabilities (say, a strained muscle, in contrast to paraplegia) cause fatigue, limit certain activities, and make the individual's life less predictable than it might otherwise be. Moreover, such limitations affect other people who interact with the person who apparently "owns" the disability. In the least complicated situations, emotions are "catching." With more serious disabilities, work loads, survival needs, and unpredictability increase for everyone in the household or friendship group.

Women in cancer treatment have been very articulate about fatigue.

> Fatigue was the most difficult aspect of chemotherapy for me to deal with. Unlike loss of hair and nausea, I did not expect it. Since I'm a normally energetic person, this was particularly demoralizing.
>
> Fatigue from chemotherapy was not like a normal loss of energy. It was heavy. It came on swiftly. It was like a bulk weight, bearing down on weak shoulders. To anyone who has not experienced the onslaught of toxic drugs, the feeling is hard to convey. I became moody, tearful and frustrated because of fatigue. In all the battles I fought, fatigue was a formidable foe that required enormous energy to overcome.[4]

Such fatigue is almost concrete in its inflexibility. Rena Blumberg, like most others in her situation, learned to rest, meditate, ask for help, and relinquish responsibilities, but sometimes that is not enough. JoAnn Kelley Smith learned to tell people, "I haven't the strength or the motivation," but she felt that they believed she was shirking responsibilities. "They have not accepted the fact that I have a mass in me that is draining my energy and will soon kill me."[5] Nancy Mairs, whose disease (MS) will *not* soon kill her, notes that she herself believes at some level that she is shirking responsibility: "I tend to ignore my fatigue until my body breaks down in some way and forces rest. Then I miss picnics, dinner parties, poetry readings, the brief visits of old friends from out of town. . . . I cannot view these lapses without shame."[6] Still, at this point she has no choice. Karin Conway, who has lupus, says that she has no choice but to budget her energy. "When one's energy is gone it takes hours, even days, to regenerate a new supply. One learns to *plan* not to overdo."[7]

If the person experiencing the fatigue is a caregiver, it often seems that even less can be done about it. "Tired people," Helen Featherstone observes, "come to take exhaustion for granted. . . . To a truly tired person, most 'solutions' look like new problems."[8] Featherstone is writing about parents of seriously disabled children. Overwhelmed with the physical demands of getting the multihandicapped child through the day, keeping medical and educational appointments, implementing treatment and rehabilitation programs, and maintaining their own work and family lives, these parents are also subjected to strong societal pressures to behave as if their lives were "normal" and not out-of-the-ordinary.[9] Like Smith, they often feel that their genuine inability to do more is negatively judged.[10] Moreover, caregivers' own need for respite is less likely to be recognized than is that of the person with the disabilities or illness. The "sick role" may, as Gliedman and Roth (1980) suggest, be handicapping for both the disabled child and the parent,[11] but it has this one advantage: it validates attention to one's own needs for rest and self-care. That our society assigns such care to a "sick role" indicates the compulsory quality of a rapid pace.

Edward T. Hall, in his cross-cultural analysis of the nature of time, points out that our American-European "emphasis on saving time, which goes with quantifying time and treating it as a noun," leads to "a high valuation of speed."[12] Rushing from one activity to another is highly valued by others and oneself. It is not surprising, then, that "supercrip" and "superwoman" are roles that the movements for disability and women's rights are ambivalent about. We deplore the apparent necessity to be superhuman (stronger than able-bodied white males) but admire people who can do it and demand as much of ourselves. Better to be superwoman than to be weak or dependent.

Frank Bowe describes several such individuals in his book *Comeback*. Robert Smithdas, for example, in addition to his full-time work as Director of Community Relations for the Helen Keller National Center, serves on a number of national and international commissions on concerns of disabled people, has earned a master's degree, is a poet, and does his own plumbing and electrical work, wallpapering, floor tiling, and so on. Smithdas is deaf and blind and highly conscious of his function as a role model. Surely most people as active as he in the public sphere would feel free to hire plumbers and electricians as needed.[13] A deaf and blind person who cannot or does not want to do so much will have a problem with such a role model.

If the role of superman is evoked for Smithdas by his disabilities as well as by his membership in the white male fraternity, it is even more likely to be required of women who are relatively able-bodied and who care for others as well as (or instead of) themselves. One of superwoman's primary traits is an accelerated or highly condensed sense of time: she must do more than anyone else in the same amount of time. When responsibility for another is added to this syndrome, the amount of compression increases drastically because so many additional activities are required and because the highly stressed individual is struggling for control. Diane Rubin says of herself during the period when both of her parents were seriously ill,

> Not for a minute did I kid myself that I was being altruistic. I was simply fighting for control. The reins were mine: I had to hold them tightly, had to keep things running smoothly, running "right." Had to keep my finger in the dike. Even then I knew, acutely, that I trusted only me. While I knew that I was overdoing, I could not believe that anyone could manage as efficiently as I. I wouldn't leave. On those rare occasions when I wasn't there to do the actual taking care, I was so obsessed with making *plans* for running things, it was as if I never left. . . . No wonder I was exhausted all the time.[14]

> Every moment of my life was spent in taking care: early morning phone calls for my parents' medical reports; rundowns on the things to get "if you have time." I'd drive Mom to chemotherapy, shop for food, cook meals in quantity and freeze them, both for my folks and my own family to cover all the nights I'd be on duty. I paid my parents' bills. I fixed a better system for their Medicare submissions—dropped off, took home, and didn't miss a visit at Magee. If Mother had a cough, I went for medicine. If she was weak, I let her lean on me. My father had to have some information on his life insurance right away. I spent five hours getting it.[15]

Both the work overload and the sense of oneself as the only resource are typical. Like Rubin, most people whose caregiving responsibility extends over years instead of weeks or months discover that in order to survive they need respite and must slow down and accept help.

## RESPITE AND REST

The need for respite care either for the disabled person or the care-giver is usually conceptualized as "time out" to permit a later return to superhuman status. We may plan respite for ourselves in the form of vacations or days off, or it may be provided by social agencies through temporary foster care and hospitalization, or by other institutions through sabbaticals. Handbooks for caregivers encourage them to take breaks from their responsibilities by reminding them that "it is important for the [disabled] person's well-being," because without respite, the caregiver may be unable to maintain the necessary patience, concern, or physical strength.[16]

Respite care, vacation, or other temporary escape from the rush is probably a prerequisite for the discovery that rest must be integrated into daily life if the fast pace is to be maintained. Sometimes, of course, rest is medically prescribed, as it is for lupus and certain stages of multiple sclerosis. But for others, even an informed decision to "practice the art of relaxation in itself will cause you anxiety when you first try to introduce it into your life."[17] For the overscheduled, scheduling relaxation is another burden. For this reason, relaxation techniques and the physiological effects of rest are often taught in clinics and workshops. Thus directly because of the disease or indirectly through education, the individual who lives with disability may consider changing the pace of her life beyond mere alternation of rest periods with rush periods. To slow down in a fast-moving culture is to become deviant; if slowing down is necessary to survival or to meeting personal goals, it is sure to promote an existential crisis—just the sort of crisis Mary Daly and others describe as central to the experience of feminist self-centering.

## SLOWING DOWN AND WAITING

Although slowing down is an important discovery associated with many disabilities, the source of the discovery as well as people's reactions to it vary considerably. There are strong variations between different cultures in pace and the perception of time. Even in the mainstream American culture to which this discussion is confined, the disability itself may be as influential as individual temperament or past experience in causing the realization "I had better slow down." People with multiple sclerosis, for example, must take longer to do each activity simply because their bodies will not work fast.[18] Blind people can move as fast, but their pace is affected by external facts—for example, that reading aloud or reading braille is slower than visual reading[19] and that walking is slower when one cannot visually scan an unfamiliar path. Caregivers to people with dementing diseases learn to slow down because the confused person may become agitated when rushed but may be calmed by a slower pace.[20] Parents of a child with cerebral palsy can foster the child's independence only by waiting while the child does with excruciating slowness some task that the parent could do easily in a few minutes.[21] In any case, the disability slows the person down to the point where she or he has time to be aware of how she or he feels, and if the disability is not invisible, this time allowance probably carries with it social permission to express some of those feelings and even to be more assertive about individual needs.[22]

Our culture gives lip service to the idea that we should "take time to smell the flowers," but there is an implied corollary: that we should do so "on our own time." This may mean *any time* for the pampered daughter of a rich man and *never* for the mother, wife, or worker whose whole life is given over to caring for others. For most of us, it means that we can occasionally slow down, when we are not "on duty." This creates special problems for those whose work and personal lives are integrated—for example, active feminists who work in women's centers, or mothers of toddlers who work in day care centers.

But when illness or accident or life with a disabled child or partner requires a slowing down, a refocusing of attention on the self, there is at least a temporary opportunity to change all that. Adjusting to a physical disability takes time. Learning to live with someone else's disability takes time. Coming to terms with grief takes time. Learning to do old tasks in new ways takes time. Trying to move too fast through such hard work is a mistake. Peter Purpura cautions parents whose children have died that they should not try to get well too soon: "It's like the scab on a wound that may heal on top but inside is still festering. Many times what appears on the surface to be a parent getting well amazingly fast will often emerge later in tragic ways."[23] Robert Chernin Cantor describes cancer patients' temporary regressions to a childlike state in which they are taken care of as "a plateau from which they are able to survey their lives." Accepting care permits the individual to use all her or his energy to reassess her or his life. Cantor says that "devoted wives and nurturing mothers" find it especially difficult to allow themselves to be cared for in this way.[24] To do so may free us to care for ourselves.

A particularly trying form of slowing down in a rushed society is waiting. Edward T. Hall contrasts city dwellers' easy adherence to clock time with the recognition by "anyone who has spent much time in the open" that "a built-in variable time sensor is necessary for survival."[25] Patients and those who accompany them through the medical thickets are forced to develop such a variable time sensor. "The worst part of the private war that the parents of brain-injured children wage," says David Melton, "is the search for medical and educational help. They suffer from . . . the hours, and the days, and the months of waiting for appointments, waiting for answers . . . waiting . . . waiting . . . then waiting to wait again. If parents of hurt children uniformly have a neurosis, it is the 'waiting complex.' "[26] Doris Lund, commenting on her life in hospital waiting rooms, says that "waiting is an illness all its own."[27] Listening to a mentally impaired person requires willingness to wait for a much-delayed response, or for no response at all. As one minister said, "I am so used to doing, doing, doing and there is nothing I can do for these people [with Alzheimer's disease]. I've learned to just sit, to just share being."[28] One of the hardest things I have learned about being with my disabled daughter was to stop trying to play with, entertain, or educate her. Now we companionably eat hamburgers and french fries together, communicating only that we are physically present for each other.

Grief, says C. S. Lewis, feels "like waiting; just hanging about waiting for something to happen. It gives life a permanently provisional feeling. . . . Up till this I always had too little time. Now there is nothing but time."[29] Waiting for death, of course, is like grief inverted, taken out of order. Again, there is a sense of reordered time, a suspension of pace.[30]

Outside of hospitals and doctors' offices and waiting rooms—and sometimes inside them—waiting, like slowing down and resting, may be the occasion for introspection. Hall observes that American-European whites think that when "nothing overt is happening, nothing is going on."[31] But of course if thinking or feeling is going on, the pause or the wait is potentially fruitful.[32] And even if all that transpires is a few minutes of quiet, a blank mind, that can be a relief; and if, instead, suffering or pain transpires during the waiting, or even the recognition of a stiff neck or a headache, that is self-knowledge that rushing about might mask or deny.

## RECOGNIZING INDIVIDUAL PACE

Disability may slow us down to the point at which we look within or reevaluate our lives. It may also require us to "spend" the necessary time to discover what pace best suits us.

Again I must warn against generalizing about disabilities. Sidney Dorros believes that people with Parkinson's disease are characteristically in a hurry and he strongly implies that the hurry is desirable.[33] I personally know of two mentally retarded adults who have compounded their physical disabilities because they would not stop walking around on injured feet.

But many disabled individuals do come to a very clear understanding of exactly what pace best suits their physical abilities. Such recognition may be simple, as when a person who uses a respirator knows she can talk freely because she has just spent several hours "hooked up," or very complex, as when Sidney Dorros's participation in an experimental drug program led him through a series of experiments with timing conferences at work and conversations with friends so that he could complete the discussions before developing physical or mental dyskinesia.[34] People with severe physical disabilities may work extensively with mechanical devices and attendant help in order to offset (by accepting) the disabilities and thus save energy for the exercise of mental strengths. Miriam Ottenberg describes Dr. Panzarella, who uses a mechanical lift, a telephone intercom recording system, attendants to push his wheelchair and provide personal care, secretaries to transcribe correspondence, a nurse to hold his stethoscope and other instruments, and carefully arranged furniture to enable him to establish eye contact with his patients. With these aids, he can practice medicine. "I live within my abilities," he says.[35]

Living within their abilities, accepting their need for rest, and setting priorities (then ignoring the lower ones) are pace-setting strategies of most of the people with multiple sclerosis whom Ottenberg describes. Because the disease is progressive and erratic, it requires continued self-monitoring from anyone who wants, like Dr. Panzarella or Miriam Ottenberg herself, to continue an active life-style without periodic disasters. Dorros's study of the way timing of his drug dosage affects his dyskinesia, a diabetic's close analysis of how food intake interacts with exercise and insulin dosage,[36] or cancer patients' monitoring of the effect of medication on their symptoms—all provide information on which to base changes in pace. They are forms of bio-feedback, sometimes very subtle indeed.

Because our culture emphasizes external, clock time as an organizing principle,[37] attempting to reorganize the pace of one's life on the basis of subtle physical (or psychological) signals is an especially difficult undertaking. However, as Barney Glaser points out in his discussion of self-pacing in research, "we are always paced by others unless we know our own pacing." When we do, Glaser suggests, and can explain the "recipe" to others, the others will usually accept it.[38] Quite apart from acceptance by others (which may, of course, come harder to women than to Barney Glaser, with his white male professional privilege), clearly articulated self-pacing should reassure the person who has thought it through. The women who wrote *No More Stares,* encouraging independent living for women with disabilities, say, "It doesn't matter how long it takes you. It's not a race. It's your life and you can choose the pace that's comfortable for you."[39] For women who have been treated as if even their bodies belonged to others, this can become a very reassuring idea.

Mary Daly has said that "women's own time" is "whenever we are living out of our own sense of reality, refusing to be possessed, conquered, and alienated by the linear, measured-out, quantitative time of the patriarchal system. Women, in becoming who we are, are living in a qualitative, organic time."[40] The individual sense of "organic time" surely begins with embodiment, a problematic issue for women in our society.[41] Physical disability makes almost compulsory a woman's coming to terms with her particular, detailed embodiment. She thus has an opportunity to react beneath the cultural layers of denial and distortion to the organic time of her own becoming.

## ROUTINE AND FLEXIBILITY

When people who have lived with disabilities write about self-pacing, they usually emphasize the importance, for good and ill, of routine tasks and daily repetition. Daily routines, especially for women in the wife or mother roles, contribute to the sense of overload, but they also provide a measure of control in an otherwise uncontrollable situation. Gerda Lerner writes that during her husband's illness, housework kept her "from going raving mad with waiting. The great cat-and-mouse game consists of the everpresent danger, the paralyzing threat, the breathless waiting for that aimless, lazy paw. It can be stayed by sweeping and straightening, precision and order and knowing exactly where everything is at each moment. Objects kept in check and balance. Edges straight, corners rounded. Chairs at correct distances apart and books straight in rows."[42] And May Sarton, describing the narrowing world of Jean Dominique as his physical disabilities increased, says that "every one of the small daily rites became more precious. What had been the decoration of life became life itself."[43] Sarton's several discussions in her journals of the dailiness and the rewards of gardening emphasize that "working at something so tangible rests and clears the mind"[44] and "balance[s] all the anxieties and tensions and keep[s] me sane."[45]

For people with complex biochemical disabilities, routine daily tasks are more basic: a measure of control over pace influences the effectiveness of drugs and other therapies. In Sidney Dorros's pragmatic book about Parkinson's disease, he says that "humans need to carry out the routines of life fairly automatically if they are to have the time and energy for creative living." For him, as his disease progressed, making the routines "fairly automatic" required both scheduling and physical effort. "For example, I would arise at the same time every day, even though there was no pressure to do so. Regularity enabled me to keep the same medication schedule each day so that taking my pills could be semi-automatic. . . . I tried to arise, eat, move my bowels, exercise, and go to bed at regular times. I also tried to stick to my schedule for medication more rigidly than in the past." Gaining control in this way "enabled me to anticipate somewhat when my best times would be . . . and to rest . . . during my worst times."[46] Again, attending to daily routines provides balance.

Like Sarton, Dorros used the part of his time that was not given over to daily maintenance for writing, but he does advise others, whose Parkinson's is more limiting, that "it is psychologically satisfying to complete some achievable tasks, however simple, each day." His example, of which May Sarton would surely approve, is planting a rose bush.[47]

Sometimes, of course, the disability or the stress of caring makes the "attention span for things nonmedical . . . only slightly longer than a blink." Sustained thought or a balanced life under such circumstances is not possible, but the dailiness of routine work still provides a measure of control. Diane Rubin continues: "The most I could manage, by then, was simply making order, sorting things but not sorting things out. Unable to make sense of things, I could at least make most things clean."[48] This is, of course, a housewife's statement about pace. In the home, Edward T. Hall observes, "particularly the more traditional home in which women are the core around which everything else revolves—one finds that P(olychronic)-time takes over." Hall believes, "At the preconscious level, M(ono-chronic)-time is male time and P-time is female time, and the ramifications of this difference are considerable."[49] Hall's emphasis on the "more traditional" home in this passage is important not only for his immediate point, but also, in a discussion of disability, for any consideration of the ways that illness or the care of people with disabilities returns one, "preconscious" or not, to the polychronic home from the monochronic workplace.[50]

Returning to the routine daily tasks of the workplace may also be healing, however. Nancy Rossi describes her return to office work after caring for her dying husband: "I could go about my work there without feeling, and it is now that I look back that I realize the routine—not necessarily the daily contact with people, which is what I was told I needed—that the predictability of the routine there is what I needed then, that that gave me the most necessary sense of 'life continues, life goes on.' That and the daily routine of caring for [the baby] had saved me."[51] All of these uses for daily routines assume that the person involved has, at least potentially, other vital work to do: writing, grieving, adapting to a changed relationship or life-style. For those who care for people with dementing illnesses, serious retardation, certain mental illnesses, autism, and similar conditions, regular, predictable, simple routines are necessary for the survival of both the caregiver and the person with the disability. "Meals, medication, exercising, bedtime and other activities" must be done "the same way at the same time each day."[52] These are cases in which there is a good deal to be said for monochronic time—and in which serious problems arise in the average, relatively unpredictable household. Institutionalization is in bad repute these days, precisely because of such rigidity, which is, however, highly desirable for individuals with these disabilities. Indeed, as institutions change to afford more freedom and flexibility, residents, staff members, and families may have grave difficulties because of the confused person's emotional distress at the loss of routine predictability.

What many people who live with disabilities find about the routines of daily life is the opposite of the conventional wisdom: "We waste our lives with trivia, and stand aghast in old age to find that time has run out and little has been accomplished."[53] On the contrary, establishing "trivial" routines may be, at the time, a sensitive, life-giving accomplishment. Hall says that in American-European cultures "we expect that things will happen fast once we have made up our minds and, as a consequence, we are apt to pay little attention to the pattern we are weaving in life's fabric or to the slow accumulation of Karma in the multiple acts of daily living."[54] It is just such consciousness of the patterns we are weaving that living with disability enables us to develop.[55]

Helen Featherstone finds that in families of disabled children, mothers have an advantage in coming to terms with the loss precisely because of their usual role as the weavers of the fabric of everyday life:

> Immersion in a child's immediate needs provides important opportunities for coming to terms with loss. The mother learns routines for caring for her child, finds help, locates services. Daily exposure forces her to confront her own doubts and to re-examine painful feelings. Frequent consultations with doctors and other professionals teach her whatever is known about the child's problems. Under favorable conditions these routines of caring build confidence and help a mother to "work through" her feelings. She becomes the expert on her child.[56]

This is a crucial psychological insight and helps to explain another common phenomenon, maternal resistance to the pressures to probe her feelings: "They used to say things to me like—do you feel guilty, (about having a retarded child)? Are you disappointed? Disappointed? Guilty? Christ, if I could just get a bottle down her. It's much more real, Dr. Jacobs. It's not all this theory. It's really not as psychological. It's . . . it's solid."[57]

## LIVING IN THE PRESENT

Another characteristic aspect of the changed pace of people who live with disabilities that is related to the shifting, polychronic time of traditional women's roles is increased focus on a present as opposed to a future orientation. When a family member is in precarious health or near death, the future orientation that enables us to plan and keeps us synchronized with the pace of the larger society becomes irrelevant. Where a person with a stable, long term disability may slow her pace precisely because she has plans for the future toward which she wants steadily to work, those whose disabilities are highly unpredictable or whose predictable short-term future is death do best to concentrate on the present day. Miriam Ottenberg found that "every achieving person with multiple sclerosis" whom she interviewed answered the question, How can you plan? "the same way: Don't postpone your life. . . . Anything that can be done now, we do now."[58] Multiple sclerosis for these individuals is not immediately life threatening, but it is highly unpredictable. To seize the day, when it happens to be a good one, is a strategy for avoiding paralysis. Suzanne Massie says of living with her son's hemophilia,

> I learned that there was only one thing I could absolutely count on and that was that I could never count on anything. Not plans, not vacations, not hopes, not anything. All of us, without realizing it, live mostly in the future. At least half of our lives is consumed in thinking and dreaming of tomorrow. With hemophilia, there is no tomorrow, at least never a tomorrow you can rely on. And certain it is that, should you begin to count on tomorrow, to permit yourself for one moment a timid confidence, the disease, as if it were malev-

olently conscious, will plot to destroy your plans and your fragile confidence—just to show its power.[59]

The unpredictability of life with any chronic illness requires the ill person and those who care for her to change plans suddenly, solely because of the demands of the disease.[60]

Where death is in sight, living in the present is compulsory. "And as my diet and my tumor have restricted my movements in space, so the probability that I shall die soon has restricted me to the immediate present in time. It has erected around me an invisible barrier that I bump into a dozen times a day. . . . I'm reasonably sure that I'll be alive a month from now, and I sincerely hope I'll be alive three months from now; but beyond that I don't know. . . . In short, I have no future any more."[61] Barbara Sourkes describes "the subjective experience of the living-dying interval" as "neutral time." "There is a sense," she says, "of being suspended in space and time, without defined movement in either a forward or backward direction."[62]

Those who are living in "neutral time" frequently describe it, in conscious imitation of Alcoholics Anonymous, as living "one day at a time." It is a strategy for avoiding overwhelming fear: "We focused our lives down into the present minute, the exigencies of the hour, and we blocked out the frightful possibilities that lay ahead next week, next year. Seen in its entirety, the calamity overwhelmed us with terror. Broken down into small steps, taken one at a time, the ordeal became manageable and endurable."[63] In this spirit, support groups for cancer patients and their families are called One Day at a Time and Make Today Count.[64]

The quality of the "one day at a time" prescription is different for those who care for people with mental illness, retardation, and dementing illnesses. Louise Wilson's doctor tells her that for patients like her son, who is mentally ill, "you simply cannot make plans. If I were in your place I would just take each day as it comes. I would get up each morning and pray for strength to get through that one day."[65] As Wilson's story unfolds, the doctor's advice proves to be entirely accurate. There is no happy ending. Indeed, there is no end. Taking one day at a time is a means of surviving trauma, not of enriching the quality of life. Karen Junker says of her life with her autistic daughter, "Perhaps this is what the child in the glass ball has taught me above all—to turn my back on misgivings that are so paralyzing, accept the day whatever it offers, and not worry about a future that might never come. Now I know it. Each day has its own sorrow."[66] There is a further problem here for the one who cares: she is living one day at a time because of the unpredictability of someone else's illness. No matter how intimate the relationship, or how necessary the caring, the day-to-day strategy may run counter to the caring person's own need for planning. Diane Rubin says, "I lived the way sages of the East suggest: one day at a time. It is vastly overrated. Living only in the now is fine for newts or snakes or cows, but not for people. Humans have to have tomorrows, too."[67] This dilemma also affects some "coalcoholics" whose adherence to the Al-Anon slogan "one day at a time" may keep them in a destructive situation that future-orientation might enable them to change or escape.

Nevertheless, for many, the decision to live in the present is a positive decision to emphasize the quality rather than the quantity of life, an emphasis that, as Robert Butler points out in his discussion of aging, "runs counter to the culture."[68] Stephanie Simonton sees the shift of attention to the quality of life in the present by the cancer patients she works with as a positive change from the cultural norm of putting off the things we want until tomorrow.[69] And Mary-Lou Weisman describes her decision about her goals for her son, Peter, who has muscular dystrophy: "What we've decided is that Peter's life can't be about anything that happens over time. It can't be about when he can ride a two-wheeler, or a ten-speed; or about when he gets his driver's license, or into Harvard, or married, or successful. His life has to be about quality—about how well, how deep, how rich—not about how fast, how many, how soon, how long." Immediately after this passage, Weisman admits that it is so abstract that she is not sure exactly what it means, but she is nevertheless committed to trying it and is well aware that the decision is counter to the cultural pressures to plan for "normalcy and independence" for Peter. Peter, after all, had a degenerative disease.[70]

Knowing that the disease is degenerative, that the crises will continue, that the patient will not get better can, despite the undertone of sorrow, enrich the present moment. Stephen Rosenfeld says, "Time is cut into ever smaller segments for the dying and for those who attend them. Dying does not stop time but articulates the flow. It does not universalize experience but conveys an ever sharper sense of the particular."[71] Even regression may have this beautiful side, as

May Sarton observes in her friend Judy, who is senile: as the old person "is able to do less, he *[sic]* enjoys everything in the present, with a childlike enjoyment. It is a saving grace."[72] Stephanie Simonton sees cancer patients' regression to the childlike condition of being cared for by others as a useful prerequisite to discovering how they will live in the present.[73] Doris Lund describes her son Eric's ability to live in the present as a gift to others.[74] Being "anchored in this hour," absorbed in "the most humdrum family business," meant "predictability, safety, daily life continuing indefinitely" to Robert Meryman when his wife was dying of cancer.[75] And Alice Massarani's discovery, as her infant son, Caleb, was dying, that "it did Caleb no good and it did me no good to think about what *has happened* or to think about what *might* or *will happen*. My time with him is *now*" enabled her to change her relationship with Caleb to one between two individuals and to make decisions for him based on his present needs, not on possible future needs.[76] As Claire Kahn says of her daughter's life with Niemann-Pick disease, "You don't cope with the future until you are there."[77]

## SETTING PRIORITIES

To savor the beauty of the moment or cherish a relationship or just appreciate being alive for this hour are positive forms of living in the present. Another is to use the time fully by setting priorities. Facing a life-threatening illness calls for a reevaluation of all of one's choices. Bethine Church said that during all of the thirty years following her husband's fight with cancer, "he had been a different person. It had been somehow easier for him to do the things that needed to be done, and let the things that did not matter go."[78] This experience is echoed again and again by others. In the initial stage of denial, people often assume an exaggerated superwoman role, but usually fatigue or a recurrence or a crisis of some kind makes them pause and face the disease.[79] The most observable immediate effect is some schedule revision and turning to others for help, but the underlying process behind these changes is a decision about what is most important. Often the individual radically revises her priorities. Ottenberg found that for most people with multiple sclerosis the first priority is usually their job, at least in the first years after diagnosis,[80] but in most cases, especially when the threat to life is more immediate, attending to personal relationships becomes a crucial priority. In either case, "Living on borrowed time—being constantly conscious of your own mortality—can lead you to sort out your life, causing you to push away what is a waste of the time you have left and to concentrate on the people and activities most valuable to you."[81] The sense that time is limited and should be used well is central to this experience.

R. R. Lichtman, in a study of women with breast cancer, found that these individuals typically give low priority (and little time) "to such mundane concerns as housework, petty quarrels, and involvement in other people's problems and high priority to relationships with spouse, children, and friends, personal projects, or just plain enjoyment of life."[82] These choices are not universal, however. JoAnn Kelley Smith felt that her

> priorities *should be* in thinking through the meaning of changing ideas and values in this experience and recording it, in spending more time trying to get 'into the heads' of our foster children, in establishing a better relationship with Gordon and working through with him a clearer understanding of my memorial service and the disposition of my body. *But these concerns are not a part of my reality any more.* They were at first, but in the intervening months the little jobs I do that affirm me as a worthwhile, contributing person have become my priorities.[83]

Whatever the top priorities are, the fact of illness gives permission to assert them and to concentrate one's time and energy on them. Stephanie Simonton observes that "patients and family members alike often feel entitled to say 'no' to others for the first time in their lives when they learn they have cancer."[84] "Suddenly they think, 'Wait a minute—I'm not going to live forever! So what are the things I've always wanted and been putting off? If I keep putting them off I'll never get to do them.' "[85] The result may be characterized by others as "selfishness." Obviously this is another form of the problem many women have with focusing on their own lives instead of trying to please others. As Simonton says, "Learning to do these things requires work,"[86] but it is work that makes sense to the person conscious of living "on borrowed time." JoAnn Kelly Smith says, "While I feel trapped by my limited life, I also feel a sense of freedom which comes in knowing that because life will soon be over, the restraints and inhibitions of our culture's value system become unimportant."[87]

The disabled or ill person is not the only one who decides to set priorities or goals and to change life around to accommodate them. Caregivers, family members, and friends usually undergo similar periods of reevaluation, and of course, the rest of us, disabled and nondisabled, realize at least superficially that we ought to reexamine our priorities from time to time. Barbara Tedlock found that the Quiché culture of Guatemala makes such awareness of one's self a daily routine: "The Quiché reality causes them to scrutinize each day and its character as it relates to their own character, their desire, and their past, as well as the tasks that lie ahead. The Quiché really do have to think deeply and seriously about the process of how each day is to be lived."[88] Such consciousness is highly unusual in our culture, which is almost the opposite of the Quiché, but this is just the kind of reorganization of pace that disability encourages.

## PRODUCTIVITY

In a study of temporal stratification in our society, J. David Lewis and Andrew J. Weigert observed that the social order is maintained by strong sanctions against disrupting the hierarchy of time in which "organizational time demands precedence over interaction time and interaction time, in turn, demands precedence over self time."[89] Disability or illness frequently inverts this sequence, which helps to account for the extreme dis-ease the process creates in others unless the deviant person can be isolated in the "sick role." If "able" people were to learn from those who live with disability how to invert the hierarchy, it would be the kind of revolutionary act Daly suggested when she advocated women's living by organic, nonlinear time, even within patriarchal institutions. To the extent that time and culture are inseparable,[90] the integration of women's culture with the complex individual cultures of those who live with disability should provide a powerful internal countermovement within our majority culture, and this is to say nothing of the different temporal organizations of other minority cultures.

The predominance of organizational time in our society is closely linked with the high value we place on productivity. As integral members of the culture, people with disabilities share that value. Robert Smithdas's superman approach described above is an extreme case.[91] Ottenberg's observation that work is the highest priority for the people with multiple sclerosis she interviewed[92] and Dorros's that people with Parkinson's disease tend to accelerate rather than decrease their "Type-A" behavior are other illustrations.[93] Indeed, society's labeling of disabled people as incompetent or unproductive makes conformity to the ethic of productivity almost a prerequisite to self-esteem for them.[94] Nevertheless, the reassessment of life-style that accompanies most disabilities and especially life-threatening or work-threatening illnesses frequently leads, as we have seen, not only to a slower pace and recognition of the value of rest but also to placing a higher priority on personal relationships and on goals other than productivity.

This is not to say that people with disabilities are not productive. Some are; some are not. Rather, productivity in our culture is so firmly attached to organizational time that a decision to assign a higher priority to personal time or to move at a different pace will be perceived as a decline in productivity. But if a person with disabilities is highly productive, she or he is no longer viewed as disabled.[95] Franklin D. Roosevelt and John F. Kennedy are the classic examples.[96] It is significant, of course, that Roosevelt's and Kennedy's schedules routinely included physical therapy and rest, which did not encounter public criticism. The presidents' success canceled their disability in the public perception. For less prominent individuals, the competency-deviancy hypothesis operates on a more modest level. That hypothesis is "that the more competence an individual has, the more deviancy will be tolerated by others."[97]

But what of people who cannot "produce" by societal standards, or at least do so too slowly when judged by organizational time? The work ethic pronounces that hard work will produce results. But if a person's brain is injured or the body cannot be "cured," no amount of work will produce the result that society acknowledges as productive. In our society, the fall-back prescription for this dilemma is that *someone else* must assume that individual's burden of productivity.[98] Parents of disabled children, for example, are expected to increase their productivity by providing educational and rehabilitative services, medical therapies, and so on in addition to their own normal work loads. As Hall explains,

> With [American-European] peoples time is an empty container waiting to be filled; furthermore, the container moves along as if on a conveyor belt. If time is wasted, the container on the belt slips by only partially filled and the fact that it is not full is noted. We are evaluated by how those containers look. If they are full, that is a strong plus. If they are full with good deeds and creative productions, then we can feel we have lived a "full and productive life"! Judged by this standard, some people are seen as more productive than others and require bigger containers while the rest of us sit back in awe of how much they accomplish in their lifetime. To have done little or nothing means no containers are filled.[99]

Parents of disabled children are encouraged to fill the children's containers as well as their own.

However, as we have seen, the parents or significant others of people with disabilities are themselves often forced by the work overload and by synchronization with the other person's pace to reorganize their own priorities. The simplest of these cases is when the mother of a disabled child quits her job so that she can implement the child's medical program.[100] More often, the parent learns to integrate respite, rest, and a slower pace into her life style so that she can continue to care for the child. In any case, she chooses (or, more often, is forced) to change her relationship to organizational time. As the competency-deviancy hypothesis applies to her, too, such caregivers are likely to deny or disguise the impact of such temporal changes on productivity. For example, when my "multihandicapped" daughter was younger, at the time when her needs made the greatest demands on my time and energies, very few people from my work and public life knew that she was disabled. I was so productive publically that my deviant absences for her medical appointments and emotional crises were not questioned; I just did not tell people where I went. Had I been less productive, my coworkers would probably have been much less tolerant.

The power of the productivity ethic can also be observed in the efforts made by people who work with severely disabled individuals to convince them and the public that they are in fact productive. Sheltered workshops are praised for "turning nonproductive lives into productive ones."[101] "Prevocational" programs are devised for people who almost certainly will not ever have work vocations in the conventional sense. And where people are so severely or profoundly retarded that they require custodial or nursing care, it is not unusual for their parents or other caregivers to make their lives "count" by writing about them or studying them.[102]

Despite or sometimes even because of these pressures, people who live with disabilities discover that limits on productivity may be more rigid and inflexible than the demands of organizational time. Recognitions that some problems cannot be solved and that both energies and lifetimes are limited are basic factors in existential crisis. Resolution of such crises is what the temporal organization prompted by disability is all about.

## NATURE

Much of what I have said here about disability and pace is based on the observation that disabilities encourage people to become aware of and learn to live with the body's real condition. Knowing when and how fatigue, drug reaction, muscle contraction, or even the hormone cycle or the pollination of ragweed will affect one's pace requires sensitivity to physical clues, some delicate, some gross, which most of us ignore. Obviously, it would be useful to all of us to be more sensitive to our bodies in this way as, indeed, the women's health movement encourages us to be.

Much of recent feminist literature on women's relationship to nature assumes that because women menstruate, give birth, and have traditionally been closer than men to illness, disability, and death, we have a more organic or "natural" awareness of our embodiment, which, however, may have been distorted by our adherence to masculine values.[103] This concept suggests that we might learn a good deal from women who are already acutely conscious of their bodies, as disabled women often are. However, there are problems with the concept of nature itself that block such communication. For example, the tendency to equate nature with the wilderness or at least the farm and to contrast it with the city, mechanization, and other "unnatural" environments poses real difficulties for people with disabilities. A person who depends on a respirator places a higher value on technology than on wildlife. A woman who uses a wheelchair has difficulty meeting other women in a meadow or wood. A woman whose body is paralyzed will experience the "natural rhythm" of her menstrual cycle in a much different way from most of us. Otherwise able-bodied people may experience back trouble after sleeping on floors or out of doors.

Of course it can also be argued that "nature is cruel and indifferent," that "death is a random, inevitable disaster."[104] Suzanne Massie found the response of fishermen to her son's hemophilia much more matter of fact than others' because they were close to "a *capricious* Nature" (italics added).[105]

So "the natural order, the corporeal ground of our intelligence,"[106] encompasses disability and death as well as birth and menstruation, the circulation of blood, the beating of the heart. This is what people with disabilities can teach us: not just how to "take time to smell the flowers," but also how respirators and microsurgery and microbes and "artificial" hormones become part of our nature, and how we can *decide* which pace is best synchronized with our physical and emotional and mental abilities.

CHAPTER

# GRIEF

Since the mid-1970s, people in mainstream American culture have believed that we know about the process of grief, thanks to the development of theories about the stages of the mourning process of dying or bereaved people. Stage theories of grief are usually based on the period of mourning that follows or closely precedes a death, but they have been applied to other major losses, including notably divorce and disability. People who live with disabilities experience grief in a different way, sometimes described as chronic sorrow. The imposition of stage models on this experience distorts it and limits our understanding of the psychology of mourning. Stage theories generally assume a time-limited "natural" progress through the stages, culminating in "acceptance," "reconciliation," or "resolution." Permanent disabilities, chronic illnesses, degenerative conditions and mental retardation or mental illness result in different kinds of mourning, which are cyclic or recurrent and which facilitate or require coming to terms with a changed, sometimes suffering self. Understanding this complex process is life changing because cultural pressures to deny its presence or to cope heroically are so strong.

The relationship between disability and grief is very complex, as it must take into account the enormous variety of disabilities and of individuals who live with them. My approach in this chapter is to emphasize the experience of mothers of children with severe physical or mental disabilities as reported in professional literature and in autobiographical accounts. This is the group about whom the concept of chronic sorrow was developed[1] and in whom the deficiencies of conventional stage theories of grief can be most readily observed. Their experience is also closest to my own experience, it has much in common with mourning over the death of a child, and it stands in contrast with the experience of individuals who are themselves disabled.

For feminists, the concept of chronic sorrow provides a way of understanding other losses in women's lives and a possible model for community-building based not on shared oppression but on relationships between women who have been changed by the cyclic deepening of the mourning process.

## PARENTAL SORROW

General agreement that mourning can be expected when parents learn that their child is disabled is based on the recognition that for the parents the disability represents the loss of the wished for, normal child[2] and, if the child is not a young infant, of the known nondisabled person. Other losses that complicate and validate the mourning include the loss of relationship or companionship (especially in cases of brain injury, degenerative diseases, and severe mental retardation), health, money, energy, sleep, self-esteem, and control. As with any loss, the mourners typically react to the initial shock with denial, disbelief, and isolation and with some combination of bargaining, sadness, and anger. The discovery of disability in childhood often includes the possibility that the child will die, so symptoms of anticipatory grief are common.

Although the mothers themselves may describe the impact

of the crisis as "like a death," the grief cannot be resolved in the same way because the disabled child not only does not die but also requires even more care than other children. Thus the characteristic advice to disabled adults—that they should take time to mourn[3]— is not applicable. The mourner takes on new tasks in contrast to the temporary respite usually accorded to bereaved persons after a death.[4] Compared with mothers whose babies died at birth, mothers of seriously disabled children who survive mourn less at the time the disability is discovered but more later on.[5] To "resolve" the grief would be to deny the continuity of the child's life. Moreover, the parent's grief is mixed with confusion and uncertainty.[6] Nor does the passage of time permit a resolution either of uncertainty or of grief. Even if the child is institutionalized or a degree of medical certainty is achieved, the crisis is not terminable by a single decision.[7]

Stage theories of grief are therefore inappropriate to these families. Recognition of such stages is useful, however. In the initial stage of shock, for example, alternation of sorrow and disbelief alleviates the trauma[8] and a subsequent period of psychological isolation[9] and/or preoccupation with loss[10] may be better understood through the analogy with grief over other losses. Most proponents of stage theories acknowledge that most people do not go through the stages in a linear progression, with a single end point; but in general they do assert that after attempting various strategies for overcoming the loss, the mourner comes to a point of acceptance, followed by resolution and perhaps transcendence.[11] In the case of multihandicapped children, these stages are as problematic and fraught with ambiguities as are the supposedly earlier stages of anger and denial.

Instead, parents' own descriptions of their sorrow (in contrast to descriptions in most professional literature) show a course of recurrent, cyclic sadness. Professionals who believe in the normalcy of a time-bound process of adjustment will see these reports of repeated sorrow as dysfunctional. In contrast, those who see "chronic" sorrow as a natural reaction to an ongoing tragic experience will offer a continuum of appropriate support services.[12] Parents themselves describe their sorrow as periodic[13] rather than continuous. The term "chronic" probably is somewhat less accurate than "recurrent," although it does suggest continuance over time.[14]

Examination of literature about "chronic grief reaction" after death demonstrates why the condition is (perhaps wrongly) considered pathological and why this judgment is inappropriate to the parents of a disabled child. John Bowlby, for example, acknowledges that the stages of grief alternate for some time in most mourners but states that eventually the mourner achieves emotional detachment,[15] surely an inappropriate resolution for the mother of a living child. Further, he asserts that the person with a dysfunctional "chronic grief reaction" is usually a person whose self-esteem and role identity is heavily invested in the lost (dead) person.[16] But mothers of disabled children are more than ordinarily expected to invest their energies and identities in the role of mother-of-disabled-child. Similarly, Phyllis Silverman describes the period of grief as taking place when a person is between roles (e.g., between wife and widow),[17] but the role of mother to a living child is continuous, even as the grieving continues. And Avery Weisman says that the grief process is completed when the factual loss of the person who has died becomes a significant memory.[18] But the disabled child is physically and psychologically present, even though the parent may have a significant memory of the "loss" of the nondisabled child (or hoped-for child). Ethel Roskies, writing about the mothers of Thalidomide children, says that their *initial* sorrow remained an "unhealed wound" several years after the children's birth and that the gradual discovery of additional disabilities postponed parts of the birth crisis.[19]

It is not surprising, then, that many occasions after birth or diagnosis evoke recurrences of grief.[20] These include developmental milestones of "normal" children (the age of school entry, graduation, adulthood, bike-riding, roller-skating, or driving a car) as well as developmental milestones associated with the disability (sucking or walking or talking, being fitted for a prosthesis or a wheelchair, being institutionalized) and events personally significant to the parent (hearing a symphony the child will never understand, seeing scenery she will never see). Although some of these events (age of majority, selection of the first wheelchair) are predictable, many are highly individual; and so it is not surprising that social workers overestimate the impact of the initial crisis and underestimate that of later grief episodes, even though they are sensitive to the chronic nature of parental sorrow.[21]

Mothers' own accounts of recurrent sadness often do focus on the same anniversaries as those recounting other forms of grief: birthdays, Christmas, Passover, graduation day. Paul Rosenblatt points out that such calendar events may be a product of Western culture. From a cultural viewpoint, he says, "it seems at least as strange that one would not note the anniversary of a significant loss in one's life as that one would."[22] Where a calendar event, such as Christmas or, in the United States, the Fourth of July, is almost universally observed by businesses and government as well as by individuals, the anniversary effect is almost obligatory. As Monica Dickens says, "Christmas is a stable landmark in a calendar gone crazy. Christmas is one of the few things you still do, of all the other things you don't do."[23] Such religious holidays as Passover and Yom Kippur, and rites of passage like First Communion or a Bar Mitzvah or Bat Mitzvah, carry a different emotional charge precisely because they are not so secularized and commercialized as Christmas but assert family and community identity in addition to their religious meaning. Further, the mother of a disabled child may be erratically stimulated to a recurrence of grief by even casual expressions of empathy by friends or professionals. Such grief episodes may be transient but intense.[24] As recurrent sorrow is in fact "a normal reaction to an abnormal situation," periodic grieving may be a strength rather than a pathological interruption of coping.[25] Just as temporary withdrawal from grief work may be a healthy coping strategy, enabling the mourner to recover her energies while performing the necessary work of everyday life and thus to facilitate the grief work itself,[26] temporary grieving may also be a coping strategy, enabling the one who does the daily maintenance work to attend to herself and her feelings and to learn that sorrow can be borne.[27] "There are some griefs," May Sarton says, "that will never heal and in the presence of them the only comfort perhaps is to recognize that fact."[28]

Where an illness is progressive or degenerative, periodic sorrow may include recurrence of earlier grief, but will also involve new losses. This fact may be obscured by beliefs that the grief process dates from diagnosis or the crisis of accepting a diagnosis. When post-polio problems affect a person who has made a long-term adjustment to the initial loss, the person may reexperience some grief over the original disability, just as every serious loss reevokes all past losses, but will also experience a new grief over a new disability.[29] Nancy Mairs says of living with MS, a disease whose symptoms are unpredictable but progressive, that "no amount of worry or anticipation can prepare me for a new loss. My life is a lesson in losses. I learn one at a time."[30] Her chronic incurable illness causes grief similar to that ascribed to the dying, but she says, "I can't be sure of the outcome"[31] and so cannot come to acceptance of what she cannot know.

In the case of grief over another person's degenerative disease, the mourner experiences the sense of unpredictability and repeated "lessons in losses," but these are compounded by repeated losses of the beloved person—or at least of the mourner's past relationship. "Just when you think you have 'adjusted,' the person may change and you will go through the grieving experience over again."[32] The person who was important to you has lost those qualities that constituted her or his self. The demented person, too, has lost a significant relationship, but does not consciously know it, so that the two bereaved persons cannot share the sorrow.

If the one with the degenerative disease is a child, the mother experiences relationship losses in an isolation that is reinforced by her role as physical caregiver and houseworker. The "trauma of eventlessness," which can be "a catastrophe of major proportions" for housewives,[33] is juxtaposed with the increasing absence of the cared-for child. Diapers must still (or again) be changed, feeding maintained, and breathing monitored as the personal relationship is gradually or periodically withdrawn. In the case of severe mental or emotional disability, even episodes of temporarily improved functioning may be occasions for grief. Since women's own identities are closely bound to the maintenance of relationships, disruption of the relationship is close to a total loss of self and requires construction of a new identity.[34] An identity based on being a mother and caregiver to a sick child is susceptible to multiple challenges as the child becomes more disabled, less available for reciprocal relationship, in need of more and more basic care, and reliant on mothering appropriate to a younger, smaller child.

## SOCIETAL EXPECTATIONS

Societal expectations complicate the process of recurrent grief in two apparently opposite ways: the requirement of mourning and the requirement of suppressing or denying mourning. People with visible disabilities and those who care for them are expected to mourn because the disability itself is seen as a tragedy, analogous to death, by the rest of society. Visible grief reassures the observers that their own values are appropriate and that their own nondisabled condition is "normal." Further, the disabled person is expected to be permanently enmeshed in the tragedy, because not to mourn would call into question the high value society in general places on health and fitness.[35] The requirement of mourning is well documented in the experience of adults with specific disabilities. For parents of disabled children, however, the expectation is different: they are expected to mourn in a time-limited process immediately following the crisis of birth or diagnosis. Like the dying or the bereaved, they cannot refuse sympathy, and if they display "inappropriate" (nonmourning) behavior, family members and professionals define them as dysfunctional.[36] Stephanie Simonton observes that "in our culture, people believe that when a life-threatening crisis occurs, we should all stop living and concentrate on grieving." The pressure on family members is to ignore the quality of their own lives in order to focus on the patient.[37] But the disabled child does go on living, requiring the mother's continuous focus, not just during the crisis but for life. Behavior that may be seen as failure to grieve during a crisis is commonly expected of an "adequate" mother during routine daily care.

Thus, after the crisis period, a requirement *not* to mourn becomes operative. And, indeed, suppression of sorrow in favor of a "heroic" dedicated mother pose may be admired and encouraged from the beginning, although pressure to bear up splendidly under tragic circumstances is more likely to be required of men than of women.[38] Our society prefers control of all public displays of grief,[39] but especially where the grief is over losses other than death.[40] When the disability is invisible or perceived as "less serious" than others, the expectation that the person who experiences it will not mourn, at least publicly, increases.[41] The idea that "good" mothers accept and love their children no matter what interacts with stage theories of grief to cause many mothers to perceive prolonged sorrow as a personal flaw. Kennedy found that mothers of disabled infants were aware of grief but hid it, considering it unacceptable.[42] Doctors often encourage crying for a brief period and then prescribe sedatives to suppress further grieving behavior.[43] Even when a death is imminent or has occurred, crying is likely to be labeled "regression" and the need for others called "infantile dependence"; mourners are urged to cheer up, look on the bright side, or permit themselves to be distracted.[44] Some religions specifically prohibit mourning,[45] our social norms deprive us of an adequate mourning period,[46] and our workplaces especially are organized to discourage attention to personal, emotional needs or even to illness.[47] It is not surprising, then, that parents are especially pressed to deny or not to recognize *chronic* sorrow, which indeed is perceived as pathological if the grief stage of "resolution" is defined as the appropriate healthy culmination of an early grief process.[48]

As all mourning is a personal process, for which "each person has his or her own calendar,"[49] the several people who may be experiencing grief over a disability are likely to have recurrences at different times and in different styles.[50] One person hopes for a cure, while another may immerse herself in the finality of the diagnosis or even pray for death; one is sad, another is preoccupied with medical decisions and relentlessly businesslike; one is depressed and one cheerful. In the case of death, where a family's grief is unsynchronized, the potential for "morbid bereavement reactions" is high.[51] In recurrent sorrow, unsynchronized grief is almost inevitable, though the people most attuned to the rhythms of caring may share some occasions of sorrow. If social pressure not to mourn overwhelms the individual's need to do so, depression and repression of all feelings are probable results.[52] When emotional reactions are suppressed, they remain latent and may be discharged as "unmotivated" depressions.[53] The mother of a disabled child may thus be chronically depressed both by the genuinely depressing nature of the child's present condition and by her repressed grief over its earlier crises. Encouraging her to cheer up in order not to depress the child compounds the mother's depression. She is a participant in the culture, too, and collaborates with the expectation of cheerfulness either by acting cheerful or by feeling guilty for not doing so. Grieving people generally try to reserve their sadness for private times.[54]

Where mourning is treated as weakness or self-indulgence,[55] there will be few or no cultural supports for grief. Thus the typical office leave of absence for funerals, if any, is extremely short, and sick leave for illnesses of family members or for medical appointments is usually nonexistent. Mothers are perceived as unreliable workers because they are more likely than fathers to take time off to care for children. To the very limited extent that we have rituals and other cultural supports for mourning, these are provided by religions, funeral homes, and family or community customs focused on death. Across cultures these rituals emphasize storytelling, repetition of traditional wisdom, sharing of food, and temporary permission to express strong feelings by laughing, crying, or singing. Mainstream American culture provides few of these ritual resources for mourning over death and none for mourning over other losses.[56]

The absence of cultural supports for repetitive storytelling is particularly harmful to those whose grief is chronic or repetitive. Therapy permits expression of emotions and storytelling, but it is usually based on a time-limited model of crisis intervention or on a stage theory of the grief process. Sometimes therapy encourages storytelling about old losses at the expense of direct attention to the present. More often it is directed toward grief work, identification of feelings, and recognition of the process that must be "worked through" to reach resolution. The storytelling rituals of formal bereavement affirm life: the life of the person who has died and the ongoing lives of the survivors. "There is a crucial difference between denying the tragedy, insisting that everything is for the best, and seeing the tragedy in the context of a whole life, keeping one's eye and mind on what has enriched you and not only on what you have lost."[57] To tell and retell the circumstances of a death or any other event that is for the teller a tragedy is to affirm its importance (in all its detail) and to affirm, as well, the storyteller's relationship to those events. Twelve-step programs encourage repetitive storytelling so that both tellers and listeners identify with the events described. Such stories are supposed to include "what we were like" and "what happened" when the drinker was drinking, for example, as well as "what we are like now" in recovery. This pattern of separation, initiation, and return characterizes ritual storytelling in many contexts.[58] Repetition of such stories is necessary for internalization, for acceptance of the reality of loss. The storyteller, along with other listeners, gets to hear her or his own story.[59] Telling it represents a commitment to facing the loss directly.[60] Each time it is retold, that commitment is renewed. But the person in recurrent grief has no ritual context in which to repeat her or his story. Indeed, it is unusual to have a close friend or therapist or support group willing to hear it again and again over many years.

There is no "rightful place" in our culture for the delivery of a living child with disabilities[61] and none for recurrent grief of family members at many points in that child's development. We do not even wear black arm bands during the weeks after the funeral,[62] so we are even more unlikely to "wear our hearts on our sleeves" when sorrow resurfaces months and years after a less definitive, more continuous loss. Therapists and parent support groups are beginning to recognize and validate chronic sorrow. The need for ritual, at least at such identifiable events as anniversaries, the point of institutionalization, or the move to independent living, has not been recognized, let alone met.

One possible argument against the legitimation of suffering[63] is that it could lead to chronic gloominess; but in fact rites of passage, like therapeutic expression of despair, have the opposite effect, permitting a return to an authentic optimism that is not based on denial.[64] The storytelling associated with funerals is not usually limited to retelling the tragic death, but provides a review of the whole life and thus allows for an integration of the sorrow-provoking episode with the rest of life. That is surely the emotional task of the one who experiences chronic sorrow.

## ACCESSIBILITY TO GRIEF

To make this review in the face of extreme cultural pressures against mourning requires a conscious decision to be accessible to grief. This is not to advocate wallowing in self-pity, although that is not necessarily a bad idea.[65] But knowing how to feel sadness without adding other emotions to dull the pain is an essential first step toward healing.[66] Willingness to experience the full range of grief-related emotions, including sadness, is difficult because doing so makes us vulnerable. That is why we have defenses in the first place. But vulnerability may be reinterpreted in a positive way.[67] It is only by acknowledging grief that we can obtain perspective on it. Phyllis Silverman, writing of the grief of birth mothers who give up their children for adoption, describes the process. The first step, she says, is "the acknowledgement that [the grief] exists and that she is . . . in mourning. . . . She must learn that she cannot be cured of her feelings and that she will never totally get over them."[68] Again and again bereaved people speak of rejecting tranquilizers because "I wanted to know what grief felt like."[69] For recurrent mourners, such openness is more difficult to attain because of the requirement of not mourning and because defenses are more practiced. But the ability to be realistic, "to know and feel and act as if you are in a bad situation; to live with that" is essential not only to successful bereavement work[70] but also to living with disability on a continuous basis.

Each episode of grief evokes remembrances of other losses. For both the disabled person and family members those losses include other episodes related to disability or illness. Marjorie Wagner says that the mourning she went through when she began using a wheelchair included not only grief over "the loss of using my legs" but also over falls that embarrassed her when she was a child, confusion over a leg operation that did not cure her, and the year of therapy she needed after another operation.[71] Such grieving makes possible the subsequent commitment to life: to using the wheelchair, in Wagner's case; to diapering the family member who used to be continent, in that of a family caregiver. Of course people can make these adaptations without mourning, but "tears cleanse. Cleansed eyes see more clearly. . . . If allowed out, the tears will usually end and the process of rehabilitation will begin."[72] I have been politically active on Jennifer's behalf periodically during her life, whenever she needed it, but retrospectively I understand that the most effective of those activities were those that followed a period of mourning. When she was institutionalized for the first time, I cried for days, mourning all the losses of her life, one by one, and some of my own losses as well, especially this latest, most devastating loss of my loved child and of my roles as her hands-on mother and protector. Only when I was accessible to grief and knew that it was appropriate and that I could live with it, that I would not die of it, could I take up a changed role as noncustodial mother and political advocate of people in institutions for the developmentally disabled.

Such mourning involves struggling to accept a fact of life, not of death, and this has the potential for an even more positive outcome in a changed relationship between the people involved.[73] In accommodating to the changed situation, the individual finds a new reality, not renouncing the past, but changing her relationship to it.[74] When Jennifer left home, I did not stop being her mother, but I did accept my own limitations in a way I never had before, acknowledging that I could not keep her safe. Her limitations deserved my sorrow; so did mine. What my recurrent sorrow teaches me is "that one is sometimes powerless in the face of one's own sadness."[75]

## COMMUNITY OF THE CHANGED

In making ourselves accessible to recurrent sorrow, we accept a state of existential crisis: "When life brings suffering to us, we must choose between the alternatives of entering the experience head on and trying to know its deepest and fullest meaning, or of turning aside from our own feelings and emotions with a denial that they exist and a pretense that we are unaffected by the dark side of life."[76] Having acknowledged a personal relationship to that dark side, the mourner may take a socially more difficult step by going public, "coming out" or speaking out as one who grieves. This is a critical period for anyone whose grief is not socially sanctioned. Admitting that we are sad when cheerfulness is prescribed is difficult enough. If the sadness is over a stigmatized disease, like AIDS or mental illness, the stigma compounds the problem. But mourning is a process of communicating feelings,[77] and locating a community in which such communication can take place is a crucial task for the mourner. That people who have experienced major losses often consider their compulsive repetitive storytelling a symptom of "craziness"[78] indicates how little this need is understood.

When mothers of children with disabilities reach the point of coming out as someone who grieves,[79] they characteristically describe themselves as having entered a community (usually invisible to others) of people who are permanently changed by suffering, by grief. People, they say, are divided into two kinds: "those who have known inescapable sorrow and those who have not." Inescapable or unassuageable sorrow changes life itself.[80] Because the sorrow cannot be changed, one's life-style and feelings have to be changed to accommodate it.[81] This is a sense of being both permanently sorrowful and permanently changed, of recognizing the sadness on other people's faces,[82] the vulnerability, the loss of innocence,[83] the recognition of our inability to control our lives or to protect our children.[84] "I know what it is," Helen Featherstone writes, "to stand powerless before the gods, to see a child I love hurt by forces I can neither name nor control."[85]

To know "that we haven't any special immunity to sorrow," that we are vulnerable, capable of suffering, and fragile,[86] is to confirm our humanness. "It has opened and enriched my life enormously, this sense that my frailty and need must be mirrored in others, that in searching for and shaping a stable core in a life wrenched by change and loss, change and loss, I must recognize the same process, under individual conditions, in the lives around me."[87]

Recognizing the others in the world who know this same thing and have changed their lives to incorporate that knowledge reconnects the isolated sorrowing person to other hurt people. Thus Susan Schiff found that her vulnerability to multiple sclerosis connected her to her parents' experience of the holocaust, Suzanne Massie's sorrow over her son's hemophilia connected her to the Russians who conceptualize suffering as a way to enlightenment, and Helen Featherstone's mourning over her multihandicapped son connected her to the other members of her parents group as well as to starving people pictured on television.[88] Albert Schweitzer said that we are not truly human until we see each other person's suffering as our own.[89] The community of persons permanently changed by chronic sorrow approaches that ideal.

It would be easy to interpret these connections as pathological or morbid, but the lived experience of connection through recurrent sorrow is a positive one. It affirms humanness by turning formerly private emotions outward.[90] It makes us, self-consciously, more nurturing; we respond to real losses by reaching out, by becoming more gentle, more kind.[91] If we can accept our own limits, we can accept the limits of others as well.[92]

The dilemma of the mother of a seriously disabled child is that she mourns the lost child even as she cares for the living one. She is both the bereaved mother whose child is gone forever and the mother whose child is fully present. "If one is to learn to live with the dead, one must first learn to live with the living."[93] That is exactly what she does, as a mother and as a member of the community of other changed persons.

Recognizing the discrepancy between their experience of sadness as a continuous background of their lives and conventional time-limited stage theories of grief, mothers of children with disabilities deepen our understanding of the implications of feminist theories about self-centering and therapeutic emphasis on experiencing one's own feelings. The mother's mental and spiritual task of living with the outer reality of the child as she is and at the same time with the inner reality of chronic sadness deepens our understanding of the complexity of holistic health. And the individual depth and rhythm of the mourning process adds texture and reinforcement to the concept of woman's closeness to nature.

CHAPTER

# MOTHER-BLAMING

Mothers of disabled children are among the most politically active advocates of disability rights and among the most articulate interpreters of disability experience as well. Our ability to learn from these women, however, is inhibited by bias against parents, especially mothers, among adolescent and adult citizens with disabilities, including disability rights activists, as well as among professionals and others in the community at large. The women's movement, which has been respectful if often ambivalent about motherhood, has generally ignored or discounted the experience of mothers of "handicapped" children. The fact that the rhetoric of the independent living movement is easily compatible with feminist thinking makes it easy to omit the complex problems of parenting multihandicapped, brain-damaged, and severely retarded children (among others). Indeed, efforts to change public policy to benefit people who can and should live independently as adults often directly harm those who require closer caregiving. Simple application of the "minority" model to disability civil rights further inhibits our ability to hear what these particular mothers tell us about their own experience.

My analysis is based on both personal and professional literature about children with disabilities and their families, as well as experience over several years with two parent groups: one of parents of multihandicapped young children and the other of parents of adults with mental retardation. My strong bias is toward crediting the mothers' own accounts. However, interpreting those accounts is complicated by the overlay of political ideas from both disability and feminist theory.

It is not unusual for people who are active in the disability rights movement to identify two groups, parents and professionals, as likely to harm the cause or to be suspect in their statements of support for disabled people. The linkage of these two is remarkable because in professional literature and in parent discussion groups, parents and professionals are frequently perceived as adversaries. "Parents" almost always means "mothers" in these discussions. When supposed adversaries are assumed to be equally at odds with the interests of a third group, and one of the groups is assumed to consist mainly of women, the situation seems ripe for feminist analysis. In fact, however, such analysis has not been attempted, even among feminists with disabilities.

In my own community, a division between two disability groups focused in part on the fact that the board of directors of the more conservative organization included no "consumers" of disability services, though it did include parents. The rival group, consisting exclusively at first of people with disabilities, eventually sought to include at least a token parent, a mother. As far as I know, none of the adversaries addressed the fact that many of the parents in the conservative group are fathers. As parental attitudes toward disabled children are frequently stereotyped under such categories as "maternal overprotection," the failure to distinguish between fathers and mothers seems significant. Informal discussion with women from the consumer group and with other participants in the independent living movement revealed a widespread, almost casual assumption that mothers of adults with disabilities want to keep their children dependent and confined.

As a feminist and the mother of three adult children, I find this highly unlikely.

"Professionals," however, have traditionally discounted mothers' experience on the grounds that mothers have failed in various ways to provide an environment that maximizes the disabled child's potential without overestimating her abilities, frequently assuming that the child's "treatment" should be the sole or central focus of the mother's life, though the mother should not, of course, be overprotective.

Far from linking professionals with parents, the pattern of mother-blaming suggests an even more improbable connection between very conservative professionals and very liberal civil rights activists, both of whom assume that mothers are to blame for problems of people with disabilities. To disentangle the reasons for these paradoxes, an examination of mother-blaming literature is useful.

## MOTHER-BLAMING BY PROFESSIONALS

Mother-blaming is pervasive in professional literature about disability, and its effects are a central theme in mothers' accounts of their experience. Anger at professionals is a dominant motif in parent support groups; the experience of being blamed is a principal source of such anger.[1] The classic case of mother-blaming is the "schizophrenogenic mother," who, as Osmond, Franks, and Burtle suggest, "should be looked upon as an iatrogenic disease."[2] Essentially the concept argues that "process schizophrenia" is caused by a "dominant, carping, punitive, generally unpleasant" mother and "reactive schizophrenia" by a "weak, vacillating and submissive" mother."[3] Theodore Lidz, an influential researcher on families of schizophrenics, found, for example, after a seriously flawed study of seventeen families, that "schizophrenia was a deficiency disease—a deficiency of the parents."[4] As we now know that schizophrenia involves a biochemical imbalance, the persecution of several generations of mothers for causing their children's mental illness seems particularly cruel. A similar situation obtains for infantile autism. Until quite recently, the mother, described as an "autistic parent,"[5] was held responsible for the psychopathology of the child.[6] Such traits as overrigid perfectionism or extreme rage were identified in the mother, and children were "treated" by being separated from the labeled parent. Today we know that autism is a biological disorder that, like schizophrenia, has nothing to do with maternal rejection.[7] Moreover, studies of autistic children's families show no significant differences between their parents and those in matched "normal" families.[8] Family problems do not cause autism, though they may result from or be intensified by the stress of raising an autistic child.[9]

Although few observers of mental retardation go as far as Maud Mannoni, who attributes the problems of retarded children to their mothers' *"fantasy"* of their lifelong dependency,[10] stories like this one are common: " Bobby was one of seven. The *father was unemployed and mentally ill*. The *parents* were said to be totally overwhelmed by the problem of looking after the children. They were unable to cope with Bobby and gave him very little stimulation. . . . although Bobby probably had limited potential to start with, his condition was made worse by the lack of a constant mother figure: *by his mother's inability to cope"* (italics added).[11] The casual slippage from "parents" to "mother" is compounded by a parallel loss of focus on the impact of the father's mental illness and unemployment. The reporter does not even raise the question of how the father's behavior may have influenced Bobby's "condition." A similar analysis of children of men who were prisoners of war in Vietnam found that the fathers were distressed and emotionally distant, that the children had many emotional problems, and that the childrens' problems were the mothers' fault because they were disturbed by their husbands' problems.[12] Although these families had no biologically caused dysfunctions, the pattern of attributing all emotional difficulties to the mother is exactly the same as that in studies of families in which the child has neurological disabilities.

Paula Caplan and Ian Hall-McCorquodale found in a survey of articles in mental health journals of the 1970s and early 1980s that mothers were blamed for seventy-two kinds of problems in their children, "ranging from bed-wetting to schizophrenia, from inability to deal with color-blindness to aggressive behavior, from learning problems to 'homicidal transsexualism.' "[13] The list includes agoraphobia, arson, hyperactivity, "premature mourning," and many others. Caplan points out that "not a single mother was ever described as emotionally healthy, although some fathers were, and no mother-child relationship was said to be healthy, although some father-child ones were described as ideal."[14]

Mother-blaming is so ubiquitous in professional literature about disability that I could easily fill pages just citing horrible examples. The commonest of these negative judgments are that mothers are overanxious, overprotective, out of touch with reality, guilt ridden, arrested in denial, malicious, indifferent, emotionally divorced, lacking in empathy, rejecting, unconcerned, overinvolved, hysterical, and/or emotional.[15] Research on which parent-blaming conclusions are based is frequently biased in terms of the questions asked, preconceptions about family dynamics, populations selected for study, and by outright misinterpretation of data.[16] For example, one researcher described maternal attitudes toward children with bladder extrophy as varying "from direct abandonment to extreme overprotection involving refusal to bear more children and slavish devotion to the damaged child."[17] There is no consideration here of the possibility that devotion might be a job requirement or that deciding not to have another child might be a normal, responsible decision.

An award-winning book by George Henderson and Willie Bryan, which is generally sympathetic and helpful to people with disabilities and their families, nevertheless includes this remarkably parent-blaming passage:

> Few parents of a child with a disability listen to their hearts. Instead, they treat their child like a book to be read, interpreted, and even marked on. Moreover, as they do with such a book, when the child becomes uninteresting or difficult to understand, parents give him or her away or throw him or her away. Sometimes a child with a disability becomes "the enemy" in the family—someone to be conquered, locked away, and guarded. In other families, a child with a disability becomes a pitiful person that parents and relatives call "poor baby." In rare, beautiful instances, children with disabilities are cared for and about as persons.[18]

Rare, beautiful instances, indeed. In my experience, in literature by parents, and in professional literature based on parents' own statements, such instances are common, the norm.

## DISABILITY AND FEMINIST MOTHER-BLAMING

The reason Henderson and Bryan's book received an award was the sensitivity they demonstrate toward the rights and abilities of individuals with physical disabilities. The insensitivity and condemnatory tone of the passage I have cited is very different from the respect with which they view other experiences of people with disabilities. It is, however, consistent with parent-blaming by some disability rights activists. This excerpt from a disability newsletter explains the bias: "If anything is a cornerstone of disability rights, it is that we have control over our own bodies, and we are in charge of making decisions about our own lives. We, disabled people. Not our parents. Not our doctors. For us, these people have for long hindered and held us back. We do not consider such people to speak 'for us.' "[19] This passage also shows why the language of the disability rights movement is easily assimilated into discussion of feminism—too easily, for the ideology of independence does not address situations in which the child or the adult is genuinely, permanently dependent. The issue goes beyond the Baby Doe case addressed later by the newsletter writer. The reasoning that because parents and doctors "have for long hindered and held us back," only people with disabilities should make disability decisions assumes that differences among disabilities are not significant and that parents necessarily will not act in the child's interests. It is not appropriate to assume that an intelligent, well-educated, articulate individual with mild cerebral palsy knows more about the needs of the mentally retarded, incontinent, 150-pound adult who has multiple daily seizures than does her nondisabled mother who has cared for her since her birth.

In the two Baby Doe cases, the parents of two infants, "Baby Doe" and "Baby Jane Doe," one with Down's syndrome and one with spina bifida, on the advice of doctors but not of persons with disabilities, chose to withhold life supports from the babies. The parents' decisions were challenged in the courts and in public discussions. Disability rights advocates argued that the parents could not give "informed consent" because they were not informed about the positive aspects of life with disabilities. Many, like the newsletter writer cited above, argued that only people who themselves have disabilities should make these life and death decisions. However true it may be that parents are inexperienced with Down's syndrome and spina bifida, the issue in these cases finally was whether the parents, whose loving attitudes toward the babies were obvious and whose lives would be directly affected by the decisions, or hospital-based medical review committees or federally empowered Baby Doe squads should make the decision.[20] Feminists have more reason to suspect representatives of hospitals and government than individual mothers.[21]

Of course, feminists are no more exempt than other people from the mistrust of mothers. Although we have attended rather carefully to the mothers' own voices since the mid-seventies, when Adrienne Rich's *Of Woman Born* was published,[22] mother-blaming has continued unabated in forms ranging from Nancy Friday's castigation of her mother for repressing the daughter's sexual expression[23] to Nancy Chodorow's and Dorothy Dinnerstein's advocacy of male parenting as the solution to the psychodynamically induced cultural problems caused by female mothering of infants.[24] What these accounts have in common with mother-blaming by people with disabilities is an underlying assumption of maternal omnipotence. It is precisely the same assumption that underlies professional mother-blaming. To assert that schizophrenia is caused by poor mothering is to suggest that mother alone has the power to form the child's personality. The remarkable tenacity of this idea among feminists who in other contexts know perfectly well that men and patriarchal institutions have a great deal to do with human options is probably a result of the fact that all of us have been daughters and only some of us mothers. Several feminists, commenting on young women's treatment of old members of our community, have observed that the older women are expected to be nurturing, supportive, almost stereotypical grandmothers. "What they want—no, demand—from me is unconditional love and service. Their efforts to control my behavior take many forms, but are often distinguished by explosive intensity or irrational anger. . . . lots of negativity and trashing. . . . I have become the Bad Mother or the Wicked Witch. Then their mirror says 'self-centered, overpowering, coercive, withholding.' "[25] "Their behavior," says Marjory Nelson, "is so similar to the ways I treated my mother."[26] Nelson, who has some physical disabilities related to her aging, carries the analysis further, as she understands that she, like the young lesbians who recoil from her weakness, has based her self-concept on strength in an effort to prove her superiority to her mother. Seeing the weak side of ourselves as victims, we develop "the habit of blaming everyone else for what goes on in our lives. The prime scapegoat in this endeavor is mother"[27]—and, for the younger feminists, the older women in the movement, especially in their roles as "founding mothers." Such scapegoating helps to account for some women's unwillingness to learn from feminists' political experience in the sixties and seventies.

Nelson's association of feminist mother-blaming with disability is unusual, as one important complaint of old women is that they are assumed to be disabled merely by virtue of age.[28] Her recognition that we blame mothers for our own weaknesses—or our fear that we may be weak—helps to explain mother-blaming by women with disabilities as they attempt independent living in young adulthood. Having experienced weakness and vulnerability in the family, certainly the safest place to express these conditions, the individual blames mother for having caused them and for perpetuating them through her care.[29] Mother here becomes the "magic momma" in two ways: she has caused the weaknesses, and if she only tried, she could cure them. Roberta Cepbo says that as a child she "must have had a firm conviction, that, if I grieved enough about my deformed feet and back, Mom would be able to find a way to change them into what they were meant to be. What a burden to lay on my dear mother—the albatross of impossible expectations."[30]

Psychoanalytic feminism attributes these impossible expectations to the internalized mother of infancy who seemed all-powerful to the baby because she provided or failed to provide for its needs. Kim Chernin, paying more attention than most psychodynamic interpreters to the mother's subjectivity in the transaction, says, "It is from the mother's own sense of failure to conform to this divine imaging of the Great Mother that the child also comes to believe in the mother's failure. And to be, therefore, unable to forgive the mother for shrinking and diminishing and frustrating."[31] Harriet Goldhor Lerner, surveying feminist psychodynamic theory, points out that whether or not it directly blames mothers, it is preoccupied with the mother-child dyad at the expense of a broader understanding of family dynamics.[32] Even where the positive aspects of mothering are stressed, this mother-focused perspective implicitly holds mothers responsible.[33] Nancy Chodorow and Susan Contratto, notwithstanding Chodorow's important role in the development of the psychoanalytic theory that Lerner describes, point out that feminist theory continues to be preoccupied with the irrational concept of maternal responsibility.[34]

The fantasy of maternal omnipotence is at the root of mother-blaming among professionals and others who are concerned with disabilities. It holds mothers responsible for the reactions of everyone else to the disability,[35] for the societal restrictions that make home care seem like the only alternative to repressive institutions, and for the discomfort of the disabled person herself. Although psychodynamic theory locates the source of the fantasy in early childhood, it is commonly acted out in adolescence. In middle-class, white American culture, blaming mother for children's difficulties is institutionalized. The child, longing to evade responsibility for her or his own life and culturally discouraged from seeing its socio-political component, turns on the most convenient and least dangerous target, mother. Erik Erikson, reflecting in 1968 on changes in his clinical experience since the 1940s, said that "at one time we cautiously tried to prove to sensitive young people that they also hated the parents they depended on," but now, in the late sixties, "they come to us with an overtly ugly or indifferent rejection of all parents and we have difficulty proving to them that they also really like them—in a way."[36] That statement was written at about the time that the contemporary feminist movement was forming. Its earliest theorists were mainly members of the parent-rejecting generation Erikson describes. In adolescence, the fact that the mother tries to enforce the cultural rules of patriarchy and that she cannot alleviate the child's emotional and physical discomforts[37] come together. Acculturated to see feminine characteristics as negative, the adolescent appreciates in the mother only her masculine qualities and depreciates her femininity; yet, as Emily Hancock points out, the stereotype of femininity is so strong that some women are unable to see that it does not apply to the mother with whom they live, who does not act out the stereotypical qualities.[38] Where feminine qualities are perceived, they are rejected; where they are absent, they are assumed to be there. Maria Lugones describes the dynamic in her own life: "I was unwilling to become what I had been taught to see my mother as being. . . . to love her was supposed to be of a piece with both my abusing her and with my being open to being abused." Lugones locates the abuse of mother in "using, taking for granted, and demanding her services," pointing out that since all other family members have the same entitlement, the mother has little left of herself.[39] As Judith Arcana points out, the dilemma for the feminist mother in this situation is separating the child's "true need/desire for growing independence and autonomy from the culturally induced denial of his mother."[40] The feminist daughter faces the same dilemma; her ability to find a feminist solution depends in large part on her ability to see her mother as also a woman and herself as one who has felt entitled to abuse or exploit that woman, her mother. It is an identification that has frequently been delayed until the daughter becomes herself a mother.

Among people with disabilities there are some complicating factors: adolescence may be extended because of the disability; departure from mother's home may be delayed by lack of accessible housing or support services; the responsibility for needed treatment and for political advocacy may fall upon the mother by design or default. The disabled adult child is likely—even, as we have seen, encouraged—to blame these facts on maternal overprotectiveness; the mother, to see them as inescapable obligations. A woman who has spent her life adapting to her child's special needs and acting as the child's advocate is unlikely to relinquish these roles easily,[41] especially if no alternatives are available without further advocacy. In the early stages of the community-centered approach to mental retardation, for example, keeping the child in the community meant, in effect if not in theory, keeping the child in the parent's home. As this created problems for the parents, they sought professional help and became stereotyped as a pathological group. When they became aggressive about finding such help and politically active on behalf of their children, "pseudoprofessionality" became part of the parental role, at least for middle-class parents.[42] Pseudoprofessionality and aggression are stereotypes somewhat at odds with traditional femininity; the mother, then, is set up as overpowering and controlling, an overwhelming maternal caricature whose influence can be escaped by the maturing child only with a fight. Instead of appreciating maternal protection and advocacy, the child rebels against it. The mother, in turn, resents the child's ingratitude: "I knew I had saved your life more than once and what did I get in return but your disdain. Far from being grateful, you resented me." Strikingly, this mother continues: "The more obvious it became, the more guilty and defensive I felt because *I know you were justified*. . . . Your behavior was a constant reminder of my shortcomings and inadequacies. I couldn't reconcile my actions with my ideas of *what a mother should be. . . . I should have been the one to protect you*" (italics added).[43] Instead of being credited for what she has done, for what the child is able to accomplish, the mother accepts responsibility for what has gone wrong, including the daughter's mother-blaming. Roberta Cepko, observing her own mother's willingness to take the blame, says, looking back, that "I never believed it was mom's fault," but at the time, she had pulled away from mother's comforting hands, "trembling with bitterness, annoyed at her sympathy and gentleness, wanting not to be comforted but to vent my rage at the person most vulnerable, the one who loved me most."[44] The daughter's need to express rage and the mother's willingness to accept responsibility lock them in conflict.

## MOTHERS' ACCOUNTS

One serious problem with the mother-blaming professional literature described above is that it is seldom written by people who have themselves mothered children with disabilities.[45] Maryellen Walsh, describing methodological problems in research on schizophrenia, points out what she sees as the most obvious and most overlooked element: "None of the researchers . . . had long-term live-in experience with a schizophrenic, watching a human proceed from apparent normalcy to evident illness over a period of a quarter of a century." Moreover, Walsh notes that the researchers were men and one woman without children, "who did not know in a practical way what it means to bring up a child."[46] Real life mothers, even of nondisabled children, suffer from children's beliefs that their mothers should be always available, always giving, never withholding, while also providing absolute freedom. Experienced mothers recognize that even if we could provide these services, we should not, because children need to learn about reciprocity and collaboration.[47] Where serious disabilities are involved, both the "failure" to be perfectly giving and the likelihood of being seen as abusive are increased. Consider, for example, the family life of a child with cystic fibrosis: "Imagine, if you will, that every day of your child's life you forced medicines upon her, although they never seemed to do any good; you required her to participate in uncomfortable regimens, which you supervised; and then, for thirty minutes or more, twice a day, you turned her upside down and pounded on her. And this never seemed to help either."[48]

Adolescents who have no disabilities have difficulty accepting their mothers' individuality and separating the real woman from the maternal stereotype; dependence is always an issue in this separation. For children whose dependence is reinforced by physical or mental disabilities, the issue is compounded. Listen to these mothers of sons:

> No matter how much I suppressed my concern and tenderness, Eric still suspected me of harboring some. He was not abusive, not overtly cruel, he simply behaved most of the time as if I did not matter and did not really exist. . . . Eric behaves as if the word 'mother' was a dirty word.[49]

> "You're no real mother," he hissed in my face. "If you were you'd do something to stop the pains. . . . You'd stop my suffering. You're not saying anything, are you? That's because you know what I'm saying is true. . . ." He called me ugly names. And when he stopped, breathless, torment and loathing were in his eyes. . . . "Say something!" he screamed, and with that he struck me with all the mixed-up fury in his plagued body, struck me violently across the face.[50]

My own experience with a daughter incorporated barely controlled violence combined with a devastating reversal of the usual process of doing less for and talking more to the adolescent. Jennifer's deteriorating mental condition meant that my years of preparing her for independence ironically turned out to be the evidence of inadequate mothering of a woman who relentlessly became more dependent. I learned this at the very time when the disability rights movement began to castigate mothers for wanting their children to be dependent and to work toward eliminating the intermediate care facilities that provide the kind of structure my daughter requires. Merely labeling her independent because she is an adult obscures her needs for protection and care.

Mothers' reports of their own experience reflect heavy physical, economic, and emotional burdens and strong societal pressures against acknowledging these. The requirement of heroism coupled with an equally strong requirement to treat the experience as "normal" and to incorporate the roles of trainer and therapist into that of nurturer are compounded by the probability of "perpetual parenthood."

Perpetual parenthood is not a possessive maternal whim for mothers of people with mental disabilities as well as many with severe physical disabilities. Not only must we provide for food, shelter, and financial management but also for physical care including diapering, seizure management, and sometimes physical restraint, and for self-protection against back injuries from lifting a heavy uncooperative adult as well as from bites and scratches and blows.[51] Even when adequate institutional placements are available, they are often unexpectedly temporary, their quality must be continuously monitored, and the need to plan beyond the mother's death is a pervasive concern.

Even where the disabilities are relatively mild, the mother's responsibility is lifelong:

> I am responsible for where she lives; whether or not she's happy, or at least given every chance to be happy; how close she gets to achieving her potential, whatever it may be. I'm responsible for getting her teeth checked and her hair styled and for keeping her in dresses and jeans and gym shoes. Forever. Whether I like it or not. . . . Secretly, I am convinced that nothing *can* happen to me because I have to take care of Victoria. An illogical concept, to be sure, and smacking of arrogance. Lonely, too.[52]

Strikingly, "perpetual parenthood" is often combined (as it is for Victoria's mother) with another status that is also unacknowledged in our society: noncustodial motherhood. Historically there have been many situations in which women have chosen or been forced to have someone else care for their children. Only a generation or two ago, parents of multihandicapped children were strongly encouraged to do so. Yet the ideology of the nuclear family in our culture is so strong that this pattern has been invisible and the variations of class and individual circumstance as well as disability have been hidden. The result has been a dichotomy between all-day-every-day-mothering and not mothering. "The horrible effect of this is that many women who come to know they cannot provide daily care for their children believe they must somehow give up being mothers altogether. There is no construct, no language for positions between the all-or-nothing duality. There is no talk of nurturing mother-child bonds apart from daily live-in caretaking."[53] To assume the significant lifelong obligations and emotional ties of perpetual motherhood and at the same time suffer the invisibility of noncustodial mothering places a woman in a classic female dilemma: denial of her own reality.

## FEMINIST PERSPECTIVES

Whether the mother-blaming comes from professionals or from people with disabilities, whether it represents scapegoating or a psychological strategy for individuation, I think feminist analysis based on believing the women's own stories would show that inappropriate analysis of maternal behavior inhibits our ability to understand what is really going on in these relationships. For example, mothers of children with disabilities often make very subtle adaptations to the biological-psychological needs of these children, a form of synchrony. The behavior that results from this experience (anticipating the child's needs and moods, forestalling out of control behavior by exercising parental management) is usually labeled "symbiosis" or "controlling" rather than synchrony. When a woman, so labeled, describes what her life is really like, she cannot be heard.

Similarly, a mother's statement that problems in the family result from stress caused by living with disability will almost always be discounted because research on families of disabled children, usually initiated because the mother seeks help, find that the families are already distressed. Only very recently have a few researchers begun to question the assumption that the family's distress causes rather than results from the child's disability.[54] Although a study published in 1972 found that parents' estimates of their child's developmental functioning coincided with the findings of psychological tests,[55] parents I have met in the 1980s and 1990s uniformly agree that their judgments in such matters are assumed by most professionals and by friends and neighbors as well to be biased, either positively or negatively.

Mother-blaming keeps the difficulty of achieving independence or remaining dependent a private matter. Even politically knowledgeable individuals who know, for example, what it takes to pass ordinances requiring wheelchair ramps or to fund adaptive equipment sometimes revert to the assumption that individuals or families choose to make independence difficult once these environmental modifications are in place. Listening thoughtfully to mothers' own descriptions of their lives prevents this simplification. Interviews with mothers of children with thalidomide-induced disabilities led Roskies to reconsider a basic premise of her research: "Our data strongly suggest that society . . . played as vital a role in shaping the meaning and course of events as did the mothers and children themselves. It was this fact that made us question whether we had not been using the term 'mother-child relationship' as a misnomer for what was actually a triangular relationship involving mother, child, and society."[56] The mother-blaming scenario obscures the responsibility of "society," by far the strongest of the three in the relationship. In the study of "thalidomide mothers," Roskies found that the records of the rehabilitation institute that defined for these mothers the nature of their experience consistently reinterpreted their behavior to discredit them: "If parents complained of the lack of highchairs, they were 'disguising their guilt.' If a mother was told that her child would be kept for one week and the ensuing hospitalization lasted six months, the mother's rising anxiety was interpreted as separation anxiety. An attempt to form a parents' group was seen as a 'reflection of guilt.' "[57] While the institution itself taught a philosophy of normalization, any difficulty in attaining normality because of the child's very serious disabilities was attributed to the mother's failure to "accept" the child.[58] Recognizing that she is indeed faced with a serious problem is essential to the self-concept of each of these mothers, so the institution's mother-blaming serves only to disguise the fact that the philosophy of normalization is faulty in that it denies the reality of the disability and its social impact.

When we assume that mothers socialize our children in a sociopolitical vacuum, we do more than render difficult the mother's life; we are implicitly or explicitly exonerating the father of all responsibility. Often the mother-blaming scenario is consciously based on the male-centered psychodynamic theory that considers separation from the mother a necessity for both sexes, "based in the notion that continuing intimacy with our mothers necessarily breeds immaturity, emotional incompetence and lengthy dependence."[59] Chodorow's and Dinnerstein's solution, involving the father in primary parenting, does not challenge this assumption. Instead, it expands the privatization of responsibility to both parents, while ignoring "the fact that almost all men are unsuited for the job by virtue of male socialization, which is, essentially, masculinity training."[60] To the extent that these theorists do recognize the deficiencies of male socialization, they attribute them to the psychological structures that men derive from having been mothered exclusively by women.

Beyond infancy, mothers are supposed to rear "well-adjusted, obedient, achieving, nonalienated," and above all independent children and to do so "in a callous and ruthless social order."[61] One reason the role of that social order remains obscure is that the process of mothering is essentially hidden in the private domain traditionally assigned to women. To devalue relationships, nurturance, emotional effectiveness, and the physical work associated with family maintenance in contrast to masculine independence, competition, rationality, and power[62] is to "set up" the mother of a child with disabilities to be unseen and unheard in the very institutions on which she depends for the child's survival and well-being. When people with disabilities blame mother, they may be redirecting their feelings of frustration and anger from the disability itself to mother, but they just as probably are redirecting it from the fathers (personal and institutional) who are perceived as more important and less safe.[63] "This blaming of the mother is not just scapegoating; it serves a more profound purpose: It allows us to avoid looking directly at the consequences of our own morality of power. By identifying ill . . .

with the relatively powerless in a culture . . . we avert our eyes from the father, the principle of power, and retreat from confrontation with our own values."[64]

A key insight of the disability rights movement is that the concept of "normality" is the source of many of our problems. Feminism would add that normality is defined by men with male experience as the standard. Devaluation of maternal experience keeps this insight in the private realm, as a substantial part of the mother's task is to normalize the child's appearance or behavior as much as possible. When the disabled child and her mother violate this obligation, they threaten the social order, forcing society to confront their difference.[65] Beth Browning suggests that this is precisely what the parents of Baby Jane Doe did as well: they challenged "the tradition of female sacrifice to the role of nurturing resource and compulsory-compensator for the inadequacies of society."[66]

Browning's analysis suggests an important function of the ethical debates over the Baby Doe decisions. They expose the usually privatized difficulties of parenting severely disabled children in the absence of societal supports. Although mother-blaming has been a prominent aspect of these debates, it has also been clear that such private solutions as adoption or foster parenting do not address the larger social problems exposed by these cases. Families do not create problems in isolation from the political and economic processes of their time.[67] Analyses of family dynamics that focus on the mother-child dyad or on the nuclear family as a closed system fail to acknowledge the realities of male dominance in the first place and the privatization and subordination of family life in the second.[68]

To address the social dimension of these problems is not to ignore the interpersonal relationships involved. On the contrary, it is by "coming to terms with the mother-daughter relationship" and "freeing the feminine qualities that the culture denigrates" that women can begin to uncover what is really going on, to stop blaming mother, and to build on women's strengths.[69] When we learn "to rage because of how terribly we have been mothered but including now in this rage our mothers as daughters with a right to their own despair: then we shall have liberated an anger that indicts not the mother but a social system that has never ceased to suppress women."[70]

The passage I have just quoted refers specifically to the mothering of daughters with eating disorders. It is important to remember that most such analyses are culturally biased, based on the experience of white, middle-class, North American women. As Linda Tschirhart Sanford and Mary Ellen Donovan point out, "not all of our mothers were miserable and unfulfilled. And not all women feel they have cause to blame their mothers." Sanford and Donovan quote a black woman: "I think this hating-your-mother trip is something for white girls who have a lot of time on their hands."[71] The serious issue of class bias in connection with the disability experience of mothers is rarely addressed but is central to the expectations placed on mothers by society. Henderson and Bryan, describing "parents who care about their child with a disability," describe an idealized set of attributes, most of which involve skillful interaction with professionals and the ability to seek out and interpret professional literature, concluding, "Caring parents tend to be well read."[72] Besides the underlying assumption that parents have extensive educational and intellectual resources, this passage reveals a still less examined assumption that *caring* can be equated with rational, intellectual mastery of facts. Not only does this assumption conflict with the cultural assignment to women of the affective components of human experience, it also denies the fact that the disability itself profoundly impacts the nature of care. Paula Caplan, who spent years working with children who have learning disabilities, observes that schools rely on mothers to provide "technical help" with the children's education "even though, *by definition* learning difficulties are not caused by motivational problems or lack of exposure to learning." When the mother, after reading "all the books" on how to teach the child to read, cannot succeed in doing so, nevertheless "the teacher says I should keep working with Jessica, but I don't know what else to do."[73] Notice that this mother tries to do the impossible task. Not only does she have the skills (including the ability to read "all the books") to permit her to attempt it, but also the willingness to cooperate with the illogical system. Judith Arcana suggests that such willingness may be in part a function of class, as middle-class women, having more access to economic privilege, are more likely to support the social institutions that support such privilege. Indeed, Arcana found that "minority mother-blaming increases as more [minority] individuals and families move into the middle-class, become educated to misogynist theories of the family, and take on attitudes of the higher status group."[74]

When we turn from a focus on maternal responsibility to a focus on society, we see political factors more clearly. For example, discrediting maternal observations of client behavior enables the representatives of state agencies to place multihandicapped mentally retarded clients in inappropriately "independent" group homes rather than more closely supervised and more expensive intermediate care facilities. In this way a liberal ideology (independence is desirable and possible for all) serves a conservative political purpose (reducing investment of state funds in a welfare client).

## DIFFERENCE

A feminist analysis that credits mothers' descriptions of their own experience and considers mother-blaming suspect whether it comes from conservative professionals or liberal disability-rights advocates uncovers issues that appropriately belong in the feminist discussion of difference. Both feminists and disability-rights activists have minimized such important differences as those between a mentally retarded adult who is inclined to physically harm herself or others and a mentally able paraplegic who requires a different kind of attendance to facilitate her living independently. Adopting the same minority rights platform from which to view these very different women's situations is sure to serve one or the other badly. Attending closely to what their different mothers tell us about what their daily lives are really like and *believing them* may enable us to see much more clearly the ways all differences interact with such key women's issues as dependence and body awareness. Moreover, such attention to specific differences will surely make our political positions on public policy more sophisticated, more diverse, and more useful to the individual lives of different women.

Feminists have easily added disability rights to the list of civil rights issues that concern us and have enthusiastically added politically correct disability language to our agendas along with verbal commitments to wheelchair access and American Sign Language interpreters. Almost immediately, however, we came up against a phenomenon very similar to that we encountered with race and class: the idea that "those women are never satisfied." Like the dilemma, the reason is the same: women are not all alike. There are significant differences not merely among their physical needs, but also among their requirements for appropriate care. Women who have visual, auditory, or mobility impairments can and do articulate clearly what they need in order to do what they want to do in mainstream society. Women who have mental or severe multiple disabilities often cannot communicate or analyze what they need in order to function comfortably in the world. In many, perhaps most, cases the people who understand them best and who are best able to interpret their verbal and nonverbal attempts to explain their needs (and goals) are their mothers. Mother-blaming deprives us of access to understanding of these different women. This is not to say that the mother's own needs are identical with or irrelevant to the daughter's, but that their often profoundly interrelated lives are different from those others on which we base our assumptions. Elly Bulkin's comments on other differences are especially relevant here: "As long as heterosexism and racism remain pressing issues only for those who are most directly affected by them, each woman remains boxed off from those women who are significantly different from her—and whose lives and words have the potential to enrich her own. Within this context, each woman suffers a significant deprivation—loss of knowledge, fear of change, separation from any but an illusory sense of connection with all women."[75]

Not only do mothers' descriptions of their own experience give us access to the individual lives of their children, some of whom cannot speak (or eat or move or even breathe) for themselves, but also—and this is a respect in which they are peculiarly inaudible—to their own lives.

An inevitable effect of mother-blaming is that the mother's own perspective, her insight, is discounted. She becomes merely a discredited appendage to the important different person, the identified minority group member, with the real disability. This fact has far-reaching political implications for all women. For example, one common "liberal" argument in the debate over reproductive rights advocates refusal of sterilization to mentally retarded women on the grounds that they cannot make an informed decision to be sterilized but have an absolute right to reproduce if they choose to. This argument is almost always used to block a mother's request for sterilization based on her experienced and realistic belief that the retarded daughter cannot adequately handle the birth and rearing of a child and that the mother herself cannot do so for her daughter.[76] To consider this daughter's "right" to bear a child without attending to what her mother's life and experience are like is to deliberately and cruelly oversimplify a crucial women's issue. It also obscures significant public policy questions: the absence of social supports for mothers with disabilities and for mothers of children with disabilities; the relative abilities of judges, social workers, and mothers (able-minded and mentally retarded) to judge child-rearing capability; the economic impact of maternal unemployment on child care and nutrition, among other things; and the lack of diverse supportive services for retarded adults who live in the community. In these cases, as in the Baby Doe cases, the mother, because she is personally involved, may not be the most "objective" judge of the ethical values involved; but as feminists I think we must seriously question whether objectivity is desirable in such a situation and whether societal institutions, even when they are implementing announced goals of disability rights groups, are more appropriate decision makers than the women who know from living with the specific person's particular disabilities what her or his life is and will be like. The fact is that there is no easy answer to a moral dilemma. But we do have good reason to believe that those personally involved are more likely to recognize the complexity and the psychological and emotional relationships involved.

Mother-blaming enables us to avoid these difficult issues and to operate out of more abstract judgments about legal rights. What we can learn about difference by attending to both the disabled woman *and her mother* should move us away from the dichotomies suggested by legal rights and wrongs and away, as well, from the notion that the person with disability is necessarily an "other" to the mother (or vice versa). We need to hear both voices; they need to hear each other; and each must *be believed* if difference is to inform our feminism (and feminism, our differences).

Strong cultural pressures cause mothers of children with disabilities to "normalize" their children's lives and to behave as if the family's dynamics were "normal." Succeeding in this form of passing renders the mother's real burdens invisible and reinforces the idea that she is merely but irrevocably identified with the role of mother. If, eventually, her child leaves her home for independent or supervised living, her status as a permanently responsible, noncustodial mother is masked by the ideology of independence and the culture's refusal to acknowledge noncustodial motherhood. Feminist views of motherhood, based as they are on a critique of the patriarchal family and of dependence, further distort our perception of the central issues in these women's lives. An "objectifying reverence for the oppressed"[77] may be accompanied by an objectifying hostility toward motherhood. A sound analysis of difference based on the experience of disability should objectify neither disability nor motherhood. Instead, we should focus on these women's difference. "Figure out what it's about, and it will give you a new idea of how things fit together. You will gain knowledge; you will gain power."[78] That there are conflicts between the perspectives of mothers and daughters and between those of people with different disabilities should not surprise us who have struggled with other aspects of women's diversity for several years. Nor should we allow the fact that society reinforces traditional role behavior in mothers of people with disabilities to persuade us that we have nothing to learn from them about women's experience and about difference.[79]

The fact that both paternalistic professionals and radical advocates of independent living engage in mother-blaming should be a clue to feminists that the mothers' own perceptions of reality are being ignored or distorted. The fact that many of us come to this discussion with our own biases against motherhood or against dependence should alert us further to the importance of examining our own assumptions. I believe, with Adrienne Rich, "that only the willingness to share private and sometimes painful experience can enable women to create a collective description of the world which will be truly ours."[80] The politics of disability are incomplete without our hearing also the stories of nondisabled people who nevertheless live with disability.

CHAPTER

# DENIAL AND
# NORMALIZATION

A curious illustration of the power of mother-blaming is the debate among parents, professionals, and members of politically active disability communities about "normalization" of mentally retarded people. Two vociferous, outspoken, and diametrically opposed groups of advocates for people with mental disabilities have developed at least partly in response to the disability rights movement. Both are critical of existing policies; both advocate "least restrictive environments"; each accuses the other of insensitivity to the rights of mentally disabled individuals. Their clearest difference is their view of deinstitutionalization. The debate over this issue derives from fundamental differences of opinion about the meanings of acceptance and denial, reinforced by the fact that most advocates for people with such disabilities as mental retardation, dementing illnesses, and schizophrenia do not have the disabilities themselves, but speak as guardians, professional caregivers, or able-minded members of the disability rights movement. That is, the advocates speak *for* but not *from* the disability position. They speak also, however, from their own experience, which ranges, depending on the individuals involved, from that of intimate, sychronous, personal caregivers through that of intellectually gifted persons with physical disabilities whose belief in access to "normal" life is extended to other very different situations.

"Normalization"[1] is problematic to feminists for two reasons: normal female roles reinforce subordination; and "mainstreaming" is usually "malestreaming," requiring at least implicit adoption of male values. To explore the interface between disability experience and feminist experience with regard to normalization it is helpful first to consider the concepts of denial and acceptance as these are used in describing the experience of people who live with disabilities.


## DENIAL

Generally in disability literature, denial is assumed to be a negative sign of maladjustment or a necessary, temporary stage that protects the fragile person after the first shock of diagnosis or accident but impedes adjustment thereafter. Nevertheless, denial of disability is socially sanctioned in that people who valiantly overcome their handicaps are idealized, and the model of good adjustment for everyone in society at large is healthy, physically fit, emotionally well balanced, and mentally alert. "Our society creates an ideal model of the physically perfect person where people are unencumbered by weakness, loss or pain; it is toward this distortion of perfection that we all strive and with which we all identify. Thus, denial of the existence of imperfections is an acceptable form of behavior and attitude."[2] The acceptability of denial across the culture disguises the real penalties that denial of disability entails. Even when passing as nondisabled is impossible, denial of the extent or the exact nature of the disability is likely to increase the individual's (or the caregivers') work, to increase symptoms and dangers, and to create barriers in relationships with others.

Strong social sanctions against being a burden to others and in favor of individualism encourage decisions to deny symptoms and attend to life as usual when we are ill. On the simplest level, we see this in workplaces and schools, where people who ordinarily attend when they have colds or other illnesses are praised for their dedication to work rather than blamed for spreading germs or criticized for not taking care of themselves. When the disability is more serious, pressure to act normal and be "productive" increases, based on a realistic fear of loss of employment as well as a psychological need to resist being seen or seeing oneself as less than able. When dying people "hide our symptoms and try to attend to work and life as usual because we are supposed to," they are responding to "social needs that are imposed on us by the mores and values of this particular society."[3] A dying person cannot meet the demands. Persons who *can* may nevertheless inappropriately divert valuable energy from their own health and other priorities and thus increase rather than decrease their problems.

An important aspect of cultural support for denial of symptoms is the pressure, especially on women, to maintain a positive attitude, actively to deny negative emotions. Yet we know that heart disease, cancer, ulcerative colitis, and ulcer disease as well as other less dramatic illnesses can be triggered (n.b.: not *caused*) by denial of feelings, and other symptoms may be exacerbated by denial or even by "a strong need to maintain an image of 'looking good.' "[4] Cancer patients who are upset by the diagnosis have a lower rate of relapse and less anxiety and depression over time than those who do not express their anxiety and depression early on.[5] In some instances, denial makes the individual sicker by encouraging self-sabotage. For example, a person with environmental illness who is in denial will not avoid substances that cause the symptoms,[6] a person whose reactions have slowed following a stroke may continue to drive,[7] or a person with cystic fibrosis may refuse therapy on which her or his life literally depends.[8] "The message you give [the body's healing system] when you put on a performance is that you don't want to recover, and the result is that your body cooperates by helping you to die."[9]

Obviously the person with the disability is not the only one susceptible to social pressure to deny. Indeed, family members and friends who do not experience the real limitations in their own bodies that the disabled person does are likely not only to increase their own activities in support of denial[10] but also to serve as enablers of the other person's denial by absorbing more and more of the necessary work while maintaining that everything is going on as usual.

Denial harms relationships by inhibiting honesty among the people involved and erecting major barriers to communication.[11] Especially when symptoms are erratic or periodic, hurt and resentment are likely to characterize relationships with family members who may seem oversolicitous at one time and unwilling to help at another, when what has changed is how the person feels, not how the person looks[12] or tries to look. Moreover, family members' denial may prevent a person from receiving necessary training and therapy[13] or even, in the case of a young child, from developing a healthy personality.[14] Such denial may be a "defense value . . . motivated by fear and aimed at supporting an illusion of psychological equilibrium . . . an antianxiety device."[15] However, it may be a deception implemented as a direct response to pressure from others. For example, family members may be advised by doctors to withhold from the patient the seriousness of the diagnosis.[16] Parents may teach a child not to show her or his emotions.[17] A nurse may tell a patient to stop crying: "You are paralyzed and will be for the rest of your life and crying will do no good. So stop."[18] Mothers of moderately disabled children may be "given far less permission to express their distress . . . the emphasis [is] more on the instrumental needs of the baby than on the affective crisis of the mother."[19] And above all, the health care community "wants the patient to give it a good fight. The sick are in a performance position."[20]

For family members, another problem is the difficulty of interpreting messages from the disabled person about his or her own level of denial. Roni Rabin, describing the experience of her father, David, with ALS, says that he resented friends' avoiding him, but they believed on the basis of his own refusal to talk about the disease that he was either in denial himself or was being secretive and trying to shut them out.[21]

A still more serious negative effect of denial is the damage it creates to the individual's self-concept. A chronic illness or disability is part of one's self. It must be internalized or its loss, through denial, becomes the loss of an integral part of one's identity.[22] Micheline Mason argues persuasively that members of the disability movement themselves encourage such denial by insisting that the distress disabled people experience is caused by other people's oppressive attitudes and not by the disability itself. Instead, she suggests,

> the distress caused by unaware attitudes is so acute that many people with physical differences quickly learn to ignore, disguise or attempt to deny the disability. . . . This minimizing of personal difficulties . . . is done at the cost of any hope that we can share our suffering, is a pattern, and should be interrupted. . . . I want to state that I fractured my arms and legs over forty times as a child, and it was no fun at all.[23]

To attribute such pain to societal oppression prevents disability groups as well as individuals from forming a clear sense of their own identity. Seamoon House addresses a similar problem in feminist groups, where unwillingness to acknowledge that the woman with disabilities is "categorically different" results in denial of a most significant aspect of her self, the fact that "I have a moderately severe disability, which has caused me to be regarded as categorically different for most of my adult life."[24]

The price for the woman of ignoring one of the most significant parts of herself is a damaged self-concept. Acknowledging its importance, though, evokes social sanctions: the discomfort of the feminists who will not see categorical difference; charges of political incorrectness from those who argue that oppression, not disability itself, is the source of pain; labeling of honest behavior as self-pity or complaint.[25] Somewhere between denial and acceptance is a slippery territory where the woman who has been attempting to pass by denial of the negative effects of the disability begins to recognize the importance of being true to herself but is encouraged by the social pressures around her to maintain a *false* denial: to keep secret her own reality.

> Slowly I began to see how, all my life, I had worked hard at being "well adjusted" and making sure that that was how others saw me. And it started to become clear what that meant. It meant smiling when I was in pain and reassuring whoever I was with. It meant only discussing my leg if I could

find something funny to tell about it. It meant accepting whatever the doctors did to me (psychologically as well as physically) with unquestioning courage. All in all it meant being very untrue to myself.[26]

Recognizing this is a step toward change, but the change violates the woman's well-integrated lifelong behaviors as well as the social mores surrounding her decisions about how to change.

In her discussion of maternal thinking, Sara Ruddick observes that "self-effacement and cheery denial" are the degenerative forms of "clear-sighted cheerfulness." Such denial, she says, is caused "by the insupportable difficulties of passionately loving a fragile creature in a physically threatening, socially violent, pervasively uncaring and competitive world."[27] When the child is disabled, these pressures toward denial increase, the child is encouraged to adopt the same defenses, and siblings are reinforced in their beliefs that some topics are unspeakable[28] and that the disability really is not a serious problem after all.

Despite all these negative effects of denial, there are some circumstances under which denial may be seen as a positive response to a difficult situation. If it is temporary, partial, or intermittent it may even be "healthy" as a way of reducing stress and managing an otherwise unmanageable situation. It may also meet the individual's need to be normal, or to seem normal to others, and in some cases it provides motivation to achieve beyond one's apparent limits. The clearest understanding of the positive qualities of denial that I have found is in literature about people with cancer. This phenomenon is interesting since cancer-treatment psychologists have developed such therapies as imaging and other varieties of positive thinking[29] that have been controversial because some see them as encouraging denial and others as patient-blaming.[30] Without joining that debate, we can observe that the idea that one may control the disease or its progress may be unrealistic and may derive from denial but still serve as a useful way of organizing life during a time of medical and psychological crisis. And even though, as we have seen, denial can have a number of negative effects, these are not inevitable. "People who believed they understood the cause of their cancer, believed they could control it, or believed they were handling it well, and who then discover their beliefs are untrue, are not worse off for having thought so. In fact, they may be better off." Discussing this idea, Shelley Taylor cites the literature on depression to argue that the ability to see things clearly can be associated with depression while the "illusion" that things are better than they are "may be essential for adequate coping."[31] Beth Meyerowitz notes extensive agreement among cancer observers that some degree of denial is a "healthy" response in cancer patients and that its absence is associated with anxiety and depression. Denial, she says, reduces distress by giving the "patient" an opportunity to control her reaction and thus the treatment and assistance she receives. She warns against therapeutic pressure to "open up," express feelings, and "face reality."[32] Similarly, Robert Chernin Cantor emphasizes the positive role of denial in providing emotional protection and safety,[33] and Barbara Sourkes encourages therapists to serve as "an advocate of the patient's defensive structure in the service of optimal coping."[34] Further, defining the defenses as *selective attention* rather than denial, Sourkes asserts that although the aggressive nature of medical treatment precludes denial that one is ill, one can actively choose to divert energy to physical survival instead of dealing with the implications of the diagnosis.[35]

The supposed denial exercised by parents of severely disabled children may also be a case of selective attention or of intermittent denial. To live one day at a time doing what is necessary for that day and not focusing on the uncertain future is functional in a medically overscheduled life, and it may serve as well to protect parents (and thus other family members) from unbearable pain.[36] Ray Barsch describes a characteristic reaction of such parents who express gratitude that the child has survived in the past instead of acknowledging how bad things are in the present and cautions against interpreting this as a form of denial that should be challenged, suggesting instead that it is a psychological buffer zone used "to insure the survival of the parent in a complex society."[37]

Temporary, partial, or intermittent denial does more than get us through the day. It protects from pain, makes it possible to use psychological and physical energy for other purposes, and gives us a measure of control over our reactions when everything else is out of control. Helen Featherstone suggests that for parents of children with disabilities, denial may be half of an internal dialogue in which the desire for hope is balanced against wary observation of symptoms that something is wrong.[38] Colin Parkes makes the same point about denial and other defenses in bereavement, where the individual, over time, oscillates between "two opposing tendencies: an inhibiting tendency, which by repression, avoidance, postponement, etc. holds back or limits the perception of disturbing stimuli, and a facilitative or reality-testing tendency, which enhances perception and thought about disturbing stimuli."[39] The point is not that the truth lies between these extremes or even that denial helps one get strong enough eventually to face reality, but that denial may become the means through which insight is available. One may gain both respite and insight "through a defense mechanism which offers the way to finally enter the realm of emotion."[40] A striking illustration of this possibility is Karen Thompson's experience when her lover, Sharon Kowalski, was beginning to recover from serious injuries from an automobile accident. Unwilling to face the reality of Sharon's condition, she accepted very gradually, as if they were temporary, the most basic disabilities. When she saw someone who was less seriously injured but who seemed to her to be worse, she realized that "denial of Sharon's real condition forced me to face my own fear and prejudice about disabled people."[41] Notice that Thompson attributes this insight not to the lessening of denial but to denial itself. Seeing how abnormal the "less disabled" person is beside her gradual acceptance of Sharon's extremely disabled, fully individualized, human self forced her to attend honestly not to Sharon's limitations but to her own prejudice.

Since denial may "contribute to the maintenance of hope" and thus enable the family of a person with chronic illness to invest in that person and in the rigors of treatment,[42] simple condemnation of denial as maladaptive may be harmful to the family's coping and to their relationships. Thompson's hope that her partner would fully recover facilitated her ability to cope and to help until she had worked through some of her prejudice and fear.

Denial originates in the need to be normal or seem normal to others. In caregivers it includes the hope that the disabled one can be or seem normal. Parents of disabled children, for example, emphasize the normal aspects of the children's development as part of the essential process of identification with the child. "Normal," then, means "like me."[43] Labeled as denial, this strategy may instead be evidence of positive adaptation. Most of us, disabled or not, deny parts of ourselves so that we fit into jobs, social groups, or our families. To reclaim those parts of ourselves does not necessitate expressing them freely in these contexts, but being aware can "give us a stronger sense of ourselves and . . . release in us the energy to move toward situations where we can express ourselves more fully."[44]

Another positive effect of denial or refusal to accept a negative prognosis is the motivation to surpass or overcome one's limitations. At best, this kind of denial provides energy for physical therapy or the drive necessary to achieve major life goals despite the disability.[45] In his biography of his mentally retarded brother, Roger, Robert Meyers attributes Roger's strength and perseverance to their parents' denial: "By denying to themselves and others that he was retarded, they unconsciously and indirectly set out to prove he was not retarded, and so gave him as many experiences as a non-retarded person would get. . . . My parents' denial . . . ironically, helped Roger develop the strong sense of self which carried him through the frustration and mockery that was to come."[46] Shelley Taylor, surveying the literature about "depressive cognitions," argues persuasively that relative to depressives, "normal" people are less accurate about their own limitations, tending to inflate others' view of them, to believe they can control objectively uncontrollable outcomes, to underestimate negative feedback, and to attribute their successes to internal causes. All of these self-perceptions increase persistence and improve one's ability to accomplish what one attempts. Taylor thus argues that nurturing "illusions" renders a person more effective in the face of threatening circumstances.[47] It also, as countless success stories demonstrate, enables people with various disabilities to become "supercrips," individuals who succeed brilliantly beyond what seem to be immovable barriers to their "normal" functioning.

When denial actually facilitates achievement, it is reasonable to ask whether it is in fact denial at all. Rather, it may be simply a disagreement with another person's interpretation of what the real disability is. The boundary between physical and social limitations is by no means as clear as we usually assume, and both disability activists and rehabilitation professionals may be wrong about how such limitations are best addressed. Ultimately, the definitions of denial and acceptance rely on individual perceptions that will almost certainly change over time.

## ACCEPTANCE

Acceptance, then, is individual. Generalizations about how realistic one should be about one's disability assume that someone (usually an outside, supposedly objective observer) knows exactly what reality is. Such knowledge, if it were possible, would require a delicate and thorough balancing of physical, psychological, emotional, interpersonal, and societal factors, some of which will be unknown to "objective" observers and to the disabled person as well. Usually acceptance develops in the person with the disability at a different rate and in different terms than the acceptance of family members and other caregivers. Guidance toward acceptance by professionals or by disability rights advocates may be helpful but is also likely to be biased by differing philosophical or psychological beliefs. Family members, friends, and members of disability groups will be further biased by their own emotional responses to the individual, her or his specific disability, *their* specific disabilities, and the social environment.

As we have seen, denial is often partial or selective, and so must acceptance be. An individual's statement about acceptance must therefore be evaluated in terms of her or his specific disability, consciousness about other disabilities, and social and emotional circumstances.[48] Nancy Frick, addressing a conference on post-polio syndrome, provides one valuable definition: "By acceptance I do not mean learning to prefer disability over being able-bodied. Neither do I mean resigning oneself to the inevitable. I am referring to the conditions that make it possible to see one's disability as other than devaluing."[49] Societal devaluation is acknowledged here as a source of denial and of the difficulty in achieving acceptance. Individual psychological devaluation is also implied; the two are obviously linked. Acceptance does not in this view require resignation to socio-environmental conditions that can be changed, but it is not reliant on the completion of such changes before one can see one's disability as other than devaluing. Although working to change others' attitudes may facilitate acceptance, their actually changing is not necessary to the disabled person's own perception of the disability as other than devaluing.

Acceptance does not require a *positive* valuation of the disability, however. As Nancy Mairs says of her life with MS: "I hate it. My life holds realities—harsh ones some of them—that no right-minded human being ought to accept without grumbling."[50] And, "If I weren't scared of this catastrophic disease . . . I'd have at least one screw loose."[51] According to one study of support groups for fathers of children with disabilities, acceptance of their children's limitations is paralleled by increased pessimism.[52] Knowledge of the real situation is appropriately discouraging. The American cultural myth that all problems can be solved with hard work and money is just that: a myth. "Losses that cannot be 'fixed' cause us to realize our finiteness and our limitations as human beings."[53] Clearly this applies to physical disabilities, but it may apply to societal handicaps as well. Carol Pearson points out that internalizing such social myths as the belief that everyone has an equal chance to succeed in our society prevents our "recognizing and accepting the pain of our oppression. Seeing the world as it is and mourning its inhumanity is a prerequisite to moving on to other paths."[54]

Pressures to demonstrate adjustment by adopting a false cheerfulness or specious normality are barriers to acceptance. Erving Goffman makes a useful distinction between "fulfilling ordinary standards" and "normification"—that is, giving the impression of trying to deny one's differentness.[55] Goffman goes on to show how the social roles expected of stigmatized people include acceptance of oneself as a normal person in order to protect "normals" from admitting how limited their tolerance really is and how uncomfortable the stigmatized person makes them.[56]

Resisting normification can signal the disabled person's acceptance of the fact that she or he is indeed different or may indicate adoption of a social role prescribed by uncomfortable normals. Acceptance, finally, involves awareness of one's real limitations, including both physical and societal limits.

Leo Buscaglia, arguing that acceptance requires individuals to do the work of discovering for themselves what their real limitations are,[57] says that such acceptance "does not mean to suggest a process of looking for compensations . . . or . . . recognizing the supposed advantages of having them, or . . . resignation to a sad fate, but rather recognizing that there will be limitations and that these limitations are acceptable."[58] Of course, some people never achieve this level of acceptance, but most do, when they come to see the limitation as only part of the self who has other accessible attributes that can be used effectively, not as compensation but for their own value. Struggling with this problem requires a transformation of values so that new goals become meaningful because they are reachable[59] and because they utilize assets that are now seen as having a higher value than they had previously based on what is lost through the disability. For example, athletes whose injuries cause them to leave the sport that has been the highest value in their self-concept often turn to education or business for the first time, revaluing intellectual competence. Even if the disability is lifelong, there will be periods when such reevaluation takes place, for example, when the improved mobility associated with a motorized wheelchair requires abandonment of an earlier higher value on moving by use of one's own muscular power.[60] Often the new value that motivates the first changes is a transformation of the old value: the person with the disability or illness decides to bear witness, to tell the world what it is like to have this condition and to provide a role model for others who have it.[61] Coming out as a public disabled person may lead to a career (for example, as a leader in the disability rights movement or as a rehabilitation counselor), but more frequently it is part of a process of finding a balance in one's life where the disability is neither denied nor made to serve as the central organizing principle of one's life. Breast cancer patients, for example, describe themselves as better adjusted than before they had any signs of cancer,[62] reflecting a belief that they have a more integrated awareness of their whole life, not merely resignation to life-threatening illness. The cancer episode challenges ego integration. As this challenge is assimilated, the woman learns not only what her new limitations are, but also the costs of those limitations, and incorporates this awareness into her larger self-concept. For disabilities that continue over time, such periodic challenges cause repeated "advances in maturity," incorporating the disability and its costs. Such insights "reopen the question of how to strike a balance between too much and too little acceptance."[63]

Finding such a balance is particularly an issue for parents of disabled children, who require enough hope to keep going with everyday life, with medical and other therapies, with advocacy for the child, and with their own health. Sometimes all of this requires denial; sometimes, acceptance. Sometimes what must be accepted is the impossibility of doing it all. For parents and for other intimate caregivers, three sometimes conflicting kinds of acceptance are needed: acceptance of the disabilities, of the *person* with the disabilities, and of the caregiver's *self*[64]—her or his life as a person who lives with this disability, this disabled person, this changed self.

One strategy that most caregivers use to move themselves toward acceptance is comparing the disability to others. Parents of children with disabilities usually perceive other child disabilities as more severe than the ones with which they live.[65] Ordinary daily life with the familiar person and the increasingly familiar disability diminishes one's perception of its relative severity and thus brings about a higher level of acceptance. This fact, based on parents' experience, is one important argument for mainstreaming children with disabilities in school and social settings. If family members become more accepting through familiarity, so may other children and adults.[66]

Familiarity is also involved in accepting the person with the disability. As the disability is part of the child's self, the parent caring for even a severely disabled child comes to acceptance of that total integrated personality to an extent that makes it impossible to imagine the person without the disability, but that also incorporates the disability as just one part of the whole person. It is easy for those with limited disabilities, however serious, to imagine that this means seeing that the disability is only a minor part of the personality and that acceptance means embracing this view, but in many cases, it is simply not true. A child with severe mental retardation and multiple physical disabilities has a personality that is made up predominantly of those disabilities and the behaviors they entail. In these circumstances, parental acceptance does not mean subordinating consciousness of the disability to other (presumably positive) traits, but acknowledging their centrality in the relationship and in the family.

For the family, despite the pressure to behave as if their lives as a family are "normal" and unremarkable,[67] acceptance involves "being reconciled to the fact that something has happened that deeply affects and will continue to affect the total family."[68] Although assimilating the change may involve a positive belief that the family can survive and cope, what must also be accepted is that the change is not temporary or even stable, but continuing and unpredictable. Helen Featherstone describes the mothers in her parent support group:

> These women had not spoken about rainbows after the storm, about families drawn closer by tragedy. They were in pain. Their eyes misted over as they struggled to describe the uncertainty of the early months, the despair with which they contemplated the future. These were not voices from "the other side" encouraging the exhausted swimmer. These were voices from the middle of the river, the gasps of courageous women who sometimes felt themselves going under. . . . I returned to my desk wondering how many people ever make it to the much advertised state of acceptance.[69]

I would suggest that for many of us what must be accepted is that there very probably will not be another side. Helen Brown, mother of a multiply handicapped daughter, acknowledging that Karen's condition may not remain stable over time, says, "My problems are never solved, nor are those of other parents of handicapped children."[70] Elsewhere, Brown describes her task during Karen's childhood as one of accepting "simple facts of life: I had a handicapped child who wasn't so nice to be around."[71] Such an unpleasant fact, an everyday reality for the mothers of many disabled children, is so inconsistent with prevalent societal belief in "poster children" and supercrips and with mother-blaming ignorance about real symptoms of real biochemical illnesses that it takes great courage to accept it, however damaging to the mother's own self-concept—to say nothing of her work load—the alternative (denial) may be. Accepting reality means being able to "perceive their responsibility in the situation without feeling the need to take too much, or too little, responsibility for what has happened to them and to their loved one."[72]

To accept oneself under such pressures may be more difficult than accepting the disability. Wanting and being expected to be an effective mother (by ordinary societal standards) under these circumstances may be an unrealistic goal, but it is difficult to give up; most of us do not give it up until the disability or the child forces us to. Accepting the disability means accepting real limitations in the child's abilities; self-acceptance for the mother means the same thing: acknowledging her own real limitations. For me as a well-trained professional, feminist, domestic overachiever, the hardest part of accepting Jennifer's disabilities has been acknowledging what I am unable to give.[73] Forgiving our own errors and shortcomings is a crucial part of acceptance, as is recognizing that the child's disability is not the only problem in the parent's life. "Acceptance means that this disability is part of your life and that, on balance, you accept your life."[74]

## MENTAL DISABILITY

To see how denial affects normalization, it is useful to examine the experience of people who live with such disabilities as mental retardation and dementing diseases.[75] As the mother of a woman with mental retardation, I am frequently surprised by the extent to which even people who work with retarded people on a daily basis engage in denial about their real limitations. It is a form of denial that is reinforced by the ideology of normalization and also by the careless pronouncements of such believers in medical self-help as Barbara Brown, who says,

> Everyone, but *everyone,* possesses the mental means to be intelligent. The chief work of the intellect is to put our observations and impressions about things in life into orderly arrangements so that the relationships among things, events, or elements can be recognized as credible. Intelligence, the faculty of thought and reason, is the capacity to acquire and apply knowledge. . . . Most people who seem to be not so intelligent can almost invariably be found to be informationally deprived.[76]

Anyone who has tried to supply information to a person in the later stages of Alzheimer's or Huntington's disease will be extremely frustrated if forced to deal with someone who believes that "everyone, but *everyone,*" can acquire and process information in an orderly way. I have singled out this passage from Brown's otherwise realistic and useful book on stress-related illness not only because it is so emphatic about "everyone," but also because it is a very common concept among people who design programs for retarded people (in the abstract; rarely among those who live with them on a daily basis) and is at least implied by some in the disability rights movement. This is denial. Many people are not capable of ordering information so that they can recognize as "credible" the relationships among things, events, or elements. Nancy Mace and Peter Rabins strongly urge caregivers to those with dementing diseases to "avoid assuming complex reasons for the person's behavior" because the person's brain cannot process information normally.[77] Further, performance is likely to be erratic, and devices intended to help people with physical limitations may be sources of added frustration because the ability to learn new skills is lacking.[78] Loss of memory, catastrophic reactions, agitation, anxiety, and nervousness are characteristic symptoms, which cannot be dispelled by explanations or verbal reassurances because the causes are not susceptible to reason.[79] To deny the reality of such profound mental deficits is not helpful to the person involved and may be devastating to caregivers. Moreover, it limits essential services. Mace and Rabins cite cases in which people with dementia are disqualified for nursing home care when they cannot be managed at home or when intermediate care cannot be funded through Medicaid.[80] And Bryan Jennett, discussing disability after head injury, says that professionals frequently underestimate the extent of disability because the person with the injury is unable to recognize personality change and denies problems of memory. Only hearing the stories of relatives and friends gives a realistic idea of the extent of the disability.[81] The denial of those who believe that societal barriers and perhaps self-esteem are the only truly handicapping conditions is a factor too. Jennett cites those who

> quote the triumph over disability of some exceptional paraplegic or quadriplegic patient, perhaps writing novels or poetry with electronic gadgetry. To make such a comparison indicates either insensitivity or ignorance, failing to recognize the profound difference it makes when the brain itself is diffusely damaged, so that the patient's personality and cognitive function are undermined—and thereby his [sic] capacity to cope with and to adapt to disability.[82]

Similarly, the stereotype of the "happy and carefree retardate" has made much more difficult the lives of people who live with unhappy, troubled, or merely emotionally labile people with mental retardation. Children with Down's syndrome, for example, are stereotyped as unusually warm, loving, and affectionate, but at least part of the stereotype derives from affect hunger[83] and the inappropriate extension of an impression from early childhood onto retarded adults. Of course, even if the stereotype were true of children with Down's, it would not apply to those with other forms of mental retardation. And people with Down's syndrome who survive into their forties often develop Alzheimer's disease, with the full range of unhappy symptoms characteristic of dementia. Arguments for rehabilitation funding and community mainstreaming for people with mental retardation may then obstruct appropriate placement for adults who have both mental retardation and dementing illnesses. Furthermore, programs that assume the ability of all people with mental retardation to meet ever-increasing goals toward "independence" express denial about the real limitations of those who may have reached their full potential or begun to decline.

Yet another kind of denial characterizes adults with mild mental retardation who adopt a "cloak of competence," strategies of dissembling so as to pretend to have intellectual skills that in fact they do not have. This may be passing or denial, or a blend of both. Difficulties with reading, writing, numbers, telling time, and handling money are common, even among the highest-functioning retarded people. To maintain denial or to pass with such social deficits requires the presence of a benefactor to provide both practical and psychological assistance. In the process, the benefactor also reinforces denial.[84]

Misunderstandings about "developmental delays" compound the problem. Parents' initial reaction to explanations about a child's delay may be to assume that the child will always be a year or a few years behind on an essentially normal developmental track. Over time, the disability itself reeducates family members on this point, and professional caregivers presumably know better. Nevertheless, the pressures to keep the child on as normal a developmental track as possible are enormous and may greatly increase the discomfort of the family and the disabled person as well. For example, I know a family whose six-year-old child, with profound mental retardation, cerebral palsy, blindness, and seizure disorder, was functioning at about the level of a two-month-old. The parents, who had never been away from the child, sought respite care from a cerebral palsy center. The center agreed to provide care only if the child was weaned from the bottle, which "infantalized" him but also provided a primary source of nutrients and his only sense of comfort. In order to obtain a few days of respite, they spent weeks with a screaming child who could not understand that being deprived of his most basic comfort was in the interest of achieving a "normal" developmental task. The traumatic impact of this change on the child and on the family did nothing to change his two-month-old level of functioning.

Pervasive in our culture is the assumption that "ultimately I am my mind and my manner of using it."[85] People with physical disabilities emphasize this idea more than most of us do, for obvious reasons. Arguing for accessible university environments, one activist explains, "If you're disabled, you can't work at a gas station or McDonald's. You have to use your mind."[86] What if the mind is disabled? Who, then, *is* the person who is defined as her or his mind? What about the fact that McDonald's has been a leading employer of mildly retarded adults and that many able-minded people and people with certain physical disabilities do work in service stations and at minimum wage jobs? Seamoon House, writing of feminists' rejection of her self-definition as "disabledminded" because of a psychological disability, believes that they accept the concept only if the disability is assumed to be reversible.[87] This idea—that mental disability can be reversed or overcome with proper reeducation—keeps people focused on changing at least the symptoms of disability instead of on realistically accepting limitations.

In the cases of mental retardation and dementing diseases,[88] acceptance is primarily the task of family members, as the disability prevents the disabled person from clearly understanding the implications of those limits.[89] She may, at intervals, accept their nature. Jennifer, for example, after years of training, sometimes accepts that her tremor is caused by her muscles and not by a defect of character for which she will be blamed, but her emotional grasp of this point varies enormously. Sometimes she thinks she should be able to control the muscles and sometimes that she has caused the problem, though she does not know how. It remains then for me and her father to accept the reality of the tremor and of the mental deficits that make it hard for her to understand. Part of our task as those who (except for Jennifer) know her disabilities best is to monitor the other supposedly accepting adults who are capable of such lapses as saying in a staff meeting in front of Jennifer that "she can control her tremor if she wants to" or believing that her ability to perform a mental task one day means she can do it another day. Both her father and I are well educated and fully familiar with everything that can be medically known to date about her disabilities, but accusations of denial are always probable if we describe what we know to be her real disabilities. The dozens of people who have come through her life to teach her to tell time, for example, have come and gone, and we remain the bearers of the bad news that Jennifer cannot retain the ability to tell time for more than a few days, or, usually, a few minutes. Those who believe that with training people with retardation can learn to tell time think that we deny her real ability to learn. We do not; we have seen her learn this skill repeatedly. We see them as denying her real limitation: inability to retain this skill. As May Sarton says of her own process of accepting her longtime partner's dementia, "It's only the relentless truth of her condition that gradually permeates everything for me."[90]

## NORMALIZATION

The concept of normalization governs most of the policy decisions for which people with disabilities and their allies have worked in the past few years. The principle is that a person with disabilities should live a life as equal to a normal life as possible, should have the same rights as others, and should be accepted "with their exceptionalities when these cannot be remedied."[91] As simple as it is, this idea has encountered a good deal of resistance, but gradually over time it has had a profound effect on access to public places and the architecture and philosophy of residential placement even of severely disabled people. The most serious problems that have followed on efforts to implement decisions toward normalization have derived from the mistake of forgetting the part about accepting people "with their exceptionalities." In their zeal for seeing individuals as "normal," some well-meaning people as well as others who are merely defending the status quo have treated some disabled people as if their exceptionalities did not exist or had no importance.

Indeed, Niels Bank-Mikkelsen, who developed the concept of normalization, said he regretted using the term because there has been so much confusion about the meaning of "normal." Instead, he prefers a phrase such as "the principle of equality."[92] In public policy, under the slogan of normalization or community integration, neglectful treatment often follows deinstitutionalization, for example.[93] I would suggest that in these cases, the principle of normalization is a sophisticated form of denial, a refusal to accept real limitations under the guise and with the vocabulary of respect for the individual. To place a retarded person in a residence in a community without individually appropriate training and supervision may actually interfere with the ultimate goal of normalized behavior because the person may not be prepared to cope with the demands of the community.[94] In the case of a person with dementia, prolonging "independent" living in the name of normalization merely increases the abnormality of the caregiver's life. Parents of children with disabilities live with their children in two cultures:

> The unclear and constantly changing amount of normality and abnormality embodied in the handicapped child makes the mothering of such a child an adventure in two cultures. At times the rules of the culture of normality are most relevant, while at other times the rules have to be taken from the culture of abnormality. Often it is difficult to predict in advance which would be most relevant. And frequently the choice involves an overt conflict between two equally valid but incongruent possibilities.[95]

For example, Roskies cites cases where children without arms could learn to feed themselves, a normal goal, by using their feet, but such atypical behavior would interfere with the social goal of becoming part of the normal community.[96]

If it is understood as meaning the principle of equality, normalization will not be so readily interpreted as being or doing like everyone else. Or at least that is the theory. In practice, women learned from the battle over the Equal Rights Amendment that many people, especially those in power, do understand equal as meaning the same. Furthermore, even the most eloquent defenses of normalization based on the notion of equality contain some conceptual traps that women rightly suspect. For example, William Bronston explains that "normalization as a methodology says 'at least as good as the average citizen.' This means that we have a reasonably common statistically occurring floor below which no human being can be allowed to slip."[97] But surely half of all people fall below the average, however it is measured. Later, Bronston argues against "overprotection" by asserting that "normalization requires that risk be programmed in to insure humanity is preserved and people will be raised to be part of this real world with all its dangers, cruelty, and discovery."[98] As the mother of a daughter whose disabilities make it impossible for her to understand money, I want her to have more protection than the average citizen against people who would financially exploit her. Furthermore, as a feminist who is well aware of how susceptible all women are to rape, sexual exploitation, and battering, I am unwilling to expose her to the dangers and cruelty that confront ordinary women who do not have her perceptual and physical disabilities, her impulsivity and socially inappropriate behaviors. To "program in" such dangers would be criminally irresponsible.

Martin Seligman and Roslyn Darling point out that not all families have equal opportunities for normalization, which requires good medical and educational services, respite and day care, accepting neighbors and relatives, financial resources, household help, special equipment, transportation, and social opportunities for the child.[99] This list of necessary resources suggests that normalization of a child with disabilities requires services to the adults whose lives are less normal because of their own relationship to the child's disability. Not only parents, relatives, friends and neighbors, but also the child's classmates and, especially, teachers need support, and seldom receive it.[100]

Mainstreaming in the schools is by now a widely accepted way of implementing the principle of normalization. Where it is realistic and accepting of the mainstreamed student's limitations, it can be effective. For example, David Luterman describes some schools that mainstream a whole class of hearing impaired children *and their teacher,* so that the regular teacher has a trained teacher of the deaf to work with her and the hearing-impaired child is less isolated.[101] Isolation is a common outcome of ordinary mainstreaming, which is based on the mistaken premise that normal classrooms are less isolating than special classrooms.[102] In fact, the opposite is more likely to be true. Another mistaken assumption is that mainstreamed children will feel less different. In fact, the perception that one is too different to be attractive to others is more acute among students who are mainstreamed. Being surrounded by "normal" classmates makes the individual more conscious of the disability[103] and more isolated.[104] The parents of mainstreamed children have more responsibility for the child's educational program than when the planning and implementation are conducted by a trained special teacher,[105] and the curriculum itself may be inappropriate for the disabled child.[106] In some cases, placement in "normal" or open classrooms exacerbates the child's disabilities by increasing confusion and distractability where a structured, more controlled environment increases the ability to concentrate.[107] None of this is to disparage mainstreaming where it is effective. My point, rather, is that denial of the child's individual limitations (or of the parent's, when the parent is the monitor of the special educational needs) may have a devastating effect on progress toward the desired "normal" role.

Another problematic aspect of normalization is emphasized by Oliver Sacks in his analysis of the refusal of educators to accept the extreme deficits of brain-injured people. Trying to make their clients, patients, or students as normal as possible in the presence of severe disabilities, professionals may deprive them of their most rewarding occupations. For example, Sacks describes Nadia, an autistic girl with great artistic skill, who was taught to maximize "her potentialities in other directions," with the result that she learned to talk and stopped drawing. Sacks quotes Nigel Dennis: "We are left with a genius who has had her genius removed, leaving nothing behind but a general defectiveness."[108] Another illustration is twins who were separated in order to normalize them. They gained the ability to be quasi-independent, under close supervision, and socially acceptable (i.e., "moderately presentable" and clean) "though their moronic and psychotic character is still recognizable at a glance." What they have lost is their extraordinary—and deviant—ability to communicate with each other numerically, which was "the personal and emotional center of their lives."[109] Sacks does not argue that twins should never be separated, clean, or "presentable," but that normalization should not be used to deprive people of the personal and emotional center of their lives.

At another extreme, widespread criticism of the Kennedy

family for their treatment of Rosemary, John F. Kennedy's retarded sister, focuses on the pressure they placed on her to be normal, as if their sincere inclusion of her in the siblings' activities somehow caused her outbursts of violence in young adulthood. Collier and Horowitz, in their biography of the family, exemplify this view: "Her inability to keep up in the contests of wit and endurance, and especially her inability to share in the social life of Kick and Eunice and go out with young men . . . left her disoriented and angry. She began to have tantrums and then rages which developed into near-clonic states during which she smashed objects and struck out at the people around her."[110] Implied in this account is the notion that a less demanding family would have prevented such violence by their relaxed attitude. There is no indication that the critics know that such outbursts characterize many retarded adolescents and adults or that they may have organic causes. Here normalization is seen as a negative influence, but the underlying dynamic of the criticism is the same: parental expectations are probably wrong, whether they want the child to be more or less normal, and the "right" treatment will enable the child to become *more* normal as she matures. The Kennedys are then blamed for their drastic intervention to control Rosemary's outbursts by a prefrontal lobotomy, which was recommended by both physicians and Catholic theologians, the experts most valued by the Kennedys. The surgery had the desired effect of ending the "wild moods" but it lowered Rosemary's overall functioning.[111] The effort to make her behavior more normal resulted in its becoming both more and less so. Their dilemma, which should be evaluated in light of the Kennedys' access to the best medical advice of the time (1941), is recapitulated today in many decisions about the uses of psychotropic drugs, which may also reduce wild mood swings at the expense of overall functioning.

Notable in Collier and Horowitz's account of Rosemary Kennedy's story is the emphasis on her female role behavior. The family assumed that the daughters would fulfill traditional role expectations; none of them was groomed to be president, though any (except Rosemary) might have been a president's wife. Similar assumptions, almost universal in American culture at the time and widespread today, handicap most women with disabilities in a classic double bind: to be "normal," they should adopt role behavior that oppresses all women.

The day my doctor awarded me my diagnosis . . . he warned me that most people with my "illness" lead practically normal lives. I imagined myself caught up in a whirlwind of bridal showers and tupperware parties and developing a sudden compulsion to wear incredibly high heeled shoes that made important clacking sounds when I walked. I saw myself assuming my place in front of the crowded mirror in the "ladies" room and applying my eyeliner with the same air of frantic determination as everyone else. I confess I was more than a little frightened by it all.[112]

Sex-role stereotyping is even more pervasive in curricula for children who are mentally disabled and behaviorally disordered than in the culture at large, precisely because it will enable them to "adjust" to normal society.[113]

Arguments for the reproductive rights of people with disabilities are often characterized by confusion of sex-role expectations with the ideas of individual rights and responsibilities. Inability to separate truly individual ability from societal beliefs about maternal fulfillment results in such polarized generalizations as: every woman has the right to decide whether or not to have a child (regardless of whether she has the ability to make other decisions); or, no woman who cannot independently care for a child should be permitted to have one. The courts, responding to parents' requests for sterilization of mentally disabled adult children, have recently prohibited sterilization, even when the parents' intention was to provide the daughter with more independence and therefore a "right" to more sexual activity.[114] Here, her right to reproduce takes precedence over her right to be more sexually active. Or, more ominously, her sexual activity is more likely to result in reproduction. In many such families, the parents rightly perceive that any child of the disabled daughter will be raised by the grandparents, already overwhelmed by the responsibility of caring for the child's mother. Here the assumptions about motherhood as a "normal" condition become hopelessly tangled: the young mentally disabled woman has a right to be a mother; her mother has no right to interfere with that "decision," even if it is no decision because of the disability; yet her mother will be expected to mother the new baby if the daughter cannot do so because of her disability; if she declines to do so both children will be neglected and she, not the involuntary mother, will be a bad mother; but if she tries to arrange for the daughter to be sterilized, she is a bad mother because for selfish reasons she wants to prevent the daughter from being a mother. This is not about reproductive rights but about compulsory motherhood. The fact that many women with disabilities can successfully raise children is not at issue here, nor is the fact that many women are unable to refuse sexual activity, but the reluctance of many in our society to acknowledge these two facts is closely connected to stereotyped assumptions about what is (and is not) "normal" for women.

If we were able to accept each woman *exactly* as she is, including a realistic evaluation of her abilities and limitations, these arguments would be neither so convoluted nor so oversimplified. A woman with mental retardation but with the ability to work well with social support services could choose to be a mother; a woman with a form of mental retardation that precludes her making safe decisions about sexual activity would have appropriate, nonintrusive supervision; a woman with mental disabilities that make her self-destructive and dangerous to others would be able to be sterilized; and so on. What is normal for each of these women is different from what is normal for others with similar generic labels, such as "mental retardation." A dangerous form of romanticizing disability is the assumption that mentally retarded people "learn just the way we do, only a little more slowly."[115] Some do and some do not. Rosemary Kennedy was not able slowly to learn not to assault her grandfather; the danger to his life was immediate, and her brain was not able to learn that lesson at any speed. An infant who could be killed by a sudden fit of rage or an excessively vigorous hug or by being thrown in a wastebasket like an out-of-favor toy cannot wait while its mother slowly learns what she did not learn in the preceding twenty or thirty years about self-control and responsibility.

In Michael Dorris's best-selling and award-winning book on fetal alcohol syndrome, he traces the development of his own crisis of conscience over the reproductive freedom of mentally impaired women. He was firmly committed to "every self-evident liberal belief" including the unacceptability of forced sterilization and the right of individuals to make their own medical decisions; he was wary of government-sanctioned genocide and wrongful imprisonment of Native American people. Yet for the survival of those same people and the prevention of widespread, multigenerational mental retardation and physical disability, he found himself tempted to advocate imprisonment of alcoholic pregnant women and involuntary sterilization of those who did not stop drinking.[116] The pain of such a confrontation with his most deeply held convictions derives from his experience as a Native American anthropologist observing the increasing mental disability of his own people and as the father of a son seriously disabled with fetal alcohol syndrome (FAS). Dorris's son was adopted as a young child and had exceptionally competent and diverse professional help, but his disabilities are extremely limiting and could have been avoided entirely by his birth mother's abstinence from alcohol. Dorris documents the multiplication of FAS disabilities among people without professional intervention, adoption, and other resources. One symptom of the syndrome is inability to use commonsense judgment (because of brain damage, not poor training), and thus birth control, prenatal care, and abstinence from addictive substances are unlikely to be used even in the presence of active treatment.

What is a good liberal like Dorris or a good feminist like me to make of such a painful dilemma? Minimally, experiencing the dilemma challenges simplistic views of "fetal rights" as a right-wing, anti-woman plot. Dorris does not resolve his conflicting beliefs over these issues; resolution is probably impossible. What we can do, however, as his book suggests, is to hold in mind simultaneously the individual seriously damaged life, refusing to romanticize the disabled person or to deny her specific limitations, and the larger societal problem of persons with seriously impaired judgment reproducing themselves.

The people who at this time are most willing to raise these hard questions are the parents, especially the mothers, of children, especially adult children, with disabilities. Michael Dorris was the single parent and thus the sole caregiver for Adam from his fourth to thirteenth years, but this role is much more frequently filled by women. When normalization for mentally disabled people is given higher value than the normality of the mother's own life, the underlying assumption is that the one without the disability will carry the ability of two people. "Normal" then means that society at large can stay in denial about both specific limitations and societal responsibility.

A number of studies of institutionalized versus noninstitutionalized mentally retarded children have shown that support of the mother by the grandmother is a critical factor in preventing institutionalization.[117] Thus two generations of women protect the child from the institution and maintain the belief that mothers can handle such children at home without help. Social programs to provide alternatives to dichotomous institution/home, family/government thinking are typically unfunded or underfunded, and demonstration programs often are canceled as soon as they begin to succeed.[118] What remains is stereotypical women's work, in which mothers are valued over institutions because "most mothers are amply supplied" with patience,[119] affection, dignity, and compassion.[120] When the mother's resources are exhausted, underpaid and often undertrained women attendants provide presumably less patient care in institutions.

The drawbacks of home care are severe: social isolation, the inability to relax or have fun,[121] continuous medical and educational appointments,[122] compromised mental and physical health of parents or siblings,[123] and poverty.[124] To assume that such conditions are "normal" and intrinsic to the mother's job is cynical, at best. Marian DeMyer, writing about the care of autistic children, suggests that "the current idea of not considering family needs when recommending hospitalization for an afflicted person is absolutely wrong. . . . The practice of withholding third party insurance if the decision to hospitalize is made on the basis of family health as well as patient need is malpractice."[125] Here public policy (or the policy of insurance companies) interacts with sex-role stereotyping to deny both the severity of the child's disability and the family's limitations. The greatest limitation where the one with the disability is autistic or has a dementing illness or other severe mental impairment is the inability to provide twenty-four-hour care. Maryellen Walsh points out that staff members in crisis houses often work two-day weeks,[126] and in institutions eight-hour shifts are normal; yet maternal workdays of twenty-four hours are commonplace and considered acceptable.

The concept of community care as most desirable because it is most normal depends fundamentally on women's unpaid domestic labor.[127] An organization called the Healing Community, designed to encourage churches and synagogues to help integrate "handicapped and alienated persons" into the community, estimates that 100 million volunteers are needed to respond to the national policy of dein-stitutionalization. They propose among other things that volunteers take mentally ill people into their homes.[128] Surely most of the volunteers and virtually all of the homemakers will be women, yet there is no consideration of the impact of such volunteer work on the normality of their own lives. The premises underlying deinstitutionalization are thus de facto sexist. Furthermore, the stresses on family caregivers often result in emotional rejection of the disabled person by the caregiver because the caregiver feels entrapped in the role.[129] Decisions about placement in the "least restrictive" environment address the "best interests" of the disabled person rather than those of the caregiver, a practice that is supported by the caregiving woman's socialization to place others' needs ahead of her own.[130]

Mothers may well be the preferable caregivers, and we certainly have usually been willing to assume the role. The difficulty here is that failure to acknowledge the woman caregiver's limitations is as handicapping and demoralizing as ignoring the disability itself. To normalize without recognizing denial, without accepting limitation, profoundly discounts disability as a women's issue. It also encourages both disabled women and women caregivers to pass as less limited than they are.

CHAPTER

# PASSING

To "pass" is to present yourself or let yourself be taken for a member of a more privileged group. The more oppressed group members are, and/or the less political, the greater their likelihood of being closeted. It is not surprising, then, that civil rights movements have pressed their members to "come out," emphasizing the harmful effects of passing both for the one who passes and for the rest of society. Yet most of us choose to pass at least some of the time if we can; and in circles less political than those who organize civil rights movements, passing is assumed to be necessary and even desirable. There may be considerable fear and hostility toward people who are "too far out" of their closets.

## LESBIANS AND WOMEN WITH DISABILITIES

Women with disabilities who pass as nondisabled experience benefits and costs that are closely analogous to those of lesbians who pass as heterosexual. As public discussion about the costs of lesbian passing has gone on longer and been subjected to more debate and analysis, it is useful to compare the experiences of the two groups. In addition to the basic minority status that makes passing seem desirable and the physical conditions that make it possible, disabled women and lesbians have in common certain other traits that distinguish them in part from others who pass. Both are likely to have been socialized in families and communities that do not share their particular stigma. As children, both are likely to have been treated like members of the more privileged group (able-bodied and heterosexual) and to conform to that group's standards of behavior and appearance. Both have available civil rights movements of rather short duration and some incentive from within those movements to disassociate from other groups with a longer history and literature about passing. Both are minorities within the political movements most committed to their civil rights. And both are women whose sexuality is at issue when their minority status is known.

Both lesbians and people with disabilities are often the only members of their families who belong to the minority group.[1] Unlike blacks, for example, or Jews, they may not know anyone else like themselves until they are adults, if then. They therefore lack not only family support but also community identification.[2] Indeed, they will very probably have spent most of their lives trying to fit into a culture that excludes them. Typical advice to a disabled child is to appear as much like a nondisabled person as possible; benign treatment of a lesbian girl assumes that she is going through a phase that she will outgrow. In contrast, a black child might be taught to adopt survival strategies in the white community but to be proud of the characteristics valued in her own culture.[3] Further, when the adult child comes out to family members, the response, even if it is supportive, is likely to be one of clearly differentiating the rest of the family from the one who is disabled or lesbian. The pressure is on the different one to prove she is still "like" her family, and can meet their behavioral

standards, for example, by dating men, by playing the family's preferred "sick role," or by "protecting" grandmother from this knowledge, which she might not be able to handle.[4]

Women with disabilities and lesbians, then, are encouraged
by both the traditional female role and their childhood membership
in able-bodied, heterosexual families to personalize their difficulties,
in contrast to members of ethnic minorities, who may learn in the
family to attribute them to racism.[5]

The gay rights movement and the disability rights movement
of the 1970s and 1980s are recent in comparison with the century-
and-a-half-long black civil rights and women's rights movements
from which, in part, they derive. Both movements build upon the insight and political strategies developed by those older movements
and at the same time derive their separate identities from the ways in
which other civil rights groups have ignored or actively discriminated
against their disabled, lesbian, and gay members. Each challenges
other minorities to adopt the new movement's causes as their own
and to change their behavior and ideology to make such cooperation
possible. Women with disabilities, for example, challenge feminists
not merely to make their meetings accessible, but also to change
their beliefs about abortion of potentially disabled fetuses. The need
for a separate movement derives in part from alienation from the earlier movements, so each movement bases its identity on being different from other identified minorities.

For parallel reasons, there has been steadily increasing pressure within the gay and disability rights movements to "come out."
First, as the literature for the 1988 National Coming Out Day makes
clear, the fact that so many are closeted means that most of the
American public has no idea how large and how diverse the lesbian
and gay population is, and how close to home. The situation is similar for people with invisible disabilities. Second, the effectiveness of
efforts for legislation and legal protection rely on making known the
number of people affected by discrimination and the impact of that
discrimination on individuals' lives. Third, consciousness raising
through the telling of individual stories to reach a political analysis
is a basic developmental tool of both movements.

Theoretically, the women's movement, because of the consciousness-raising model and the movement's continuous struggle
with racism, and thus with other -isms, incorporates in its agendas

the concerns of both lesbians and women with disabilities. Theoretically, the gay rights movement, because of its preoccupation with legal and social discrimination against homosexuals, incorporates the concerns of lesbians. Theoretically, the disability rights movement, through its focus on accessibility and on work-force and housing discrimination, incorporates the concerns of disabled women in general and disabled lesbians in particular. In practice, however, lesbians and women with disabilities have experienced outright discrimination, minimization, or unconscious exclusion in all three movements.

Finally, simply because we are women, the assertion of an identity based on sexuality (as by a lesbian) or on physical characteristics (as by a person with chronic illness) reinforces the sexual objectification to which all women are subjected in our culture. Even people sympathetic to the women are likely to assume a proprietary or parental advice-giving attitude on how to disguise the "handicap" through the exercise of feminine behavior.[6] Less benign interpreters will generalize the perceived sexual or asexual quality to the whole person and refuse to attend to any other traits.[7]

Lesbians have by now developed a substantial body of coming out literature and have recovered or decoded a longer literature about lesbian passing. Disability literature by women has only recently developed as a genre focused specifically on women; the genre is derived at least in part from lesbian coming out literature. A longer tradition, as yet only partly decoded, of personal narratives about particular disability experiences is also available, as is sociological and rehabilitation literature about disability in general, which sometimes differentiates women's and men's experience. My analysis is based on these materials.

## BENEFITS OF PASSING

One of the difficulties with discussion of passing is that if passing is successful, it is literally invisible, so we know about it only when it fails, when the actor decides to make the deception public, or when family members or friends share the secret with outsiders. We are less likely to know the benefits of passing, because our detailed information comes retrospectively from people who have a special interest in discussing the costs.

Some of the reasons we pass are survival reasons: for safety, for security, for comfort. But there are political reasons as well: passing increases the possibility of being accepted as an individual; it provides opportunities for reaching people who would "tune out" if they knew the person trying to communicate belonged to a devalued group; it protects other closeted people; and it reduces the amount of hassle.

Usually people who pass fear both physical and psychological losses that may come with exposure. Loss of employment, for example, entails not only such risks as homelessness and hunger, but loss of medical insurance, the ability to afford protheses, such tools as computers and adaptive telephone equipment, and the social reinforcement that comes from being accepted as "normal." Lesbians may be more susceptible to "gay bashing" when they are not closeted and to other kinds of sexual harassment (e.g., from those who think heterosexual sex, or even rape, will "cure" them). These are not unrealistic fears.[8] Laws prohibiting employment and housing discrimination do not extend to sexual preference, and those that protect people with disabilities have limited application where the worker is perceived as missing too much work or is unable to meet standards of appropriate appearance (for example, smiling, acting enthusiastic). Dolores Klaich, describing "lesbian survivors" from the 1940s, and 1950s, says, "We had learned to play society's closeted game; we had endured and we had survived. So many of our friends had not."[9] And Irena Klepfisz says, "As an adult I have nurtured what I consider to be a mature, healthy paranoia, one which I cling to as an important means of survival."[10] These are open lesbians; paranoia is obviously greater among those who pass, whose code is "Be selective. Cultivate normalcy. Stress sameness. Blend in. For God's sake don't pile difference upon difference. It's not safe."[11]

Sharon Stonekey describes the alienation she experienced as she moved back into the closet at an Alcoholics Anonymous meeting in the small town to which she and her lover moved after being threatened and harassed in another neighborhood where they were out as lesbians. They have chosen to pass in order literally to survive. Stonekey's survival also depends on recovery from her disease, alcoholism, for which she seeks a "program of honesty" while blatant homophobia prevents her from being honest. Furthermore, her ability to move, to escape a dangerous situation, obviously relies on employment, to which admission either of alcoholism or of lesbian identity can easily be a threat.[12] A Dublin lesbian describes the effect of her being out as a lesbian in her workplace:

> In a normal working day at that time, nobody would exchange a pleasantry with me. Worse, they taunted me about my gayness. Whispers, giggles and tension when I was around began to occur with increasing regularity. In short, I was isolated at work.
>
> My work suffered as a result. I began to concentrate less and consequently make more mistakes. I was frequently called to the manager's office and asked to account for my behaviour. The mistakes were idiotic, something a child with decent writing skills wouldn't do, but they were becoming a feature of my work. This situation lasted for about six months at which time I was expecting to have a nervous breakdown. It was at this time that I had my final interview with the manager. He assured me that I didn't have a future with the company. That my "sort of person" didn't "fit in." He offered a fairly large financial settlement and asked that I resign.[13]

Having such experiences or hearing or reading about them reinforces the belief that passing is desirable. Sometimes it is literally required by the employer.

Women and men in the military or in government service will be discharged if they are known to be gay or lesbian[14] or if they fail to pass periodic physical examinations, including weight and fitness checks. Obviously these regulations do not keep the services free of people from the targeted groups, but they do keep them in the closet. Indeed, the physical requirements can be harmful to the employee's health, as they lead to crash dieting, fasting, and overexertion. For an individual in a military career to choose not to pass is merely a self-destructive way to quit her job.

The benefits of disability passing are most clearly illustrated by the most stigmatized diseases, AIDS and cancer. Although it is not legal in the United States to fire someone for having antibodies against HIV, people are losing their jobs for this reason, and the U.S. Department of Defense removes personnel discovered to be HIV-positive "from sensitive, stressful jobs,"[15] thus providing a model for private businesses to do likewise. Not only does this affect an increasing population of women, especially black and Hispanic, but it is a pattern familiar to women, many of whom have lost jobs after mastectomies and other cancer surgeries.[16] Although the use of a prosthesis or the pretense that the illness was less serious or less stigmatized may not prevent the illegal discrimination, it is understandable that the affected individual sees passing as a survival issue. In addition to needing employment for food, shelter, and self-esteem, her ability to obtain the medical care needed for her physical condition depends on her being employed.

In a culture such as ours that has a "body code," economic survival depends on passing.[17] Indeed, Shulamit Reinharz asserts that "in some situations, if one's body does not meet the body code, the woman is retained only if she can pass. When women attain the symbolic meaning of 'physically unattractive' (to men) they may be pushed out of visible areas or forced into retirement regardless of their skills."[18] When this is true of physical attractiveness (to men), women whose bodies are unreliable because of chronic illness or disability or those who are not interested in appealing to men are at risk. Since all women in the culture are expected to attempt to meet the body code through clothing, cosmetics, mannerisms, shaving, and plastic surgery if necessary, expecting further sacrifice of health or psychological well-being seems almost "normal." Community programs to improve employment opportunities for people with disabilities emphasize socially acceptable appearance and behavior.[19]

George Henderson and Willie V. Bryan describe the penalties that are typically enforced by employers and coworkers

> when individuals deviate noticeably from established societal and agency norms. First, their supervisors and peers direct an increasing amount of communication toward them, trying to change their attitude and behavior. If this fails, one after another of their coworkers abandons the perceived troublemaker as hopeless. Gradually, communication ceases. In the end, the would-be change agents are ignored or excluded from organization activities.[20]

Henderson and Bryan are addressing the problems of individuals who are working to include people with disabilities in the workplace. The process of exclusion they describe helps to account for the emphasis many disability rights activists place on normalization of disabled workers. The movement does not advocate passing, but its stress on productivity and even on resisting discrimination may reinforce individual decisions to pass in order to maintain employment and to avoid social isolation like that imposed on the "would-be change agent."

In addition, there are some disabilities that are literally unmentionable in mainstream American society, principally those having to do with sexuality or elimination. Until very recently mastectomies and colostomies were not subjects of public discussion, for example. People with such disabilities were expected to keep them secret. As Erving Goffman observed, such people "are forced to present themselves falsely in almost all situations, having to conceal their unconventional secrets because of everyone's having to conceal the conventional ones."[21] Lesbians, whose "deviance" also involves sexuality, have a comparable experience of presenting themselves falsely in most situations.

Lesbian and disabled women who are mothers have additional reasons for passing at work and elsewhere in the community. Custody suits frequently cite the mother's "unfitness" for parenting either because of her life-style choices or because of her physical or mental disabilities. These cases are often publicized in lesbian and disability publications, where people who are weighing the decision to pass are likely to see them. Moreover, children bring their families into contact with schools, day-care centers, and social agencies where heterosexism and ableism will very probably cause difficulties for both parent and child.[22] If the child has special needs, the agencies and programs may involve medical and psychological necessities. In any case, social acceptance is a crucial issue for children and their families. The mother's willingness and ability to meet the extra demands, energy, and money that may be required by refusal to pass must be taken into consideration, as must her assessment of the child's hardiness under such pressures.

Family members are stigmatized by association with any member's disability[23] and in response (or anticipatory fear) frequently try to pass as a group, enforcing secrecy on all members.

This too is realistic. It is perhaps most vividly seen in the families of people with mental illness. Maryellen Walsh interviewed a hundred families that included a member who was labeled schizophrenic, most of whom "told me they never mentioned the illness unless they were pressed, unless someone 'had to know.' They were afraid of losing friends, afraid of increasing their social isolation, afraid of making an already difficult life worse." One mother told Walsh that "she was sure anyone who found out wouldn't hire her."[24] Similarly, mothers of people with AIDS have told me that they fear their own coworkers' finding out because they know of other family members who have been isolated and victimized at work, even after the affected child had died.[25] Lesbian coming out stories often cite family members' concerns about preserving their own anonymity as relatives of lesbians, as if this, too, were an infection, a virus, a contagious disability.[26] The families in Walsh's study, mothers of people with AIDS, and parents of lesbians frequently do choose to pass, however loving their relationship may be with the stigmatized person. Sharing family membership, they share the stigma.

Furthermore, being one step removed from the issue, they may find it easier to pass and are more likely to perceive the benefits as outweighing the risks.[27] The person who actually has the disability day by day is more likely to feel the strain of maintaining the deception. The lesbian who lives part of her life in a community or a relationship in which she is accepted as she is will be likely to experience discomfort where she is hidden. Even so, many individuals choose to pass despite their realistic understanding of the costs. The perceived benefits include several political considerations.

First, people who choose to pass often say that they are doing so temporarily, so that they will first be accepted as individuals before the stigma is introduced, when it will become more difficult to see beyond the "perceived focus"—the "normal's" preconception about "the sphere of life-activity for which an individual's particular stigma primarily disqualifies him [sic]."[28] The passing woman, who knows, for example, that lesbians are often seen as *only* sexual, or that people with chronic illnesses are seen as *unable* to keep up with the work load, chooses to establish, first, that she is a person with many skills and interests or someone who always completes her work on time. She assumes that once this is known, others will see her sexual choices or her particular illness as just one of her many characteristics. Myths and stereotypes do in fact strongly influence acceptance of individuals. This perceived benefit of passing is closely aligned with those involving safety and security, but it also implies at least some intention of moving out of secrecy once the goal of the passing, to become known as an individual, is met.

A second political benefit flows from the first. The person who passes assumes that she can advocate the causes of her own and other minority groups more effectively if she is not stereotyped as one of them. This is a frequent subject of discussion among lesbian teachers.[29] In view of the amount of open homophobia in our class-rooms, it is probably realistic to assume that many of the things we might teach about the situation of women and men in our society will be "tuned out" by students who know from the outset that the teacher is lesbian. Similarly, it is argued, women who dress and be-have in heterosexually approved ways can be heard with less auto-matic resistance when they criticize American standards of beauty or heterosexism in general. The political stance, here, is that one can undermine the patriarchy from within only if one can pass. The same argument is advanced for publishing novels with mainstream pub-lishers rather than as "gay literature"[30] and for the writer's passing as heterosexual so that readers will not interpret the whole work as sex-ual. One writer Dolores Klaich interviewed was openly lesbian in her everyday life but chose to be anonymous in the interview because "there are people who read my books, I'd hate for them, or others, to read my work always bearing in mind my private sex life."[31]

The same basic argument can be made for persons with disabilities. Particularly now that disability access (at least for wheel-chair users) has some general societal acceptance as an understand-able cause, it is relatively easy to introduce other access issues into casual conversation, particularly if one is not seen as having an ax to grind or a weakness to be exploited. As an apparently able-bodied person, I begin group activities by suggesting several ways in which people may need to allow for their physical and psychological needs in our work space. These will be heard as neutral statements if I am not first seen as someone who is incapable of meeting the rigors of my work life without special arrangements. If a person with a chronic illness anticipates some days when she cannot work, or cannot work comfortably without frequent breaks, she may try to structure these into everyone's work life before telling anyone that her condition is chronic, assuming that by the time they find out they will understand that different physical needs can be accommodated in the work environment, that these are not special arrangements for a person who lacks ability. Anne Finger describes a form of disability passing that involves acknowledging the disability but not its negative aspects because listeners will hear only the negatives and miss the presentation of such positive qualities as the ability to find a community or to overcome self-hatred. Finger chose after such an experience "never again [to] say anything about self-hatred, except to other disabled people."[32]

A more difficult political/personal benefit of passing is protection of someone other than the passing individual herself. I have touched on this in the discussion of family members' passing. It is common for family members of a lesbian who comes out to them to ask her to protect them by concealing her lesbianism, at least from certain people, and it is common for family members themselves to pass, if they can. Where this situation becomes a political choice is where the family member herself is at a known risk. For example, a parent may work for a church that considers homosexuality a sin, or the lesbian partner may hold a job from which she will certainly be fired if her lesbian identity is exposed. Teachers and people with military jobs are frequently in this situation. The partner may also be closeted for personal reasons. One of Dolores Klaich's respondents explained:

> There's also another reason, perhaps at the moment the most important. The woman I'm living with—her family doesn't know about her lesbianism, and since she's very close to her family, and I know her family, it would be cruel if they were to put two and two together from this interview if they happened to see it. This is no way to treat a family you're close to. It has to be done—if it's done at all—face to face.[33]

An analogous situation for someone with a disability occurs when the illness is or is perceived to be contagious (as in the case of relatives of people with AIDS) or familial (as in Huntington's disease). It may also occur where the relative or partner is expected, accurately or not, to have to give extensive physical or emotional support to the person with the disability. In a workplace in which mothers routinely use their own sick leave to care for sick children, being known as the parent of someone with a chronic illness may be a serious handicap.[34] The relative with the disability then may choose to pass in order to protect the nondisabled person.

If the disability is indeed familial, and one relative has been passing, another's decision not to pass may be seen as a direct attack on the first's life choices. When Dolores Klaich decided to publish her book on lesbian relationships, a woman who had been closeted for thirty years reprimanded her for writing the book: "She has spent thirty years creating her double identity. She refused an invitation to be interviewed about her life, even anonymously. . . . she did not welcome entrance of what she termed 'the leering public' into her life."[35] Notice that the closeted lesbian sees another woman's public activity as threatening her own secret.[36] For a disabled person, the threat is in part exposure of the personal life, in part work-force discrimination, and also in part disclosure of real limitations that may have been disguised by such devices as schedule manipulation, workspace organization, and outright deception (for example, when hospitalization is treated as a vacation or an incomplete report is filed as if it were finished).

Still another political motivation may be simply to reserve energy to fight political battles elsewhere. If, on balance, the stress of passing seems less than the stress of being out, the individual may choose to pass without compromising the political intention of working to achieve change in conditions that make passing desirable.[37]

This benefit of passing—saving energy—draws our attention to the theme that pervades discussion of all of the benefits, the extreme societal pressure to pass, to act normal, to conform. "OK," says one woman, "I know what you're getting at. I pass. I pass beautifully. And if you pass, society—people let you be."[38] For people with chronic illness, balancing the different kinds of energy depletion may itself diminish survival resources. The energy spent keeping a secret might better be spent on healing;[39] the energy spent coping with people's negative responses might better be spent on finding appropriate help.

Pressures to pass include economic and legal sanctions; cultural standards of beauty and social acceptability; the fears of family members, partners, and other passing women; and outright threats of job loss, isolation, withdrawal of friendship, or loss of insider status. In addition, there are some pressures to pass from inside the very social movements that otherwise encourage coming out.

In the women's movement, sensitivity to and acceptance of lesbians, especially in leadership positions, was a serious, divisive issue in the early 1970s, one which was fortunately resolved in favor of active advocacy of lesbian rights as well as the parallel development of a diverse lesbian feminist political and cultural community. Still, it is not uncommon even in 1989 to hear feminists publicly advocate that lesbians pass for the good of the feminist cause, or at least that they dress and act in heterosexually attractive ways in order to be more readily accepted by those who resist the label "feminist."[40]

Such pressures evoke anger or frustration from women who have fought these battles before, but they may be very influential on women who are deciding whether or not to continue passing. Further, lesbian groups may encourage passing either directly, by reciting the dangers of being out, or indirectly, by being so militant about political correctness that women who have fears about the dangers of exposure are alienated and seek to hide from the political lesbian community as well as from homophobic society. Further, the women who stay in such political groups may be dis-couraged from addressing their internalized homophobia.[41] To achieve an informed and thoughtful decision about passing requires considerable self-knowledge, particularly about internalized oppression.

When a community develops a hierarchy within the group, in this case ranging from totally closeted to "public lesbians," individuals will place themselves along the continuum because of their physical or sociological or emotional characteristics and either ignore the other possibilities or consider them antithetical to their own best interests. For example, a lesbian who must support a child and avoid a custody suit may be alienated from a public political demonstration. Having made this decision, she is less likely to join the group on another issue, or when she changes jobs or her child is grown. That such hierarchy exists may not be a deliberate agenda of the lesbian group, but it functions to preserve homophobia.

Similarly, in the disability rights movement, hierarchies have developed between disabilities, which serve to reinforce passing among those who can precisely because others are urged not to pass.

Thus, birth-disabled and newly disabled individuals resist working with each other; the movement gives physical disabilities higher priority for support than mental or sensory disabilities; self-supporting individuals are valued over those on welfare, and those who look less disabled are valued over those who look more so.[42]

All three movements have at times pressed people with mental disabilities to pass within the disability group itself.[43] All develop norms within their own hierarchy under which members of less acceptable groups are expected to be silent or compliant or even to match the group's ageist or ableist stereotypes.[44] Until disability rights movement groups explore internalized ableism, cooperation is problematic, and those who are able to pass are unlikely to be fully committed to the needs or agendas of those who cannot. Barbara Bechdol clearly states the disability agenda: "In my mind, disability is about oppression and overcoming or working around it. The oppressors' attitude may be internalized or externalized. If it is internalized, then you work on yourself. One way to do that is to realize that you are not the only one experiencing the oppression. In fact, oppression is a cross-disability phenomenon."[45] The pressure to pass in this movement is enormous because of the unjustified historic exclusion from the work force of those who can work. As the "Declaration of Principles" printed in the *Independent Living Advocate* states, "Society has consistently belittled individuals with disabilities by equating the term disability with the traits *weak and unproductive* and assumed that these individuals cannot *compete* with their fellow citizens" (italics added).[46] The movement then seeks to prove its members strong, productive, and able to compete. This effort to demonstrate productivity, the training to be socially attractive, and the emphasis on mainstreaming and normalization, while they are designed to bring people with disabilities out of hiding and into the public work force, serve simultaneously to encourage them, once there, to pass if they can.

## COSTS OF PASSING

I have presented the benefits of passing at length because so many of us do pass despite the overwhelming criticism the process receives. Similarly, although imaginative literature about black people's passing as white emphasized the extremely harmful effect on the passer's physical and mental health, hundreds of thousands of Americans had done so by the 1960s, presumably because access to jobs, cultural activities, decent or at least neutral treatment, and other forms of social acceptance were worth it.[47] As long as the penalties for being an open member of a minority group are severe, many individuals who can pass will do so. To the extent that they succeed, we are left to deduce their evaluation of the benefits from the negative evidence of penalties against those who fail to pass and the retrospective stories of those who have decided that the costs are too high.[48] Literature about the costs is extensive.

Deception is demoralizing, anxiety provoking, and harmful to the passer's health and relationships. It also deprives society as a whole of knowledge about our diversity. Passing involves adopting the values of the privileged group; it causes "emotive dissonance"; it is harmful to mental and physical health; it makes the secret the central focus of the passer's life; it harms relationships with those who know the secret and with those who do not; it makes it difficult to know who your friends or enemies are; and it maintains the very repressive system that causes it.

First, the one who passes adopts the characteristics of the privileged group in order to get a job or avoid punishment. The decision may be as simple as wearing a business suit and thus making a nonverbal statement that you accept the values of the corporation. Wearing the uniform is a condition of employment. But the testing of your commitment to mainstream values continues: "After the uniform, will you also stand for off-color humor? will you accept stories of sexual conquest? will you join in on racist jokes? . . . The point of the test is that a true token never threatens or deviates from the norms of the dominant culture."[49] Judy Grahn describes an episode in her own life when someone told a homophobic joke: five of the six who were laughing were gay. She concludes, "The walls of the closet are guarded by the dogs of terror and the inside of the closet is a house of mirrors."[50] When we choose to pass, the consistent danger is that we will forget the purpose of the deception, that it will stop being a deception because we have become believers. Thus, a woman with a "kidney problem" describes herself as "frantically, deliberately, DETERMINEDLY not disabled" and almost completely closeted as a disabled person because "inactivity is a known contributor to kidney failure in cases like mine." To me, the striking thing about this account is her assumption that by definition being openly disabled means to be inactive. The societal stereotype overrides knowledge of her own physical needs and she sees her choices as being either to perceive *herself* as nondisabled or to be inactive and thus at risk for kidney failure: "a fundamental self-deception," she says, "but it works."[51] The danger, of course, as Michele Cliff reminds us, is this: "I know who I am but you will never know who I am. I may in fact lose touch with who I am."[52] Mary Daly reminds us of the "doublethink" discovery of George Orwell's Winston Smith, that "if you want to keep a secret you must also hide it from yourself."[53] It is a habit women know well, resulting as it does in our inability to see ourselves at eighty as old women, so thoroughly have we absorbed the cultural value on youth by passing as younger than we are.[54] Despite the many costs of passing, "many closeted women have become institutionalized like long-term prison inmates, and would not leave the apparent protection of their psychic prisons even if given the opportunity."[55]

Even without fully assimilating mainstream values, women who pass are forced to maintain a divided and dishonest sense of themselves. "We find no honor in our self-assessment as a dishonest person."[56] The double life, Judy Grahn says, "means that the gay person can never simply stand flat-footed on the earth; there are always two people operating in one body, and one of them is a liar."[57] The cost, ongoing as long as the lie continues, is " 'emotive dissonance'—the discordant emotional penalty paid by a person who is 'maintaining a difference between feeling and feigning.' "[58]

Such doublethink, dishonesty, and discordance are themselves stressful enough to contribute to physical or mental health problems. Passing is quite harmful to the passer's health, especially if the initial reason for passing was a disability. For example, an individual with a heart problem may attempt tasks that exacerbate the condition, or a person using carefully timed medication may skip or postpone a dose. Because the disability is hidden, the person may be quite unrealistic about its seriousness.[59] Further, when symptoms do appear, they may be treated as insignificant or emotional by observers who then encourage the individual to minimize or ignore her own body's signals. Potentially this situation could lead to further disability.[60] Even when the results are not life threatening, the physical penalties can be severe. Berenice Fisher and Roberta Galler describe

Barbara, who "after making her way to work through severe winter weather . . . would sit alone in her office and cry from the pain in her legs," and Alison, who periodically had to withdraw for periods of recuperation after keeping up with her nondisabled friends.[61] Laura Brown, writing about post-traumatic stress disorder (PTSD), describes "the negative synergy of trauma and silence, abuse and secrecy, that would lead women to feel and act crazy, when in fact it was mainly the context in which they were forced to operate that was pathological."[62] Although the passing environment may be less openly abusive than the violent experiences that produce PTSD,[63] the conditions of "trauma and silence, abuse and secrecy" may well be replicated in the lives of disability passers. Susan Brown, Debra Connors, and Nanci Stern describe physical effects of disability passing at two extremes: endangering physical health rather than admitting the need for help, or acting out "supercrip" behavior and thus alienating oneself from other people with disabilities who do not succeed in (or aspire to) that role.[64] Robin Norwood, describing the effects of trying to lead a "normal" life while suffering from depression, says, "It is trying to keep the secret that makes us sicker and letting it go that helps us to recover." She describes perfectionism as a natural outcome of compensating for the secret disability, and being unaware of or resistent to the need for rest as increasing the symptoms.[65]

Lesbians, too, may experience stress-related illnesses and attract psychiatric labels as a result of passing. Lee Zevy and Sahli Cavallero describe traits produced by "invisibility and deception": "incongruent body language, cues, and signals; trouble establishing intimacy; and tremendous anxiety, woodenness, rigidity or anger about revealing secrets about lesbian identity. Based on these traits, lesbians are often misdiagnosed as narcissistic or borderline personalities."[66]

One ironic outcome of passing is that, far from reducing the secret to the status of just one feature among many in the passing woman's life—a principal goal of passing in the first place—it makes the secret the central fact. "When a person must constantly be vigilant in order to deny his [sic] disability it becomes the central focus of his life. He may resort to partial social isolation in order to help conceal his defect and thus fend off possible discussion."[67] Wendy Chapkis quotes "Kathay," a woman who considered the fact that she was fat so crucial to her identity that she perceived herself at 130 pounds to be a fat woman passing as thin. So preoccupied was she with her discredited identity that, she says, "I did really weird stuff when I met new people." Unable to imagine that other people did not recognize her deception, she would freeze: "I thought that if I was absolutely quiet, they might not turn and look at me and realize I was fat. . . . I would just freeze like an animal sniffing a hunter."[68]

Needless to say, this obsession is harmful to her personal relationships. Passing interferes with all of an individual's relationships, from superficial ones like Kathay's new acquaintances through coworkers, friends, intimate partners, and other members of the lesbian or disability community. By keeping relationships distant, the passing individual limits time spent with other people and thus avoids obligations to divulge information.[69] At the same time, of course, she prevents herself from making new friends and may, as well, undermine the working relationships that passing was meant to protect. At the same time, the habit of reticence reinforces the "layers of hiddenness, the masks, the false faces" endemic in feminine role conditioning and thus limits the capacity for friendship. Madonna Kolbenschlag, who describes this as a problem for many women, cites Kierkegaard's description of the fundamental quality of a spiritually whole person, "transparency."[70] Transparency certainly is a quality a passing woman must avoid. Baba Copper, writing about generational barriers between women caused by age passing, describes the hostility generated by passing: "When we pass easily, we gain comfort knowing that we do not have to identify with the woman who, in our view, is not passing. 'I am not like her' translates easily into 'I am better than her.' "[71] Thus we dissociate ourselves from members of our own group. One of the participants in Dolores Klaich's research describes her dilemma as a closeted teacher in dealing with students who may have been lesbians. She was not, she says, worried about her job, but was "really torn up" about her responsibility to them. Uncertain about how to handle the situation, she changed the subject, thus of course leaving them "very troubled" and with "nowhere to turn."[72] Other closeted women are defended against any suggestion of obligation to come out. Sasha Gregory Lewis quotes "Viv": "Look, Bev and I are about as closeted as you can get. So are our friends. That's a kind of security for us. When you do hear from these radical lesbians, they're always trying to get you to come out. I've lived my life in the closet and I'm going to stay there.

And I certainly don't want to be around anyone who's going to start telling me to come out; I simply am afraid of them. I don't trust them."[73] As Judy Grahn says of gay people who actively persecute open homosexuals, "There is no safety in this behavior."[74]

The segregation of passing women from those who are "out" works both ways. Politically active lesbians resent the loss of energy, money, and moral support they believe the closeted women could bring to the cause. Even in the family, a potentially intimate network, those who believe in honesty about the stigma may refuse to associate with closeted family members whom they believe should be more open. Barbara Grier, for example, chooses not to associate with her sister who is "totally in the closet." "I do have the option," she says, "when it comes to my own flesh-and-blood sister to decide that what she is doing is morally reprehensible to me, unconscionable, and cannot be stood. And that, therefore, I have the right to decide that I will have nothing to do with her."[75] Divisions over the issue of passing isolate the passing woman from those who might provide her with support if she were not so protective of her secret.

Isolating themselves from other lesbians, those who attempt to pass as heterosexual are unable instead to form close relationships with heterosexuals because acceptance by them is based on a lie.[76] Further, the passing woman cannot be sure the "normal" acquaintance does in fact believe the lie. Leo Buscaglia describes nondisabled people who "believe they are making it easier for persons who are disabled if they avoid *seeing* their impairments. They act as if they do not realize the other person's *secret.* . . . This attitude loudly proclaims the view of disability as stigma and usually results in causing both parties to feel uncomfortable to the extent that future normal interaction is avoided."[77] I have been in this situation with a closeted lesbian friend and a friend with a chronic illness. In each case, I lost several years of what might have been a valuable friendship before both of us got honest. As Karen Thompson says, "When you can't share the most important things going on in your life, your relationships remain shallow."[78]

Erving Goffman shows how friends may not only help the individual to pass but may disguise from her the limitations of her passing. "They can in fact serve as a protective circle, allowing him [sic] to think he is more fully accepted as a normal person than in fact is the case. They will therefore be more alive to his differentness than he will himself."[79] Protecting my friends from "knowing that I know" thus handicaps them and denies them valuable feedback. Yet I protected them because I believed (rightly, as it turned out) that they wanted me to help them pass. We encouraged each other's deceptions and thus deliberately constructed an unreliable and dishonest relationship.

Without a circle of friends (and, in the case of disability, of professionals), the passing woman is likely to put an exhausting and perhaps intolerable requirement of support on her intimate partner or those few family members or friends who know the secret. If these people are also closeted, their own needs for support, information, and feedback on their situation will also be confined to the partnership, family, or friendship, further increasing the stress.[80] "Louise," having described the dishonesty, fear, and confinement of her long-term closeted relationship, concludes, "Over the years I think it wore on us. All of our human feelings were loaded into those few hours when we could be ourselves. The rest we repressed. I think even some of the feelings for each other got repressed too."[81] And another woman describes a similar discovery: "I began to see what being closeted had done to us. It had made us totally dependent on each other for every kind of emotional gratification. It was a kind of slavery. *All* we had was each other. So neither of us could make a move that didn't threaten the relationship."[82]

To further compound the stress on her primary relationship, a woman with chronic illness will probably pass at least some of the time with her partner. Raven describes her own behavior—sneaking aspirin so her lover will not know how often she has headaches, saying she wants to be alone so she will not have to admit to needing a nap, telling her lover to leave when she is really in pain and wants her to stay. Their communication is tangled, she says: "How could I separate my unnecessary emotional neediness from my real physical needs?" She says she "has internalized the societal message: sick is bad . . . and the alternative culture message: of course I could be well if only I got my head together."[83] Such passing may in fact alleviate some strain on the relationship in that protecting the lover from "too many" demands may respect her need not to be overwhelmed by her partner's illness, but only at the cost of a basically dishonest relationship, which of course increases the stress for both women.

Finally, a major cost of passing is to society as a whole. We are kept from knowledge of our own diversity and of our heterosexist and ableist bias because so many lesbians and women with disabilities are literally invisible to us. Disabled women are deprived of role models and contributions of women with disabilities go unrecognized.[84] Our understanding of our own history is distorted by the suppression of knowledge about lesbian experience, and our cultural bias prevents our decoding the evidence that is there.[85] Family members and coworkers believe in stereotypes about lesbians and people with disabilities because they are unaware that they know members of these groups. "Social suppression of gay culture is reflected in such statements as 'No one cares what you do in private, just don't flaunt it,' that is, don't express it, make it public. But without flaunting there is no culture; there is only the imitation of heterosexual culture and the illusion that one culture exists. Closets exist to maintain this illusion."[86] And the illusion, as Judy Grahn says elsewhere, is "a big false bubble of [the heterosexual culture's] own invention."[87]

## COMING OUT

The benefits of passing have to do with avoiding persecution, the deprivation and pain inflicted by heterosexism and ableism in our communities. Maintaining these prejudices is certainly not desirable, and since passing serves to support them, the question that confronts those who pass (and all the rest of us) is how to maintain personal integrity while passing and how gradually to come out of that condition.

I am interested here in people who are self-consciously past the first stage of coming out: to themselves. Having chosen to pass, and aware of the costs as well as the benefits, they intend to avoid assuming the values of the community that makes passing necessary. This requires maintenance of a double consciousness and willingness to keep clear one's own identity even while acting a different role.

Although there is a substantial body of literature about the coming out process for both lesbians and people with disabilities, I have found very little about strategies for maintaining personal integrity while deliberately choosing to pass when we would prefer to do otherwise. My information on this subject has come mainly from personal informants and workshop participants, though after I had accumulated a list of these strategies I began to see them occasionally in the literature. Again, a problem with coming out literature in this respect is that it is retrospective and thus usually written with a bias against passing.

I call these "survival strategies," not in the sense that passing itself is for economic survival, but meaning that they are chosen to enable the disabled or lesbian self to survive during the performance that passing requires. The actors use essentially the same devices that people who are less closeted use in the process of coming out, though they use them more privately. These include the use of symbols to help the passer to remember who she is, humor, reading, analysis, controlled use of language, writing, and the personal resources of home life, the lesbian or disability community, and deliberately planned "time out."

If passing is seen as a temporary condition, the passer's resources for maintaining honesty with herself are not experienced as life threatening if inadvertently (or unconsciously) they make passing a partial condition as well. If the goal is to move toward more openness without exposing oneself to inappropriate dangers, a gradual process toward partial disclosure permits testing the safety of each step.

For example, several women report the use of a talisman or symbol as a reminder for themselves.[88] Jewelry with a female symbol, a labyris, a pink triangle, a wheelchair symbol, and buttons for disability rights organizations are among these devices. Recognizable to other members of the minority group, these symbols are also usually known only to those who are "wise" and at least politically supportive of worthy minority causes. They may nonverbally identify other closeted people. The meaning of the talisman to the outside observer can to some extent be controlled. I wear a goddess pendant which shows Hera with a labyris in one hand and a pomegranate in the other. When I am asked what she has in her hand ("wise" people do not ask; they know), I say it is a double-headed ax, which is a symbol of transformation, and a pomegranate, which is a symbol of sensual delight. They usually respond with enthusiasm about pomegranates. Most users of these devices escalate their use as they begin to feel safe with the minimal level of disclosure. A talisman may, however, be completely private, and can be used for purposes other than disclosure. A lesbian may wear pearls (or "straight beads") to remind herself that in this situation she is "in costume" as a straight woman. A particular article of clothing is perceived as a disguise, hiding not merely a brace or some other clue about disability status, but also the stigmatized condition itself.

Reading, writing, and analysis are tools to clarify for the passer herself what is going on and how it is related to her situation as a member of a discredited group or as someone who finds it necessary to pass. The use of movement literature is typical. Some women report literally keeping it in the closet. Writing a journal or poetry or stories makes specific the nature of the problem and reminds us that the oppressor's perspective is not the only one, is not "true" for us. Storytelling, the telling of the individual stories of each of us, of all of us, is the basic tool of consciousness raising. As Suzanne Pharr reminds us, "All of the stories are of equal importance and must be heard."[89] First, we must hear them ourselves.

What we are talking about here is a process of unlearning. Having dedicated some energy to learning how to conceal her stigma, the individual now sets out to reverse the process.[90] Like the learning, this is a risky, dangerous-feeling endeavor. Increasing one's own clarity about why it is necessary is essential, and much of this learning comes from introspection. Simultaneously, the reading, writing, and thinking involve raising to awareness the unconscious aspects of passing,[91] so that we know and can name the ways in which we act out the heterosexual, able-bodied role and how those actions have privileged us. The passing cannot be unlearned until it is conscious.

Having some areas of one's life in which one is deliberately, thoughtfully honest is crucial. For most this is home life. As we have seen, however, personal relationships are endangered when home is the only place perceived as safe. It is also essential to have some contact with a supportive community. Resources include feminist and disability organizations, support groups for specific disabilities or for disabilities in general, twelve step programs, book discussion groups, and so on. Time out, away from the places in which passing is necessary, is very important. A lesbian retreat or concert or music festival, a disability rights conference, or a weekend in the woods with intimate friends can help to restore perspective on the temporary nature of the passing condition.

Finally, an indispensable technique for maintaining integrity is controlling our use of language. The ability to name our own experience, accurately and with care, is vital to our empowerment. It is also a way of knowing that we are being honest about the truth of our experience. For someone who is passing this may involve being manipulative or selective; however, the purpose of linguistic precision is not primarily to enlighten the other person, but rather to remind oneself. We tell the truth so we do not have to see ourselves as liars; we control the way we do so in order to protect ourselves from abuse. Neither of these is a discreditable motive.

Both lead almost automatically into the next stage, strategies for moving beyond passing, for coming out. Again, these begin with physical nonverbal signals, often a change in clothing style. Particularly for women with disabilities, this can enormously simplify one's work life, as the trappings of heterosexual attractiveness often interfere with mobility and comfort. Unless there is literally a work uniform, a gradual change in this direction is easy to accomplish (and often a relief to everyone, not just those who are passing). Talking about such changes contributes to the process: "I decided never to wear high heels again; I want to be able to move around more comfortably." "I decided that pleasing Mr. Brown is not worth having tired feet." "I think being required to smile all day is harmful to my health."

Beyond this point, the effort to control the speed of disclosure becomes a preoccupation of the passer. Although it is certainly possible to avoid repeating comments that provoke a negative response, this is a period during which recognition of one's powerlessness over other people's reactions becomes crucial. Always when one is passing there is the possibility of disclosure, either by someone who knows the secret or by the "betrayal" of one's own body. The summer sun darkens the black woman's skin,[92] a woman with asthma has an attack during a meeting, the woman with MS can no longer climb stairs. Sometimes also a "wise" person can recognize behaviors or appearances that are invisible to one less knowledgeable and will simply break the silence. "The decoding capacity of the audience must be specified before one can speak of degrees of visibility."[93] But the deliberate, gradual reduction of passing behavior activates the desire for control and perhaps the fear of being out of control.[94] The fact is that we can control only our own part in the transaction, so the intention of gradual disclosure must be very clear.

Most of the strategies for gradually moving beyond passing have to do with talk. Women begin to refer to outside sources to say things they are not yet willing to say directly: "I saw a woman on 'Donahue' who said that people with chronic illnesses may harm their health by keeping the illness secret." "I read a book about how corporations are changing to accommodate workers with disabilities." "I have a friend who says that Mr. White is incredibly homophobic."

Part of the purpose at this stage is to test the other person's response; part is to educate her or him. Olivia Espin, summarizing stage theories about the coming out process, points out that the final stage (after passing and after rigid separation) includes "an ability to synthesize the best values of both perspectives and to communicate with members of the dominant group."[95] Thus educating a friend or colleague about disability or lesbian issues in the context of your shared experience of the passing situation clarifies both participants' ability to think and communicate across the two cultures (or at least across the two individual experiences).

Bringing the analysis of homophobia and ableism into office discussions serves both to test coworkers' attitudes and to make one's own visible. To say that the joke was not funny because it was homophobic is to "come out" as a decent human being, not as a lesbian. To point out that unventilated conference rooms cause breathing problems is to identify with humans generally, not just the disabled. And then, eventually, to say that one has difficulty in that room because of one's asthma becomes merely a part of that human condition.

Openness about one's home life, too, evolves in informal discussions. The passer's care about language ("I went to a concert with a friend") gradually becomes more specific ("I built a ramp to my porch because my roommate uses a wheelchair"). Simply refusing to make up fictitious stories about how one spent the weekend is a coming out gesture.[96]

Another strategy used by a surprising number of women moving out of passing is publication in the form of letters to the editor, columns in specialized publications, even interviews or columns in local newspapers. For example, one woman I know was interviewed about her participation in a demonstration for women's rights and made a point of telling the interviewer that she had also participated in gay rights demonstrations.[97] Another wrote articles about local independent living facilities and eventually said in print that she was interested in disability because she has a hidden disability herself. These women expressed relief at having broken silence, but for others the publicity is problematic. Sonny Wainright was an open lesbian and made no effort to hide her struggle with cancer, but when a radio station broadcast an announcement of her need for platelet donors, she said she was "embarrassed by the publicity—breaking the societal rule of keeping illness invisible."[98] Such embarrassment is much greater for those who have been passing.

Public statements may or may not be seen and understood by people with whom the individual has been passing, but they indicate a willingness to risk being known[99] and they represent a source of social support for coming out: increased and gradually more public participation in community civil rights, lesbian, and disability organizations. Increasing the size and kind of community in which one is comfortable and able to be honest facilitates coming out to oneself and then to others. "Powerlessness . . . is associated with silence and the 'speechlessness' that the powerful impose on those dispossessed of language. In a sense, then, contemporary lesbian feminists postulate lesbian oppression as a mutilation of consciousness curable by language."[100]

Delighted with the process of renaming or reclaiming language that we see in feminist books, we have sometimes lost sight of the many stages between speaking the oppressor's language and creating our own.[101] These passing women, working self-consciously toward moving beyond passing, try to find ways to use language very gradually, to "cure" their condition in ways that accept and acknowledge their vulnerability and their right to protect themselves.[102]

bell hooks reminds us that "we have all . . . acted in complicity with the existing oppressive system. . . . The compassion we extend to ourselves, the recognition that our change in consciousness and action has been a process, must characterize our approval to those individuals who are politically unconscious."[103] I would add, to those who are becoming conscious. We may accept that "when people have found their authentic self they will not want to lose it. And when they sense that something is being demanded of them to which their whole being says no, they cannot do it. They simply cannot."[104] But it is a mistake, I believe, to assume that a person who has found her authentic self will never choose to pass or feel forced to pass. Our lives differ; our risks differ. Sometimes passing is a matter of survival. None of us can make that judgment for another woman. I agree with Suzanne Pharr, however, that "what we can ask of ourselves . . . is that each of us continuously push the limits of our safety in our risk taking: that we not be content with each level of visibility but keep moving ourselves forward to freedom."[105]

CHAPTER

# NATURE AND TECHNOLOGY

Since the mid-seventies, feminist theory has given increasing attention to women's problematic relationships with nature and with technology. Adrienne Rich's *Of Woman Born,* published in 1976, suggested that we separate ourselves from the patriarchal institution of motherhood by "thinking through our bodies," recognizing them as the "corporeal ground of intelligence."[1] By 1978, when Susan Griffin's *Woman and Nature* and Mary Daly's *Gyn/Ecology* were published, the ideas that men associate women with nature to the detriment of both and that women in fact have a closer relationship to nature which may save the world were widely accepted among feminists.

Women's supposed closeness to nature is both problematic and attractive to feminists as we struggle with biological, sociological, and ethical issues. Defined by our menstrual and childbearing capacities and excluded from male-defined "culture," we have cared for children and people with illnesses and claimed, renamed for ourselves, a positive relationship with cycles of growth and death.

Such closeness to nature may be seen as negative, as it excludes us from culture, power, and control, or positive, as it connects us with the environment and dissociates us from weaponry and chemical pollution. Thus we may be tempted to seek access to technological work on an "equal" basis with men or to withdraw romantically to the "natural" landscape to the considerable discomfort of our sisters who need respirators and ramps.

Women who live with disabilities have more reasons to understand the "corporeal ground of intelligence" than do the temporarily able-bodied and able-minded. They understand it in a way that illuminates women's relationships to nature and technology by providing or forcing a closer and more direct awareness of both.

## NATURE

The dualistic notion that nature is the opposite of culture and that it is the special province of women as culture is the province of men[2] has been discussed, disputed, and disclaimed by feminists—and sometimes embraced. Dualism itself is patriarchal or masculinist, yet our acculturation and the languages in which Westerners have learned to think have historically restricted our access to male-defined culture (and politics); at the same time, our work as mothers, midwives, and caregivers has made us aware of and responsive to the body and its rhythms, its needs.

The term "natural" is a cultural construction implying its opposite, the "social."[3] The idea that women's reproductive capacity and child-rearing activities make them "natural" has been used to confine women to the private, domestic sphere in contrast to men, whose ability to "reason" supposedly fits them for the political world.[4] Because the capacity to give birth is equated with a biological imperative to nurture children and others, political equality and workforce equity become by definition "unnatural." Thus women are required to participate in the patriarchal institution of motherhood, a profoundly social construction justified on the basis of our "natural" biological role in perpetuating the species.[5] White male fear of nature has repeatedly led our culture to identification of blacks and women with the body and with sexuality.[6] Physical disabilities are similar to racial and sex-role handicaps in this respect, as they evoke a similar fear of what is "natural";[7] they remind us that we are all, vulnerably, embodied.

The nature-culture dichotomy is by no means an outdated oversimplification now irrelevant to enlightened people. It has shaped not only our public policy, academic disciplines, and the organization of family life, but even—especially—our language. "These dichotomies are empirically false, but we cannot afford to dismiss them as irrelevant as long as they structure our lives and consciousnesses."[8] Even Jacques Lacan, whose theory some women consider a psychoanalytic model compatible with feminism, "puts the father on the side of culture and the mother on the side of nature" in his analysis of the Oedipal struggle, directly associating culture with language as an expression of social law.[9]

In light of this pervasive and discriminatory use of the nature-woman connection, it is not surprising that a significant amount of female energy has been used in demanding access to "culture" as defined by men and from which women have been excluded. It is equally predictable that women revaluing and renaming our own experience should take a romantic stance toward our identification with nature, especially in view of the negative, life-destroying aspects of male dominance over nature and the human interactivity of our caregiving, birthing, and child-rearing activities.

Ignoring the masculine Victorian concept of nature "red in tooth and claw," many feminists seem closer to the concept presented in "Tintern Abbey" of Wordsworth's sister as the emblem of the calm and peace that nature brings. Thus in Sally Gearhart's popular feminist science fiction, the characters live in a "sentimentalized nature, nature which is reliably benevolent and supportive as they themselves are benevolent and supportive."[10] Acknowledging that we do in fact bleed and die, the back-to-the-land feminist sees these facts as part of our affiliation with a benign natural world, whose cycles men seek to control in contrast to women's ability to cooperate with their flow. In contrast, Annette Kolodny's work on Americans' response to the frontier experience shows men as the ones who fantasized a harmony of man and nature based on the experience of the land as an embodiment of the female principle and women as the ones who literally cultivated the land, making gardens instead of embracing the wilderness.[11] While romantic William Wordsworth idealized his sister's peaceful relationship to nature, romantic Charlotte Brontë presented women characters who were not blessed by nature: Lucy Snowe and even Jane Eyre on the moors.

Autobiographical literature by women whose lives have been reshaped by someone else's disability or illness reflect an unromantic awareness of nature's arbitrariness. When Gerda Lerner was told by her husband's doctor that "nature respects the brain and is kind to it by numbing it first so one does not know," she responded, "But I'm watching it happen and writing it down. So nature is not kind to me."[12] And Suzanne Massie, whose son Bobby had hemophilia, appreciated the unsentimental attitude of fishermen to Bobby's disability: "They accepted Bobby's problem as another act of a capricious Nature—a nature they lived with and whose power they did not question. What had struck Bobby was the bolt of lightning that singles out one tree and not another, the wind that suddenly comes up from no one knows where, or the calamity when one fisherman and not another accidentally falls off his boat and sinks to the bottom like a stone."[13] The feminist retreat to a "natural" (nonurban) environment is fraught with more perils than insect bites and poison ivy for women with disabilities. I once participated in a feminist gathering where sleeping on the floor of a remodeled barn symbolized our lack of class distinctions—and created serious problems for those with even mild arthritis or back problems. After each Michigan Women's Music Festival, the letters column of *Off Our Backs* is full of letters about the problems that rural retreat causes women who use wheelchairs or respirators.

Recent feminist literature is full of warnings against romanticizing nature at the expense of political action. Janice Raymond, who herself has advocated an "ecofeminist" perspective, warns that "this emphasis should not be at the expense of avoiding the world of human affairs or of romanticizing the world of Nature, pitting the latter against the former or characterizing the world of public institutions and human artifacts as inherently patriarchal."[14] Rayna Rapp reminds us that nature is, after all, "a cultural product, continuously reinvented as part of the rhetorical strategies defining and defending slavery, empire, and technological triumphalism."[15] Mary Gordon, expressing her uneasiness about some feminists' argument that "surrogate" motherhood is "unnatural," warns that "simple-minded romance about the 'natural'" will prevent us from understanding, analyzing, and making laws in order to allow "certain groups like homosexuals and older couples to have children in ways that are satisfying to them."[16] And Bonnie Zimmerman, raising the question of whether lesbian separatism is "a white middle-class luxury," reminds us that "tempting as this dream of free lesbian tribes may be, we must consider that tribal cultures have fared poorly under the onslaught of advanced capitalism and imperialism."[17] In a similar political analysis, Charlotte Bunch asserts that we "must not romanticize pre-industrial cultures as the solution" because a viable plan for the future must be based on "what has been both useful and problematic in capitalist and socialist industrialization, as well as in agricultural societies." Bunch warns against such individual solutions as buying "health" foods or "going back to the land, where earth mothers again end up doing all the work from scratch."[18]

"Ecofeminism" is based on women's biological relationship to the natural world, a relationship women are thought to experience more directly than most men because most women menstruate and many of us raise children or care for people who are sick or have disabilities. Celebrants and mourners at the connection between birth and death, we see ourselves as participants in a natural rhythmic cycle. Yet our role in the celebration or the mourning, is human, is conscious. The mother giving birth may wish it were a vegetable process. Babies "should be picked up and held/root end up, soil spilling/from between their toes—/and how much easier it would be/later returning them to the earth."[19] The idea that birth and death are part of a natural process in which humans are participants but not in control may indeed come easier to women who give birth or attend it, especially since between birth and death caring directly for the body gives a sense of growth and change and of our intimate reliance on plants and other animals for our well-being. Such organic awareness nevertheless comes to us partly, perhaps entirely, through culture, as we know whatever it is we know about it through language and memory, which are culturally mediated. As Jane Caputi reminds us, "We have never fully known the organic or the natural, only the filmed version."[20] Similarly, a number of feminists have described the birth experience in Western industrial societies as less a bodily experience for the woman giving birth than an experience of her objectified body *being seen* by the observing doctors, nurses, fetal monitors, and sometimes the child's father.[21] Female bodies, then, "are symbolic/material constructions, and reproduction is political."[22]

We may indeed be especially aware of the closeness of life and death to each other as we give birth or attend to the dying, but fixation on these two events as the "central defining moments" of life discounts the ongoing process of living itself, "the woman who is as she is."[23]

This is where the daily experience of body-aware authentic women who live close to the body's illness and its health, its disability and its individual ability, can clarify our sense of what being natural, in nature, means.

## BODY AWARENESS

If menstruation, childbirth, and caring for people with disabilities place women closer to the rhythms and processes of nature by promoting awareness of our own biology and showing us our relationship to other organic, living, dying, cyclic things, then disabilities that alter the body have the potential for increasing that connection as they increase body awareness. The problem with this theory is that it is by no means certain that women and people with disabilities (in mainstream Western culture at least) are in fact aware of what is really going on in their bodies. A substantial amount of literature, some of it feminist, has been published in the past few years about women's negative self-concept based on masculine objectification of the body, cultural standards of beauty, and various psychological or sociological pressures to change body shape. Eating disorders, inappropriate or harmful use of drugs, and denial of biological reality are common responses to these pressures. The closer the connection between self-image and body image in our culture, the greater the probability that the individual will define herself as worthless or worthwhile on that basis.[24] Unfortunately such congruence is rarely based on a genuine comfort in one's body, whatever its shape or size or abilities. Thus women's body awareness is likely to be acute but negative because societal or masculinist standards for beauty are so restrictive and beauty is the body characteristic most desired for women.[25] As Wendy Chapkis has observed, a white, Western, wealthy standard of beauty is increasingly being adopted throughout the world.[26]

Such body awareness is likely to focus on perceived defects in the body and not on a realistic assessment of its qualities. Many of our body processes are socially unmentionable or the subject of jokes; some are the source of shame. Most of our individual features are "wrong" by external cultural standards. Across American society both men and women feel "depersonalized," "which means that there is literally a sense of not being intimately unified with one's body— of regarding it with some detachment."[27] Indeed, women's objectification of their own bodies is sometimes so extreme that they undertake disfiguring surgery to change a body part. For example, 300,000 American women have had their breasts surgically enlarged, and 15–20,000 each year have their breasts reduced.[28] Stomach stapling, anorexia and bulimia, and chronic dieting are familiar symptoms of voluntary self-denial in North American society.[29] So is compulsive fitness training.[30] Self-denial is a psychologically accurate term. Linda Tschirhart Sanford and Mary Ellen Donovan found that most of the large number of women they interviewed had negative body images "because they saw themselves inaccurately" in terms of size, shape, or supposedly distorted body part.[31] This distorted perception of the woman's own body is grounded in gender duality.[32]

In light of the extreme negativity toward normal women's bodies, it is not surprising that women with disabilities react with even more negativity to their disabled bodies. Erik Erikson found that "in cases of morbid ego identity and in cripples, dreams occur where the dreamer tries to hide the painfully spotlighted body part, and others in which he accidentally loses it."[33] Like Erikson's "cripples," women who become ill see their bodies as the enemy and not as a partner with the mind in working toward health or toward management of the illness.[34]

"Patients," people whose illnesses or disabilities require medical care or other therapies, are usually objectified in the process to the extent that they perceive their bodies as literally belonging to someone else.[35] The experience reflects that of young children whose bodies, only recently separated from their mothers', are physically tended, moved, and interpreted by adults and told how they do and do not feel. Their bodies are often treated as psychological and physical possessions of their parents, just as the "patient's" body is treated as the possession of the doctor, physical therapist, or even an abstraction such as "the hospital."[36] As parents give childhood illnesses more attention, both negative and positive, than other behaviors,[37] adults with disabilities may relive both the guilt and the psychological boundary loss that go with the childhood experience.[38]

Nondisabled married women in body image therapy groups have described themselves as not owning their bodies, which they experienced "as utilitarian machines which gave birth to and nursed children and which sexually served their husbands," and then discounted "resentment at not owning their bodies as silly, trivial, or selfish."[39] To this culturally induced dissociation of the female self from her own body and her emotional reaction to its loss, the woman with disabilities adds pain, medical treatment (and sometimes medical abuse), surgeries, diagnostic procedures, and chronic unpredictability. She is likely to feel that her body has betrayed her and that it is an enemy very different from "self."

Physicians reinforce dissociation by ignoring information patients give about their own bodies, assuming that individuals know less about their own bodies than the "experts" do. Injuries and accidents to such physically fit people as dancers and athletes often result from training methods based on the concept of the body as adversary.[40] We are thus encouraged to ignore the body, to dissociate from it, even to abuse it; yet "highly generalized body awareness" such as that developed during severe childhood illnesses is strongly correlated with strong artistic, literary, and creative interests.[41] This fact provides a clue to the positive contribution that women with disabilities can make to feminist theory about our relationship through our bodies to nature.

Barbara MacDonald describes her changed relationship to her body as she recovered from a temporary disability: "Thus I healed myself and became whole again, connected to my aging body, wanting to live out my life in partnership with it, without feelings of humiliation because of its difference, and without the fear that I would so want to disclaim it that I would fail to protect it."[42] Partnership with her body prevents dissociation and enhances her sense of herself as a whole person whose aging, increasingly limited body is integral to her very positive self-concept. Feminist theory is full of discussions of the relationship between body and mind, especially in the contexts of sexuality and motherhood. Haunani-Kay Trask summarizes this literature as being about "the necessity for women and men to come to terms with the body's connection to the mind in the hopes of arriving at an intelligent, life-encouraging synthesis between mind and body, form and spirit."[43] What is different about MacDonald's statement is that it comes out of an experience of disability. The ideal of the physically fit, strong, active young feminist as the integrated physical-mental whole woman is transformed into a woman who is whole in her awareness of and acceptance of herself as someone whose fallible, human, aging body and mind are partners engaged in caring for her self. Positive body awareness thus comes not from striving for an ideal but from accepting the reality—that we age, change, become ill or disabled, and will die. MacDonald says, "I have this second chance to feel my body living out its own plan, to watch it daily change in the direction of its destiny."[44] Several of the contributors to *With the Power of Each Breath: A Disabled Women's Anthology* describe the profound acceptance of their bodies that has been part of their living with disabilities. An eloquent example is Stephanie Sugars's: "Watching how I live in the world in my body, I see how incredibly far I have come. I am coming to trust my body's integrity. . . . My body is such a sensitive indicator of my being. If I refuse to respond to my intuition, my body steps in with pain/discomfort/illness. I have a gate to my unconscious mind through my body."[45] So important is this kind of awareness that Stephanie and Carl Simonton have built a major cancer treatment strategy on training patients to respect and respond to "valuable feedback from their bodies."[46] Their patients' use of mental and spiritual strategies is firmly based on awareness of the body. Similarly, the Diabetes Self-Care Program, which has radically changed the treatment of that disease in the 1980s, is based on participants' learning through repeated blood tests to adjust their own insulin dosage based on awareness of their body's own characteristic reactions to changes in diet, exercise and stress.[47] And individuals with chronic pain are taught to know exactly the relationship between the pain and the environment, schedule, rest, food, clothing, "self-talk"—in short, to know how the body is related to all the other details of one's life.[48]

These holistic therapies are based on the concept of body

awareness as awareness of *process,* a concept that is closely related to the idea that our female body processes are linked to the processes of growth and decay in "nature." Biofeedback for stress management does much more than teach us to continue to live in a harmful world. It helps us overcome cultural conditioning that "deprive[s] the self of the information it should have about its body— and mind—state."[49] With or without specific training, women with disabilities who stop fighting the body as an enemy or dissociating from it learn to access this information and use it. Fritz Perls believed that Gestalt therapy could give us such wisdom: "With full awareness you become aware of the organismic self-regulation, you can let the organism take over without interfering, without interrupting; we can rely on the wisdom of the organism."[50] What is missing from Perls's suggestions is the experience of people with illnesses or disabilities that require some medical or technological interference or interruption. Still, before such interventions can be integrated, acceptance of the biological self is essential.

Feminist celebration of the erotic and reproductive capacities of our bodies is a beginning. This "return to the body" sees the mother-daughter experience of infancy as "the time when love is learned through intimate care of the body."[51] By extension, intimate caring for another's body through nursing or attendance or caring for one's own body in daily living becomes part of our positive body awareness and of holistic female bonding, which includes physical and emotional ties. When such caring incorporates the use of prostheses, medication, or machines, there is potential for bridging the supposed gulf between nature and technology.

## TECHNOLOGY

Even as disability requires body awareness and sensitivity to pace, rhythm, and process,[52] it requires reliance on technology as simple as typewriters and as sophisticated as dialysis machines. Specialized computers for people with hearing impairments, visual impairments, and cerebral palsy enhance communication and self-care. Braillers, tape recorders, hearing aids, special telephone equipment, motorized wheelchairs and carts, ramps, wheelchair lifts, adapted automobile controls, and many other devices are becoming ordinary parts of the lives of many people. Reproductive technology positively influences most American women's lives. Aerospace engineers work one on one with disabled people to devise new equipment to improve their daily lives.[53] Respirators and apnea monitors are readily used at home to save lives, and hospitals are full of life saving and life-maintenance equipment.

The use of technology also has negative consequences. These range from neurological impairments that may be caused by mechanical ventilation of newborn children[54] to lung disease caused by exposure to asbestos or miscarriages caused by video display terminals. Electronic fetal monitoring sometimes causes fetal distress and frequently results in probably unnecessary caesarean sections.[55] Common industrial chemicals impair male fertility. Diethylstilbestrol (DES), formerly given to prevent miscarriages, causes reproductive abnormalities and cancer. The intrauterine device (IUD) greatly increases pelvic inflammatory disease.[56] And so on. Feminists have been among the most vocal in pointing out these problems. Science and technology are among the most conspicuous products of masculine values, so we are skeptical about their use and cautious about integrating them in our lives.

But women with disabilities and women who give care to people with disabilities rely heavily on technology to enhance and simplify daily life—and often just to survive. For these women, the issue is not whether to use technology but how best to integrate it with self-concept and with body awareness.

An interesting example is the experience of mothers of "thalidomide babies," who came into conflict with rehabilitation specialists about the use and interpretation of prostheses for the children's deformed or missing arms. The goal of the professionals was to integrate the prosthesis into the child's body image so that the child would feel that the device was part of the self. But the child's body image was already whole, so the prosthesis was experienced as a deformation. A more suitable goal would have been to see the prosthesis as a tool, useful only for specific purposes.[57] The psychological task the mothers were assigned was to convince the child that her or his body was not whole so that the technology would be seen as completing it. The mothers' response was to confuse themselves and the children and to frustrate the professionals by using the prostheses erratically and at random in terms of tasks to be performed.

In her research on people's responses to ambulatory devices, Caroline Kaufman's preliminary results found that individuals did not include the devices in their self-images, but maintained able-bodied images of themselves.[58] The prostheses are not, in fact, part of the body, however helpful they may be as tools. Similarly, a respirator is not part of the body, though it may breathe for the individual whose body will not survive without it. What we can learn from disability is how to incorporate the technology not into the body image but into its environment, so that it is experienced as "natural" in the same way that other aspects of the environment, positive and negative, are. When we remember that the mind is part of the body, is embodied (even as the body is part of nature), and is natural, it is not difficult to see how a respirator—the product of human intelligence—can be as integral to the breathing self as is the allergen-laden south wind.

Susan Griffin suggests that one reason sexuality is so disturbing to people in our culture "is that in the sexual experience one is taken back to a profoundly physical state in which one can no longer deny that one is very deeply a part of nature and is therefore a dependent, mortal person."[59] I suggest that this is also what is disturbing about disabilities. What the disability tells the person whose relationship to it makes her fully, bodily aware is that she is a natural self, unseparated from the rest of nature. As Griffin says, "We breathe, we are born, we die, we eat, we get cold, we are part of the biosphere."[60] We also think and use tools, some of which enable some of us to be born, to eat, to breathe, to be our natural selves. When this is the case, and we can feel it in our bodies and implement the partnership with our minds, that sense of being inseparable from the rest of nature while highly individually aware of the embodied self is a spiritual experience that includes the technological support.

To use technology in such a framework is to reshape the values by which it is made. We have been wisely suspicious of a technology made by men in opposition to nature, as we have been suspicious of other dichotomies. Technology that is used for control "first obscures the connective tissues that sustain us and then excises complex decisions from an ethical context."[61] We need not use technology merely because it exists,[62] nor must we use it to manipulate and control biological realities.[63] As the "thalidomide mothers" discovered, the value system that produces and interprets "correct" uses of technology is not based on the wisdom of the body, but that does not mean that such values cannot or should not be developed.

In some American Indian and African cultures, health is harmony with nature, a balancing of physical, emotional, and spiritual factors. To live in harmony with nature is to accept it and to take from it only what is needed to live.[64] If technology were developed in or if its uses were determined by such a culture, presumably its use would be much more cooperative with nature than is the case in industrial societies such as ours. Sometimes a technological device may be what we take from nature because we need it in order to live. Women, dissociated as we have been from masculinist American-European culture, have been the carriers for that culture of physical and spiritual values. When we are body aware, as some disabilities enable us to be, we may be able to bridge the dichotomous gap between nature and technology.

Our experience not only with our female bodies but also with their illnesses and disabilities forces us to criticize the romantic view of nature (we need electricity at the music festivals and beds at the feminist retreat) and technological values (we need prostheses only as tools for our already complete bodies). We need to include technology and intellect in the politics of our cooperation with nature and the body. Our natural, living, breathing, dying, tool-using, whole selves are thus integrally a part of culture and nature.

CHAPTER 10

# CAREGIVERS AND DIFFERENCE

Disabilities bring an individual into contact with a variety of medical, rehabilitative, and educational caregivers and increase the individual's reliance on intimate caregivers. Because any single disability involves a number of such caring relationships and because most disabilities are not single, disability itself creates a circle of caregivers whose relationships to each other may range from indifferent to troubled. The disability is thus the center of a network of diverse women, a situation that provides an opportunity to examine the feminist discussion of difference in a particularly focused way.

Jennifer has a number of disabilities but no major medical problems. In her twenty-seven years, she has had, in addition to her ordinary doctors, teachers, and baby-sitters, these care providers: psychologists, social workers, a physical therapist, nurses, a neurologist, a neuropsychologist, an orthopedist, a cardiologist, an ear-nose-throat specialist, an audiologist, a family doctor, an eye doctor, a dentist, an orthodontist, three surgeons, special education teachers, school counselors, vocational trainers, psychometrists, sheltered workshop coordinators, several houseparents, and nine or more attendants each day for seven years. People with more severe disabilities have many more such caregivers. Many of these people participate in Jennifer's life in an ongoing way. Most of them have ideas about what I should do; most are women.

Jennifer stands at the center of this system as the focus of their attention. I stand beside her, her legal guardian, her advocate, her mother, but not her double. Each of the others has a direct link to one of us and to one or two others. We form a complex web based on our care for Jennifer. By no means do we agree about what is best for her. Neither she nor any of the rest of us is sure whom to trust.

In this chapter I propose to shift the focus from the person with disabilities to the web of caregivers in order to examine three issues: the relationship of caregiving to women's role conditioning; the likelihood of class barriers between caregivers; and the possibility of using caregiving networks as the basis for further feminist discussion of difference.

## ROLE CONDITIONING

Women's role conditioning strongly reinforces our behavior as caregivers, encouraging us to be devoted and self-sacrificing, to subordinate willingly our own needs to those of the person we care for. The rapidly increasing literature on "codependence"[1] clearly illustrates the harm to individuals and relationships caused by overinvestment in another's welfare at the expense of one's own identity. When disability influences a relationship, overgiving or overidentification becomes even more problematic because societal barriers to the independence of the person with the disabilities and the nature of some disabilities themselves inhibit reciprocity.

In assigning caregiving to women, our culture assumes that it will not be a balanced or reciprocal relationship. Girls are pressured to become nurturers, especially of men, though they are under-nurtured themselves in comparison to boys.[2] Women are expected to nurture both men and children; to ask for reciprocity is unrealistic.

Haunani-Kay Trask, writing of the imbalance in women's caring for men, says, "The positive value of women's capacity to nurture, to care for or with another human being in an intimate way, is often abused by the prevailing belief that such sustenance is natural, requiring no nurturance of its own. Women are caught by their desire and capacity to 'give' precisely because men are not psychologically and emotionally equipped to reciprocate."[3] In the case of disability, the person cared for is usually not expected to reciprocate, either because of the nature of the disability or because of institutional or cultural handicapping.

Again, the caregiver is essentially forced into an unnurtured condition. For example, the assumption by some members of a caregiving network that the person with the disability is the *victim* of her "handicap" increases the pressure on her primary caregiver to become her *rescuer*. To the extent that the individual is indeed a victim (of ableism if not of a disease or disability) or the caregiver is indeed a rescuer (if only from institutional red tape or barriers to access), it becomes imperative that they maintain the individually dysfunctional roles. "The victim/rescuer relationship is a hard one to break. Each person is threatened, even unconsciously, by the other's possibility of becoming a whole person on her own."[4] A physically or mentally "dependent" individual may fear not merely abandonment but even death if the codependent caregiver becomes so independent of the relationship that she can leave it. The caregiver, in turn, seeing that such fears may be realistic, is likely to resist separation by adopting an overgiving maternal role. Lucy Fischer found in her interviews with daughters who gave care to their disabled mothers that they referred to themselves as "mothers" to their mothers. "Through that analogy, they described their sense of entering another all-consuming role—a role in which they had taken total responsibility for the well-being of another person. In this way, parent caregiving is a quintessential woman's role."[5]

The association of mothering with caregiving and the assumption that being responsible for another's well-being is both "natural" and required here combines with disability-related dependence to encourage an inappropriate equation of the aging parent with a helpless infant. Even in cases where a dementing disease causes childlike behavior, the analogy to infancy is inappropriate and undermines the possibility of reciprocity.[6] Yet the analogy between infancy and dementia, based as it is on female role conditioning to provide nonreciprocal nurturing, provides a way of seeing self-sacrificing devotion as normal behavior on the caregiver's part.

The notion that women are naturally self-sacrificing because they are biologically equipped to be mothers undermines relationships among caregivers as well. Not only do women assume guilt when they feel that their giving is inadequately selfless, but they project blame onto other caregivers for this same failing. Barbara MacDonald reminds us that the patriarchal family is the source of the myth of the mother whose purpose in life is to serve the child. "This is not woman's definition of motherhood," she reminds us. "This is man's definition of motherhood, a male myth enforced in family."[7] To reject the morality of self-sacrifice is by no means a denial of the ethic of responsibility identified by Carol Gilligan[8] and Nell Noddings[9] among others as especially characteristic of women. Rather, it permits us "to give careful consideration to one's own needs and take the interest and needs of others into account."[10]

Patriarchal conditioning to a feminine, maternal role asserts that being selfless is in our own best interest. The value of selflessness, it is said, "lies not so much in the help given to the beneficiaries as in *liberation from ego* on the part of the one who served."[11] Such a view of altruism implies that sacrificing oneself to others is the only alternative to sacrificing others to oneself.[12] Social systems such as hospitals and welfare agencies reinforce such dualistic values by rewarding altruism and projecting blame onto such caregivers as family members, attendants and even nurses for not being altruistic enough—for being unnaturally un-self-sacrificing. The societal imperative for women to be nurturing altruists is so powerful that never-married women who care for aging and disabled parents see themselves as socially legitimated by this caregiving role, as they have missed "the traditional nurturing assignments of wife and mother."[13] The problem here is that nurturance and self-sacrifice are confounded. Since the mid-seventies feminist discussion of nurturing has attempted to restore a positive valuation of maternal and caregiving activities either by redefining the words to exclude implications of self-annihilation[14] or by renaming the process as, for example, attentiveness.[15] Nevertheless, in mainstream culture and, despite the theory, in feminist communities,[16] nurturance and self-sacrifice are bound together.

The idea that self-sacrifice is intrinsic to nurturing mother-hood has a corollary: that women *love* self-sacrifice. Therefore, serving others at one's own expense is defined as an act of self-love, as doing what we love to do. "Serving others *can* be self-fulfilling, but only when it is a choice, not mandated by a gender role. Otherwise, a self-sacrifice can become a partial psychological suicide."[17] In both the nineteenth- and the twentieth-century women's movements, positive evaluation of character traits considered feminine has been advocated as a source of self-esteem, but deriving high self-esteem from femininity becomes impossible when one of the most highly regarded feminine traits is self-denial.[18]

Because female nurturing and self-sacrifice are so routinely reinforced wherever care is needed (and, indeed, where it is not), "thoughtfulness" is a primary female virtue. As Janice Raymond has pointed out, this is "a kind of thoughtfulness that is really lacking in thought" because it is "given without thinking about the conditions under which it is extended."[19] When participants in a caregiving net-work require such unthinking thoughtfulness from each other, there is little possibility of changing the circumstances in which care is given and even less of removing the barriers to independence and self-care for either the disabled individual or the caregiver.

As women we often remain silent about our own perceptions of the experience of caregiving because role conditioning has taught us to respect authority and put others' needs first. We also have a realistic fear of not being heard. Mothers of children with disabilities frequently report that they repeatedly told doctors and teachers specific information about the child that the professionals simply ignored because it came from the mother. I once took a psychologist with me to one of Jennifer's planning meetings so that she could repeat the information I gave to the teacher and social worker and attendants, who literally could not hear it when it came from me. Although these professionals did not entirely silence me, they made it difficult for me to be heard.

## CLASS AND STATUS

In my everyday life, I have upper-middle-class status because of my professional credentials and white-skin privilege. In the meeting with Jennifer's providers, the role of mother changed my status so that I had to bring another professional with me to acquire some derivative status from her. Part of my problem in that conference was the assumption by most of the people involved that those who are most directly involved in the everyday lives of their clients are the least qualified to understand them. Both class and status are involved in these judgments. Families with disabled members are more likely than others to experience severe financial distress because of medical and access expenses. The work of giving care to a severely disabled person frequently requires one family member, usually a woman, to be unemployed or underemployed in the paid work force.[20] And costs of home care, generally unsupported by insurance, frequently leave the caregiver destitute.[21]

Employed caregivers whose jobs enable or require them to be closest to the person with disabilities are likely to have low incomes and to come from ethnic minority groups. These attendants, nurses' aids, and houseworkers spend more time with the individual than do such professional caregivers as social workers, psychologists, and physicians. They may also be of a different social class from such intimate caregivers as mothers, daughters, wives, or lovers. But all three groups are socialized as women to be caring, nurturing, responsive to others' needs—and perhaps critical of other women's "inadequacies" in meeting these needs. Moreover, the definition of what constitutes adequate nurturing behavior is a class-biased, middle-class ideal in which femininity requires caring behavior that involves middle-class time, knowledge, and skills. A deficiency in any of these care requisites is interpreted as a flaw in the woman's basic gender identity.[22]

Because the disability makes the "patient" an identified appropriate recipient of care, any impulse to nurture the other caregivers is likely to be suppressed, as is the caregiver's willingness to identify her own needs. Differences in rendering care based on class or culture—for example, definitions of appropriate cleanliness, speed of response time, use or avoidance of eye contact—may be seen as evidence of inadequate caring or even inappropriate closeness. Professionals may literally not know what it is like to provide direct care, yet professional training programs serve not to make them aware of such details but rather to strengthen their role as experts who educate or give directions to direct care providers but do not work alongside them. Berenice Fisher found that human services professionals "did not seem to have a clear picture of people who worked below them" because of the structural pressures of the bureaucracies in which they work.[23]

This problem is compounded by the fact that attendants or nurses' aids are seen as having no valuable information. After my daughter was institutionalized at age fourteen, the representatives of the "direct care staff" who attended her planning meeting were never those who knew her best; their status was too low to qualify them to attend staffings. On those rare occasions when such people did attend, they were effectively silenced by their lower status; they contributed their extremely valuable information only if I was able to consult them outside the meeting. Parents are also seen as biased, potentially emotional and undereducated contributors, so transmitting information from such informal contacts is a chancy strategy at best. Parents, siblings, and other relatives who know disabled children's daily activities, moods, and strengths frequently are seen as mere adjuncts to professional agendas for improving the child's condition or skills. Teachers sometimes are rewarded for transferring teaching activities to parents and encouraged to blame parents for being inadequate teachers. The "failure" of intimate caregivers to implement physical therapy or educational programs may be attributed to poor parenting or weak skills rather than to the cultural environment and physical or emotional work loads of family members. The superior status of professionals, derived from masculinist values, carries an assumption of inferior caste for others, including even other professionals whose illness, disability, or parental status recasts them in the role of "patient."

In short, there are many barriers to mutuality, friendship, or even communication between members of the caregiving network. Whether primary physical care takes place in the family or in the wage-labor workplace, "most caregivers are members of subordinate groups, who provide care from compulsion and obligation as well as warmth and concern."[24] Where the person with the disability is of a higher socioeconomic group, services are usually purchased from those in lower groups—until the financial resources run out. If the person comes from or is reduced to a lower socioeconomic class, the care is more likely to fall on the lowest paid staff members in public institutions[25] or on the family member whose income is most marginal. Where lower-class clients are served by higher status workers, the caregiving is likely to involve less personal service and more social control.[26]

Although this discussion can be presented in sex neutral language, in practice it is very much a women's issue. Most nursing home patients are women and by far most low-paid direct care staff members in institutions of all kinds are women.[27] Daughters and daughters-in-law are the designated primary caregivers for aging people with disabilities.[28] Low-paid basic caregivers often are untrained and rarely are helped to resolve their personal feelings about working with sick or disabled people[29] or to see the socialization of women as relevant to their own or the family members' situation. They work in a society with negative attitudes about women, disability, and personal service. Furthermore, sex-role stereotyping reinforces the objectification of caregivers, as when nurses, social workers, and dieticians are called "the girls" by patients.[30]

In an article on care of the frail elderly, Janet Finch and Dulcie Groves apply a feminist analysis to some of these dilemmas. When a feminist becomes disabled, they suggest, she will not want to interrupt her daughter's employment or exploit her as an unpaid worker; nor will she be comfortable with low-paid, sex-stereotyped female staff in a nursing home, though she will almost certainly prefer female to male caregivers.[31] Feminist or not, women care providers often recognize the implications for themselves of the conditions of the women for whom they care. In danger of depleting their own financial resources to care for family members, or underpaid and lacking fringe benefits as paid caregivers, they foresee their own future dependence on similar care.[32] Elizabeth Clarke, the "in-home companion" of a woman with multiple sclerosis, concludes her description of her friend's dilemma ("She will die too young and too alone") with the question, "How will I survive, unskilled, underemployed, without any foreseeable pension when I am older?"[33]

A final class-related factor for caregivers is the serious physical toll that caring takes on the caregiver. Because poor people and members of racial and ethnic minorities are especially susceptible to disability and chronic illness,[34] and family providers for the frail elderly themselves are usually older women,[35] caregiving may lead to disability and chronic illness in the caregiver. Among these documented costs are ulcers; colitis; chronic headaches; knee, hip, and

back pain; high blood pressure; exhaustion; depression; sleep distur-
bances; eating disorders; bursitis; and degenerative osteoarthritis.[36]
Those who can buy help to avoid some or all of these costs may have
little awareness of how high they really are for the unpaid or underpaid caregiver.

## BREAKING SILENCE, ACKNOWLEDGING DIFFERENCE

In part because they are composed almost entirely of women, all
three groups of caregivers (professionals, service workers, and family
members) have been unable to change the political situation in
which caring takes place. They also are unlikely to be heard, even by
each other, when they describe their own experience of disability.
Precisely because their individual stories often conflict with each
other and are spoken out of different frustrations, fears, and satisfac-
tions, combining them and acknowledging their differences has a
potential for moving us toward political change. The contemporary
women's movement has taught us the power of women's coming together to listen to each other's stories. The outcome in case after
case has been political action.

Consciousness-raising (CR) groups and speak-outs, collections of personal experience narratives and essays, are based on the
assumption that when many of us tell our individual stories, we will
see what they have in common and will begin to work for change.
After the euphoria of the first CR groups and speak-outs on any single
subject, we develop first frustration and then (relative) sophistication
as we recognize the diversity—the differences of race, class, and
culture—among those speaking and among those who have been
silenced. Only when our differences are named and respected can we
"deal effectively with the distortions which have resulted from the
ignoring and misnaming of those differences."[37]

Because issues of race, class, disability and female role conditioning are all involved in caregivers' inability to hear each other's
stories, political sensitivity to language is an issue.[38] So is the pressure to choose among competing "truths" instead of doing the more
difficult work of accepting and working with difference. It is helpful
to see the diverse experiences of disability and of care with what
Marilyn Frye calls "binocular vision" and Janice Raymond, "two

sights seeing"[39]—that is, to see the patriarchal foreground and the woman-centered background at once. Women who already understand their marginality as women or lesbians or members of the working class or of racial minority groups may find it easier to understand what happens to communication as we confront difference, because they are already accustomed to seeing from two cultural perspectives at once.[40]

> Difference—whatever it is, inborn or chosen, that locks you out of simplicities and generalizations and forces you to find your own way and your own language—provides many of the keys. Being different in some ways does not miraculously allow you to understand all forms of difference. It can enable you, though, to realize that there are women whose ways you don't know at all; it can remind you to be flexible, empathic—to listen with care.[41]

Listening to other women's truths without discounting them, as Audre Lorde and Marilyn Frye, among others, remind us, enables us to put difference in the center of our awareness, so that we can understand the experiences of these interrelated caregiving women and gain an idea of how the diverse experiences fit together. The creative function of difference, in Lorde's view, renders interdependence unthreatening and gives us the power to effect change.[42] Interdependence involves acknowledging different strengths, perceiving them as equal, and using their interactions as juxtapositions to generate creative ideas that would remain invisible to a single viewpoint based on only one woman's perspective.

Just as Lorde urges us to put difference at the center of our awareness, Janice Raymond asks us to place women's friendships there.[43] When a shared experience of caring for a particular disabled person results in a friendship between those who care, the result may be an enhanced understanding not only of their similarities, but also of their differences. Thus we may find that the more intimate caring relationships have a higher priority in our understanding of both disability and care than do more distant professional areas of expertise. Or we may see creativity flourish in the passionate friendship of mother and nurse or of social worker and physical therapist. The diverse experiences of caregivers are already focused on one subject:

the person with the disabilities. This focal point provides a means of organizing individual stories that are otherwise very different from each other. In turn, the process of comparing and seeing connections among these experiences presents an opportunity to see past the self-sacrificing or codependent or controlling individual to the social and political issues affecting the women as a group and the forces that require self-sacrifice, codependence, and control to maintain the present system.

The starting point is the activities and feelings of each individual caregiver. In the case of compulsory or at least culturally rewarded self-sacrifice, each of us must stop ignoring and misnaming her own experiences related to the disability itself and to the person with disabilities. Although as women we have been trained to be sensitive to the feelings of others, this is a selective sensitivity directed at the feelings of men, children, "patients," and "clients." There is a cultural myth that women know about and have freedom to express our feelings (in contrast to men). In fact, however, "the numbers of women turning to therapy has been an acknowledgement that while we may be more attuned to and involved in the world of emotions, we need to learn to center ourselves on our own feelings and to focus on those we find hardest to express."[44] Clearly this is the first and perhaps the hardest step toward effective consciousness raising, but it is closely linked with another: being willing to hear and not to misname the feelings of the other caregivers who do not have the automatic "right" to sensitive understanding that supposedly accrues to the central figure in the caregiving drama—the recipient of care.[45]

Blaming each other for inadequate nurturing and feeling guilty about giving too little are linked. The social context in which caregivers will inevitably give less than is needed is the connector. The process of telling our individual stories and hearing each other requires, first, acceptance and articulation of our resentments. Here it is useful to look at the idea from Gestalt therapy that guilt is projected resentment. "Expressing resentment is more taboo for women than men. Traditionally we are expected to love and serve ungrudgingly; the result often is that our resentment comes out in indirect ways."[46] At the same time, projecting resentment (or guilt) on other caregivers (or the "patient") instead of acknowledging that it is resentment of our own situation prevents us from either knowing or communicating exactly what that situation really is.

Here we can profit from the experience of other groups of women who have spoken out on other emotionally charged and female-specific issues. The first moving stories of rape, incest, battering, alcoholism, the exploitive nature of housework, and so on never presented the whole picture; never were they free from guilt or clear about the most appropriate targets for resentment. The first analysis in each case was incomplete, class and race biased, homophobic, and even sometimes women-blaming. But as the stories accumulated, both language and analysis changed. Starting with each individual woman's situation as it is at the time she tells her story, we may see the whole web more plainly than we do when we read "objective" summaries of experiences that have been prioritized by academic researchers.

Carol Gilligan and others after her have reminded us of the extent to which women's thinking is narrative and contextual and of the frequency with which we describe ourselves as being in relationships with several others, wishing to be at the center of a web of connections and fearing to be too far out at the edge.[47] Nel Noddings, expanding on Gilligan's concept of care, emphasizes that women think of their situations in concrete detail rather than abstract categories.[48] Thus a direct caregiver learns to understand and accept the body's limits through specific close care of an individual body, not through anatomy lessons or projected goals of therapy. Such close care often occurs in isolation, even though several intimate caregivers may have connections to a single care recipient. It is only through direct verbalization to a careful listener that the isolated caregiver can achieve some reciprocity of connectedness. The best example that I know of is Margaret Hackman's account of the caregiving circle for her friend Bobbi, in which Hackman learned to ask for help for herself as she coordinated, consulted, and collaborated with a circle of other caring women. By describing her own situation and developing another caregiving circle for herself, Hackman was able to maintain the reciprocal caring of Bobbi's circle.[49] Similarly, Sandy Boucher, creating a healing circle for herself on the evening before her biopsy, learned from reflecting on the disabilities and sorrows of each participant in the group that she was not isolated from those who cared for her, that each woman in the circle was dis-eased, in need of healing, and that each was giving what she could to the others.[50] Group members were thus both care providers and recipients of care. Their reciprocity was multidirectional. And Barbara Rosenblum, explaining her illness to the caregiving circle who would help her fight it, recognized from their attentive listening that she was "only the first among our friends to have cancer."[51]

It is no accident that many of the members of these personal caregiving circles are lesbian feminists: having already come to terms with some of their own differences from hetero-patriarchal society, they were in a way prepared for the additional differences that illness brought to their communities. Having developed "families" of choice, they had already formed caring networks that could be reorganized to provide new forms of care.

Unfortunately, most primary caregivers are more isolated. Over 70 percent of caregivers to the frail elderly in the United States, Europe, and New Zealand are women; 40 percent are elderly themselves.[52] Bringing these individuals into reciprocal, verbally communicative groups would probably be not only healing but politicizing. As mothers of children with disabilities commonly discover, the responsibility "requires not only the culturally sanctioned female roles of caretaking and selfless giving, but aggressive independent [political] action."[53] Groups of such caregivers frequently engage in overt political action as well as provide psychological support for each other.

Such groups as the caregiving circle for one woman or a support group for otherwise isolated family caregivers represent a model that can be enlarged to include professional care providers, hired helpers, houseworkers, attendants, and others. The problem, of course, is how to cross the boundaries between groups and how to sustain their contact with each other. Family caregivers organized to protect themselves from or to change the behaviors of paid caregivers are unlikely to hear their stories with compassion or even understanding. Nurses or social workers frustrated by family caregivers' resistance to their advice or their agencies' policies are likely to misinterpret the relatives' stories. Nurses' aids and attendants may literally not speak the language of their employers and will not readily trust those individuals' efforts to hear them.

My own experience has been that communication across

these barriers has only occurred when somehow the woman on the other side has seen me as another woman, whose life somehow mirrored or touched on her own. Once a nurse who was extremely angry at Jennifer's behavior and who blamed it on my inadequate mothering suddenly softened, becoming protective of me and kind to my daughter, when I cried and told her I knew that Jennifer was hard to handle and that was why I could not care for her at home. An attendant who blamed me for not taking Jennifer home for holidays, as she believed a good mother would, abruptly ended a three year campaign to change me when I told her in vivid detail what had happened on Jennifer's last holiday visit at home so that she saw how harmful the visit was to Jennifer and how disruptive for the family. This disclosure only became possible when I had listened attentively to her story about what she believed Jennifer's visit to her own family for Christmas would be like. When I spoke to her as one ordinary mother of a family to another, she could imagine what Jennifer's disastrous holidays were like for our whole family. Once she saw me as a mother, she stopped seeing me as not good enough and recognized me as like her, a woman doing the best she could for her daughter.

These were isolated instances, dependent on the accident of my striking the right (anguished) tone to break through the other's defenses against seeing me as like her (a woman) and yet different from her (in the ways I care for Jennifer). What I am suggesting now is that opportunities for such hearing can be structured in ways that involve less anguish and less chance.

Assembling the caregivers' stories and listening to each other's truths might ideally happen in intimate gatherings like Boucher's ''healing circle'' or the earliest consciousness-raising groups. These activities could happen in team planning meetings for an individual client and her family, provided that the agenda were not ''professionalized.'' For most of us, however, neither of these structures is possible. Perhaps for the discussion of difference it is not even desirable, as such groups have tended to be relatively homogeneous at least with respect to race and class. We can also tell and receive truths in speak-outs, public forums, printed media, and informal conversations. We can read and hear from caregivers similar to but perhaps more verbal than our own. We can be willing to find out what another woman's experience is, especially when it comes in contact with our own even peripherally. We can read and write and talk and think as we have begun to do on other issues. If we are caregivers our-selves, we can ask open-ended questions within our own networks. We can choose to be responsive, not merely responsible,[54] to each other and not solely to the person being cared for.

Formal opportunities can be provided to begin the process. Members of my parents' group describe their experiences with care-givers in neonatal intensive care during "grand rounds" at Children's Hospital. The caregivers in the audience of these presentations are encouraged to learn to listen carefully to parents by the medical school faculty member who introduces their presentation. The par-ents, in turn, learn to see the situation from the professionals' per-spective as they try to communicate more effectively with them. In another context, my daughter's social worker arranged an "acciden-tal" meeting with a psychologist I had trouble communicating with in formal staffings. And I have used my time in Jennifer's planning meetings to describe the experience of an attendant who was not present at the meeting. Laurie Shields suggests that if each caregiver were to describe her own situation to at least one public audience, we would see sudden, dramatic changes in public policy.[55]

So far, such efforts have been dependent on the interests and skills of a few individuals. In such circumstances, there is often an adversarial or woman-blaming attitude, for the reasons discussed above. Sometimes it is possible to make such attitudes the subject of discussion. Formal opportunities for breaking silence, however, are more likely to be created through feminist organizations and their various standard practices: papers and workshops, CR groups, panel discussions, edited publications, speak-outs—whatever a given organization usually does. Because the focus of these groups is already on women, the articulation of caregiver experience from a women's perspective properly belongs there. This in fact is beginning to happen. *Women Take Care* originated in the CR groups and politi-cal organizing of the Older Women's League.[56] Volumes such as Emily Abel's and Margaret Nelson's *Circles of Care* began with papers from women's sessions at professional meetings. Disability sessions at women's studies conferences frequently become speak-outs. In par-ent support groups such as the one I facilitate, recognition of gender issues follows from the pooling of our stories as parents. In feminist organizations, recognition of disability issues follows from the col-lection of women's own stories. Without formally organized groups, calls for papers, and public forums, this collection process would be as random as my tears in the nurse's office. Such connections go unrecorded and unshared; we need stories in numbers sufficient to spark our creativity, to make change.

Having made these suggestions, I am uncomfortable with their preliminary qualities, their lack of specific political strategies.[57] That of course is the point. Storytelling and speaking out are not goals in themselves but preliminaries to action. Pervasive woman-blaming and horizontal hostility among caregivers has not prevented political organizing on behalf of certain people with disabilities, but it has inhibited the coalition of efforts on behalf of caregivers. The most effective caregiving circles have been those developed within already existing personal or community networks (e.g., Bobbi's support circle and the various AIDS coalitions). To extend their model to a wider community, encompassing greater differences and defocused from the disability itself, proves extraordinarily difficult, as the movement of AIDS activism into communities other than those associated with gay men and public health has shown. For feminists, each concentric circle that is added to a caregiving coalition or a personal support group requires another round—or several—of consciousness raising. It would be arrogant for me, whose caregiving is increasingly managerial and decreasingly personal in the sense of daily responsibility for physical care, to assume that I understand the caregiving of a houseparent or trainer who spends hours of her workday providing direct care to Jennifer and her peers. But it is plain to me that these care providers are women whose whole lives as women must have something important to do with the ways in which they respond to Jennifer and to each other. When my attention shifts from Jennifer to this other woman's life experience, there is a possibility at least that I will see what her needs as a caregiver may be from her own frame of reference and not simply from my own.

The differences in power among the three groups I have identified, their conflicting beliefs about the meaning of ''care,'' and their interconnected needs for support services must be addressed with or without consciousness raising, but feminist analysis relies, always, on attention to our collective and diverse individual stories. Here in our communities our analysis begins.

As women have told our stories about other life experiences, we have initiated a process of institutional change. Seeing them in a feminist context, with the condition of being a woman at the center, we can stop judging each other for imperfect caring and look instead to the question Audre Lorde tells us to start with: "WHO PROFITS?"[58] If we do not rank-order differences but respect the plurality of perspectives, we may be able to contextualize power, seeing the relationship of institutions to individuals, and to conceptualize the changes necessary to humanizing the web of relationships. Sandra Harding reminds us that feminist theoretical categories *should* be *unstable*.[59] Maintaining that instability by keeping our discourses open to different voices and changed minds is essential to the process of change. Our experience shows us that we need major institutional changes before Gilligan's "mature integration" of justice and care is possible.

Happily, this requires not only the hard work in hard places that change always requires but also the friendship, joys, and sorrows of women's community.

CHAPTER

# CODEPENDENCE AND IN/DEPENDENCE

Codependence is a concept that helps to explain some of the problems in relationships between people with disabilities and their
caregivers. Their experience also provides an opportunity for others
concerned about codependence (especially as a women's issue) to
see how such problems can be resolved in situations where dependence is an issue not merely because of female role conditioning but
also because of intractable physical or mental disabilities.

Women are acculturated to be codependents: people who
base their identity on caring for other people, meeting others' needs,
and pleasing others to the detriment of their own needs, even to the
extent that they no longer (or never) know who they are outside of the
relationship. Thus a relationship between a woman with disabilities
and her intimate friend, lover, caregiver, mother, or attendant is

designed to reinforce the dependence and codependence of both. Societal handicaps reinforce these traits by exacerbating the dependence of the one with disabilities and the belief of both that the self-effacement of each in protection of the other is essential to the physical or emotional survival of the person with disabilities to a degree that justifies each in forgetting (or never knowing) her own real needs and personal traits; each feels she must defer always to the superior status—or neediness or reliability—of the other.

Further, our culture's excessive emphasis on independence leads to a frustrated and frustrating belief by both parties that at least an illusion of independence for the disabled person must be maintained regardless of the expense to the quality of her relationship with the one or ones on whom she depends.

Fortunately, this uneasy condition is often modified by the requirements of the disability itself. For example, living with a degree of independence appropriate to the individual requires a realistic, pragmatic evaluation of the limitations imposed by the particular disability. To accept these and figure out how to work around them, when to accept help and when to maneuver past an obstacle, requires mutual cooperation that can only be obtained by skillful communication. And the communication is only possible if each individual first knows herself and then can clearly state what she needs, what she wants, and how to distinguish between the two. Then, if the quality of the relationship is valued, both individuals have to figure out how to get the needs met from a variety of resources, not solely from an enmeshed, codependent other. We know, for example, that it is virtually impossible for a lover to provide personal hygiene for an incontinent adult and then feel sexually aroused by that person.[1] If the sexual relationship is valued, other sources of personal attendance are needed.

As a result, in part, of the disability rights movement, women with disabilities are increasingly able to make such distinctions, to ask for help when needed and to decline help when it is not needed. Often the process of learning this is accompanied by considerable anger and rupturing of relationships. As these crises are worked through, it is possible to achieve something like "recovery" from the underlying codependence of both women.

To address the efficacy of this process, it is useful to reexamine the concepts of dependence and independence, and reciprocity as well as certain problems inherent in the notion of codependence itself.

## DEPENDENCE

To see dependence as a negative trait is realistic in our society, as it is attributed to subordinates and used to devalue the contributions of the person so labeled. Dependence limits mobility and is economically disastrous in most cases. Moreover, as Debra Connors points out, negative valuation of dependence masks serious class issues: people who can purchase goods and services are believed to be free of dependence, while those who cannot are criticized for being dependent.[2]

Even apart from direct social devaluation, the effects of dependence are manifold and serious. Of particular interest in relation to codependence are the effects on self-concept and on relationships.

Where self-concept is based on autonomy or strength, dependence seriously undermines it: "I sometimes feel my disability betrays my sense of myself as a strong woman. If there's a leak in the roof, I want to be able to get up there and fix it. And in recent years I don't trust my vision enough. My sense of the sort of risks I'm willing to take is less than it used to be, and part of what I associate with being a strong person is wanting to take risks."[3] To "accept" such a lack of strength or even to replace it with a different one is only a partial solution to the dilemma of injured self-concept, in that dependence encourages passivity, which easily spreads to other aspects of one's life. Michelle Cliff, speaking of the socially induced disability of "speechlessness" (which is, incidentally, a primary characteristic of chemically dependent families although that is not Cliff's subject), illuminates this point. Speechlessness, she says, "begins with the inability to speak; this soon develops into the inability to act. . . . Speechlessness is always directed against the self, never directed outward, except indirectly." It leads, therefore, to depression and literal or symbolic self-annihilation.[4]

In the simple case of the woman who cannot safely climb on the roof, hiring a worker or enlisting the help of a friend activates other dependencies: on the worker's reliability, on the friend's goodwill; and these in turn affect the woman's self-concept as a wage earner (if she is one) or as one who has inadequate financial resources to pay for help; as someone whose resources may seem inadequate for reciprocity with her able-bodied friend. If she turns to professional help for financial aid or vocational training to improve her ability to repair roofs or for therapy to help her substitute a positive evaluation of her other strengths, still other series of dependencies are likely to ensue. Seeking help gives the woman a measure of control over her leaky roof but it is an indirect control, and her ability to repair the damage to her self-concept as a strong person is equally indirect.

In the face of such a struggle, it is not uncommon for disabled clients of rehabilitation services, for example, to "become apathetic and uninvolved" and to "develop attitudes of inferiority and incompetence" in direct opposition to the stated purpose of such programs: increasing the independence of the clients.[5] Not surprisingly, depression is a common symptom of people whose disability conditions are degenerative or result from accidents. Mary Pat Newman describes her initial reaction to blindness resulting from a shooting accident: "I decided soon after my accident that I'd rather be dead than dependent."[6] And Judith Witherow in a similar reflection on the impact of multiple sclerosis on her life says that without security and stability, both of which are undermined by the disease, "a good self concept is almost an impossibility. If you lose control of your life and all your hopes, dreams, goals and accomplishments are erased almost overnight, your first question tends to be 'do I really want to live?' "[7] Both Newman and Witherow eventually found other sources of self-esteem and, presumably, security if not stability, but the depression they describe is not unusual, nor is it always an *initial* response. Elizabeth Bouvia, paralyzed since birth with cerebral palsy, petitioned the courts to allow her to "starve," with pain killers and without forced feeding, because, she said, "I choose no longer to be dependent on others."[8]

Less extreme than suicidal depression are some of the other common effects of dependence: a tendency to be manipulative; placement of blame on others; and feelings of shame, guilt, and anger. These responses characterize both individuals with disabilities and those who care for them. Manipulative behavior, for example, evolves naturally from the passivity that dependence may create. "If your whole life is totally dependent upon others, and your security is determined by others, to say nothing of your survival, then it is perfectly natural to be manipulative."[9] Gliedman and Roth associate manipulative behavior with a view of interaction that is common in our society, but exaggerated by the dependent situation:

> Because the disabled individual finds the sociological deck stacked against him *[sic]* in many childhood and adult encounters, he may seek to overcome this disadvantage by a subtle manipulation of those remaining cues which convey competence that are under his control. The ways this can be attempted are legion. But whether the tools used are an authoritative tone of voice, a tendency to manipulate language in aggressive ways, or an exaggeratedly dependent and apologetic manner . . . the tools are in the service of a view that sees interactions as contests.[10]

Such a view of interactions is common between subordinates and dominants. Passive-aggressive manipulation is often attributed to women in relation to men. Manipulative strategies "are used to seize power within the relationship without assuming the responsibility for it."[11] Sarah Hoagland's analysis of vulnerability "as a strategy to obtain some limited, individual control over those who have power over us" is relevant here. "Even in the best of contexts," Hoagland writes, "to use vulnerability as a tool is to take a 'short cut' through another's personality to control the outcome of the situation by limiting the other's options."[12] In short, manipulative behaviors are always interactive. To blame either the manipulative person or the manipulated one is to miss the role of the dependence (and thus the disability) itself on the interaction.

Similarly, the shame and guilt expressed by people with disabilities or caregivers may express a dynamic in the relationship, but disability-generated dependence is integral to that relationship. The mentally retarded individual's shame and guilt may be expressed in resistance or in passivity, both of which complicate her or his relationship to those on whom she or he depends, but the feelings originate in consistent failures.[13] Another example is this exchange between Kathryn Ryan and her husband, Cornelius: " 'Damn, Katie, I'm sorry,' he said brokenly. 'I can't get up to go to the hospital.

You'll have to get me dressed and go with me.' I helped him with his bathroom chores and tried to soothe him. 'I'm so ashamed,' he kept saying. 'So ashamed.' 'Of what?' 'Of being helpless.' "[14] Thus, each of the individual, intrapsychological effects of dependence, from suicidal depression through shame at needing help in the bathroom, affects interpersonal relationships.

In the simplest cases, mothers with severely disabled children, disability undermines the relationship by the very protective bond that brings them closer. Mothers of thalidomide-disabled children believed that the "protective alliance" would keep the child very close to them during adulthood *or* that "discovery of the etiology of the handicap would create a gulf between mother and child."[15] In either case, normal adult affiliation is not in the picture. Indeed, prolonged adolescence is often a result of dependence on mothering, involving not only the loss of appropriate adult status markers (such as economic independence and marriage) but also the emotional lability, conflicts with parental authority, and inconsistent behavior characteristic of adolescence.[16] If the disabled person is reliant on her or his parent for intimate personal care, the situation is compounded by lack of privacy: "I was coming to resent [my mother's] participation in my care as a gross and humiliating intrusion on my body, as an assault to my spirit . . . I felt as if I were being repeatedly violated."[17] Rebelling against such care is terrifying, since it may feel to both participants as if basic survival is at stake. Equally powerful is the fear of loss of the most basic stable (or relatively stable) relationship.

Besides being damaged by adolescent behavior on the part of the dependent one, the relationship may be harmed by the very responsible role of the one who cares. "Even the most loving care soon is subtly transformed from offering what the dependent asks for to imposing what the donor believes the other person should have (for his or her own good). . . . The very need for care seems to discredit their competence or even their right to live their own lives."[18] The recipient of such care may internalize the message of incompetence or rebel against it, in either case rupturing the relationship.

Hostility toward and rejection of the people on whom we are dependent may be an expression of the desire for independence, but such rejection is likely to be interpreted in other ways, even by the angry one.[19] "Too often, in our pain and confusion, we instinctively do the wrong thing. We don't feel we deserve to be helped, we let guilt, anger, jealousy, and self-imposed loneliness make a bad situation even worse."[20] The situation is compounded by the necessity for the one who is helped to express gratitude.[21]

For the caregiver the burden of the relationship also undermines its quality. While the dependent daughter experiences her mother's help with her bowel care as a humiliating intrusion, the mother is hardly likely to enjoy the experience herself. Even if she is wrong about the daughter's inability to learn to manage alone, she is likely to feel heavily burdened by the responsibility. However willingly the burden is assumed, it is likely eventually to be transformed into physical symptoms, withdrawal, depression, criticism, or anger.[22] Where both parties are expressing (or trying to suppress) such negative feelings, the relationship may be maintained out of necessity or duty, but its quality is deeply undermined.

In light of the negative effects of dependency, it is remarkable that it is often encouraged and reinforced by caregivers, professionals, and society at large. Reasons for reinforcement range from the convenience or self-concept of the caregiver through the disabled person's own self-concept to government policy. The major societal and interpersonal reinforcers are the roles of child, of patient, and of woman.

The rhetoric of professionals who work with people with disabilities usually stresses independence to the point of reinforcing denial, yet their actual practice often encourages dependence. In the early 1970s, Evelyn Ayrault, who tended to blame mothers for teens' dependence[23] and who insisted that the disabled child must be given realistic information about the disability, nevertheless stated that "it is not advisable for doctors, therapists, and parents to discuss the teenager's condition in front of him [*sic*]. He may not have the mental reasoning ability to understand complex conversations concerning his own welfare or he may be too emotionally immature to handle realistically what is being said about his future."[24] Ayrault does argue emphatically for encouraging the teenager's independence, as did others throughout the succeeding decade, but usually in the context of blaming parents, professionals, or both for having made the person "too" dependent in the first place.[25] In the 1980s, the language of independence was pervasive, but advocates of independence generally argued, still with an implied adversary, against the "overprotective" or dependence-promoting parent or professional. Thus in the debates over deinstitutionalization, advocates of institutions for some people under some circumstances found it difficult to be heard, yet the process of deinstitutionalization itself was administered and advocated by people who took for granted that they knew what was best for the disabled individuals whose lives they were changing without consultation with those who knew their clients best.[26] An interesting presentation of this "I know better than you do what is good for you" dynamic is Miriam Greenspan's discussion of therapists' interpretation of a client's request for more therapy as representing infantile transference feelings. Instead, Greenspan suggests, it can mean "a more mature or adult sense of what she need[s] in order to take care of herself." By denying that a client may need more care, the therapists' approach actually infantalizes her. "Despite the intentions of traditional therapists to minimize their patients' dependency needs, such needs are actually *prolonged* through denial. For there is nothing more likely to provoke and perpetuate a patient's infantile dependency needs than infantalizing the patient."[27]

Where several agencies or institutions are involved in providing resources and services to the person with disabilities, official policies are likely to encourage dependence. These may begin in training of service providers to "do for" rather than "collaborate with."[28] The organization of medical services into a large number of specialized functions and the resultant routinization of tasks also contributes to the treatment of "patients" as if they were interchangeable, with "no control over which members of the hospital staff have access to them, while their own access to staff members is limited."[29] Moreover, the actual dependence of many "patients" on private donations of blood products, transplants, and money forces the recipient to be "grateful," to behave in a subordinate way, to the donors. "Nobody likes to beg for charity. . . . It destroys pride and independence. The people in our society who proclaim in booming voices that private charity is the answer to preserving pride and independence are always the donors, never the recipients."[30] Moreover, just as social security limits the income a recipient can receive, Medicaid eligibility requirements often force working disabled women to stop working in order to receive the services they require.[31] Even volunteer work may be prohibited because of policies on transportation costs (where only medical transportation is funded).[32]

In every case where dependence is inappropriately encouraged, the dependent person is cast in a subordinate role. As Jean Baker Miller reminds us, subordinates are encouraged to develop personal characteristics pleasing to the dominant group, and are said to be unable to perform the preferred roles, and thus to lack a realistic evaluation of their own capacities and problems.[33] The subordinate roles most frequently imposed on people with disabilities are those of children, patients, and women.

Frank Marsh traces Western philosophical tradition about the subordinate status and dependence of children through Hobbes, Locke, Mill, and British and American law. The point historically is that the right of parents and the state to make decisions for others "was premised on the presumed incapacity of minors and the actual incapacity of idiots and lunatics to protect or care for themselves."[34] Marsh himself argues that decisions made on behalf of a child must involve "equal respect and concern which dictates that the child (once having acquired rationality) will accept the action as the best thing for him [sic]," and that the uniqueness of the individual must be taken into consideration.[35] Nevertheless, the strong historic association of mental disabilities with childhood functions in society as permission to treat both as incapable of acting in their own behalf. Further, it spreads to people with other disabilities. To give just one example, a child of short stature is often treated by others as if she or he were a toy or baby doll, thus undermining parents' efforts to socialize the child toward independence. A child who is treated this way is likely to behave as a dependent at home as well as with others.[36] This tendency is reinforced by the fear, either of parent or maturing child, that the relationship will be threatened by responsible, adult behavior on the part of the child. There are, after all, "benefits in staying dependent, avoiding responsibility, and making demands on people accustomed to meeting them," not the least of which is the nurturing relationship itself.[37]

> Closely related to the role of child is that of patient. In fact, the psychological situation of an ill person in some respects is parallel to that of a child, especially in their position as

minority groups. Should the patient not follow through with the treatment plan, one becomes annoyed as one would with a child, or patronizingly scolds him which is but another expression of underlying devaluation. It hardly occurs to us that in some measure the childish behavior of a patient may reflect his childish treatment.[38]

Even where the express purpose of "treatment" is to move the patient toward independence, the role of patient itself may undermine that intention, as compliance, pleasing the caregiver, deference to the authority of expertise or rank, and weakness—indeed, dis-ability— are expected of patients and are the behaviors most frequently rewarded. Even where rewards are specifically structured into efforts to teach independence, the patients' sense of what is being rewarded is likely to be focused on pleasing the trainer.[39]

When the patient is a woman, the emphasis on these traits (a.k.a. codependence) is familiar, basic to female role conditioning in our society. Beginning in infancy, girls are handled differently than boys, treated as more fragile, "protected" from real or imagined threats to their safety, comforted more frequently, "consistently reinforced in the notion that they can achieve only with the help of others."[40] As Collette Dowling says, "We carry dependency within us like some autoimmune disease."[41] Because women are also acculturated to help and give to others unselfishly, women who care are encouraged to deny their own feelings in the interests of "helping," thus assuming that the one being helped is dependent and needs rescuing. In this dynamic, the passivity of the victim is reinforced by the inauthenticity of the rescuer, whose own needs are suppressed.[42] The interaction of two nurturers, where nurture requires self-sacrifice, is a dynamic of codependence. Ageism (old women are likely to become patients at some point) reinforces this dynamic with still greater pressure to be both nurturing (as a stereotypical grandmother) and dependent (as a feminine patient).[43]

The culmination of female role conditioning in marriage provides an ironic twist on education of disabled women for independence, as there is an increasing movement to encourage marriage among retarded people and others formerly considered too handicapped for marriage.[44] Yet marriage itself as it has been traditionally defined requires dependence of the female partner and even creates severe illness and disability in some cases.[45] "Marriage to a normal man may place the woman in a role relationship that reduces her displayed competence."[46] To advocate marriage for someone whose disability has already defined her as dependent, socially or financially, is then to reinforce that dependence. Old assumptions that disabled women will not be able to marry may thus be replaced with the hope that they will marry and thus be cared for and protected by a husband,[47] or provided a sense of "normality" through case managers' provision of support for traditional role behavior.

## INDEPENDENCE

It behooves feminists, then, to encourage independence of women with disabilities in a way that does not reinforce their dependence as women. Indeed, societal pressure toward independence is now a basic and very public tenet of both feminist and disability organizations' philosophies. Not only does independence appear to improve self-esteem, it is assumed to improve relationships as well. It also reinforces societal (masculinist) values.

Frank Bowe, who is one of the most respected advocates of independence for people with disabilities, asserts that "it is possible for virtually every disabled person who is at least minimally alert and who has some degree of mobility, even if only of a severely restricted kind, to work. Of the sixteen million non-institutionalized disabled persons of working age, perhaps as many as fifteen million are potentially employable. They, like millions of persons over 55 years of age, can become independent, self-sufficient tax payers."[48] The emphasis Bowe places on employability and, more broadly, on work characterizes much of the disability literature advocating independence. Slighted or actively avoided in such discussions are the other million "non-institutionalized" disabled people who are not "potentially employable." Probably Bowe's statistics exclude persons with chronic illnesses (he is not entirely clear on this point) and certainly he ignores those whose medical conditions are degenerative. To notice the omission is by no means to discount the importance of what Bowe is saying for the fifteen million potentially employable persons with disabilities, but to underscore the cultural assumption that employability establishes independence and that denying employment coerces dependence and, Bowe says, causes physical and mental illness.[49] Natalie Spingarn, writing about people who live with cancer, describes the pressure in the United States to be independent and concludes, "Such a culture is particularly hard on hanging-in patients. It tells us to act strong and certain. Yet we live with uncertainty. We do not know how long our disease will last or how it will affect us."[50]

As the disability movement achieves change in media coverage of disabled people, the pressure toward independence and its corollary pressure to deny weakness and inability increases. Although pitiable poster children have not entirely disappeared, we are more likely now to see disabled people who have "overcome their disabilities." This situation increases pressure to behave independently, regardless of the specific limitations associated with particular disabilities. It also, as Debra Connors observes, masks "the fact that we are legally defined as unemployable and that unemployment characterizes most of our lives," with the result that dependence on social welfare programs "is beginning to be perceived as a choice."[51] The person who triumphs over adversity becomes a model against which those who cannot do so are measured and found wanting—indeed, they may be accused of having chosen to be dependent.

In the case of mentally disabled people, then, the goal of education or habilitation is achieving independence: "This process is continuous throughout life and always involves experiences which lead from dependence to independence. This begins with early developmental tasks in infancy and proceeds through adult self-sufficiency in vocational success and social adaptation."[52] Nothing is said here of those who cannot be self-sufficient in either vocations or social adaptation. One consequence of the omission is that programs that adopt unrealistic goals are forced constantly to fabricate illusory progress toward those goals, to blame the "client" for failing to progress, or to invent such euphemisms as "independent living" for inadequately supervised care or "capable of managing her own medication" for someone who can take a pill when it is placed in her hand by someone else. These are very serious problems, especially because they often control access to funding.

Equally serious is the impact on relationships.

As long as dependence is arbitrarily disvalued in interpersonal relations, independence becomes distorted as a goal. What happens, for example, to the warmth and friendliness between parent and child when the parent is imbued with one mission—namely, to get his [sic] child to eat alone, dress alone, walk alone? There is no doubt that these are important goals, but when independence becomes virtually the dominating guide for parental behavior, the cost in emotional security is unjustifiably great.[53]

Beatrice Wright made this statement in 1960 before "independent living" became the rallying cry of the disability rights movement. Today, pressure on parents and educators to make independence the "dominating guide" is much greater and so may be the negative impact on warmth and friendliness of such single-minded valuation.

As our culture has defined such traits, warmth and friendliness are women's values, while independence and autonomy are men's. When women, as mothers or as professional caregivers or educators, adopt autonomy as their primary goal, they may be implementing a value system in which they do not believe. "Women do not really *want* to become autonomous in the way that men have been. They do not wish to become competitively embattled against others, or to see their own individuality as contingent upon the renunciation of their needs for intimacy or family."[54] Miriam Greenspan is speaking, here, about women's own values in the paid work force, but the internal conflict she describes applies as well to the one who assumes the responsibility for helping another person to become independent. As Greenspan says, "The words 'dependence' and 'independence' themselves betray the masculine bias against female attributes." Female dependence, she says, is in its extreme form subservience, and male independence is "a kind of autism, a denial of the ways in which men depend on women for emotional nurturance, as well as a refusal to acknowledge the very real ties that bind all of us to one another."[55]

Obviously such extremes are not the necessary or even the usual forms of dependence and independence, but the fact that sex-

role acculturation encourages such all-or-nothing ideas makes independence extremely threatening to many women. "The problem
was that Jane saw only one alternative to the helpless, dependent
person, the person she dreaded being. That was the totally strong,
self-sufficient person who was freed forever from weakness or neediness, and, most of all, from the *effects of other people*."[56] As Jean
Baker Miller points out, women do lose relationships when they
become strong, independent individuals, but men's relationships are
not threatened by autonomy.[57] The fear that autonomy or independence will harm relationships is realistic when those relationships
are based on traditional role behavior, whether the role involved is
female or "handicapped," and especially when it is both. The dynamics of the traditional doctor-patient relationship, like those of the
traditional husband-wife relationship, make dangerous the subordinate's development of independence. They also reinforce the temptations of the role of superwoman or " 'supercrip' which, however much
it embodies strength and courage is, at bottom, a reaction to the
unspoken, strongly felt insinuation that there is something wrong
with you and your disability."[58]

A further, extremely damaging, effect of all-or-nothing beliefs about dependence is the belief by a disabled woman that she
must prioritize her needs, "some as absolute and life-sustaining and
others as 'luxuries.' "[59] At its extreme, this may result in situations
like the one described by Rebecca Grothaus where a severely disabled
woman who is living alone may not report a rape. "She may fear re-
institutionalization . . . more than she fears rape."[60]

Clearly such polarized thinking is not healthy; and in fact
when women achieve an understanding of both dependence and independence from a more woman-centered—which is to say, a more
self-centered—perspective, both are seen as interrelated and a balance of their more positive definitions becomes possible. Usually
such self-centering is possible only in relationships with other people, but not in subordination (or dominance) with them.

## CODEPENDENCE

On the surface of the word, codependence would seem to mean
"being a partner in a dependency,"[61] a useful and perhaps accurate

description of how interdependent relationships might function—and function well. However, the word as it is commonly used today is neither as simple nor as nonjudgmental as that. It is part of the jargon of chemical dependency treatment, where it originated as a description of the partner of an alcoholic who has become enmeshed in the substance dependence of that person to the extent that the dependence harms both individuals and becomes a systemic "disease" in their family or group. Expanded as understanding of the problems deepened, the word has been variously defined by many people.[62] For my purposes here, the most useful definition is Robert Subby's: "An emotional, behavioral, and psychological pattern of coping which develops as a result of prolonged exposure to and practice of a dysfunctional set of family rules. In turn, these rules make difficult or impossible the open expression of thoughts and feelings. Normal identity development is thereby interrupted."[63] The rules that govern traditional feminine behavior and those that similarly confine people with disabilities constitute such a set of dysfunctional rules within the family or the social system.[64] Prominent among them are several that especially apply to the disabled-caregiving relationship: "It's not okay to talk about problems. It's not okay to talk about or express our feelings openly. . . . Unrealistic expectations—Always be strong, always be good, always be perfect, always be happy. Don't be selfish."[65] If we add to these, or support them with, injunctions to derive one's self-esteem from helping others and to place the welfare of others above one's own, we have a description of the codependent relationship most characteristic of women caregivers and women for whom they care. The relationship reinforces the negative aspects of both dependence and independence by rewarding self-sacrifice and encouraging boundary confusion. To cite just one other definition of codependence, it "is a pattern of painful dependence on compulsive behaviors and on approval from others in an attempt to find safety, self-worth and identity."[66] Consider the situation of someone whose "safety," whose *life* in the case of someone with cystic fibrosis, for example, depends on intrusive, vigorous care. The need for "approval from others" may be a matter of life and death. Similarly, for the caregiver (often the mother), the "rule" about always being strong may in fact be necessary to the survival of the one for whom she cares. That she should base her identity on such rules follows not only from their normative status for women, mothers, and nurses but also from the basic physical reality of her situation as the "respon-sible" person in a life-and-death situation.

Disability increases codependence for both women in the relationship. Berenice Fisher and Roberta Galler found in their inter-views with disabled women that both roles, female and disabled, increased the women's "determination to make social interaction run smoothly" by taking a disproportionate responsibility for inter-action with any nondisabled person. This phenomenon, which is also true of others in minority situations (including, notably, women with men), is reinforced for those with disabilities by the importance of helping the other person to see beyond the disability to the person herself.[67] Not surprisingly, women in an intimate relationship with someone in this situation often add their communication skills to those of the disabled friend, to strengthen the possibility of a suc-cessful outcome, while simultaneously undermining the other per-son's appearance of effectiveness on her own behalf. This is a classic codependent boundary violation.

Those who "treat" codependence give considerable attention to "boundary issues."

> By this we mean a person has a difficult time defining where he or she ends and another person begins. We have an un-clear sense of ourselves. For instance, we may find it difficult to define the difference between our feelings and someone else's feelings, our problems and someone else's problems, our responsibility and someone else's responsibility. Often, the issue isn't that we take responsibility for others; it's that we feel responsible for them.[68]

If a woman "cares for" a child on an apnea monitor or one with asthma, an adult on a respirator or one who cannot manage her own sanitary pads or diapers, she is *really* responsible for that other per-son's well-being or survival, however much she may become confused about that person's ability to make her own decisions about when or how she needs help. Such a situation seems, often, to require self-sacrifice, even from a woman who may have rejected the idea that women should sacrifice themselves to please husbands or lovers. The independence of the caregiver may then be subordinated to the de-pendence of the disabled person, even as that dependence is reinforced. Thus both become codependent literally and in the treatment definition as well. The anger of both, whether or not it is openly expressed, is an almost inevitable result.

In a completely different context, a discussion of relationships in the lesbian community, Sarah Hoagland discusses the boundary problems that result from both egocentrism and self-sacrifice: "In the case of self-sacrifice we cease to have a distinct sense of ourselves. In the case of egocentrism we cease to have a distinct sense of the other."[69] The charge of egocentrism is frequently made of people with disabilities; the requirement of self-sacrifice, of their friends. The loss of identity that accompanies such boundary problems leads, Hoagland suggests, to a need to control the other person. "For example, if she is ill and the self-sacrificing friend invests her own identity in helping her recover, the friend may go well beyond helping, to attempting to control her choices. . . . And in exercising such control I may not be allowing her time to heal in her own way, on her own terms, by her own means."[70] To see how insidious this problem becomes, consider the common dilemma of parents of adolescents with diabetes, who may take control of their own insulin by not using it when it is needed. A parent who insists on monitoring the medication interferes with the independence of the "young adult"; one who does not may well deal with life-threatening complications or future lifelong dependency from those complications. The difficulty of maintaining a clear personal boundary or distinguishing between our responsibility and someone else's responsibility is dramatically evident in such a case. The dichotomy between selfishness and altruism[71] is at issue here for the codependent who cares: Is it selfish to want the disabled person not to become more dependent on care? Is it altruistic to care by interfering in the disabled person's right to make decisions about her own medication?

Bernie Siegel cites studies of people with AIDS that find that the persons with the best chance of long-term survival are those who answer with *no* the question, "Would you do a favor *you didn't really want to do* for a friend who asked you to?"[72] In other words, survivors are not codependent. To say this is not especially helpful, however, to people trying to work out relationships that involve disabilities. For example, the woman with AIDS who increases her survival time by not helping when she does not want to may need help from other people, some of whom do not especially want to do what is needed. Stephanie Brown suggests that "there's such a thing as healthy dependence—being able to rely on someone else to do what they say they'll do. . . . The codependence label is anti-needy, anti-dependent; it's very isolating. . . . It encourages rejecting others, being unkind and ungiving, and it's antagonistic to good, healthy altruism."[73] Brown is a leader in treatment of adult children of alcoholics and thus speaks from inside the chemical dependency treatment field, where the negative interpretation of codependence is generally assumed.

The definition with which I began this discussion of codependence specifically addresses this dilemma in its last sentence: "Normal identity development is thereby interrupted." The emphasis on identity permits a distinction between healthy dependence, reliance on the dependability of the other person, and unhealthy self-sacrifice. Where the boundary between two people is absent, identity is also missing. To achieve identity, one must look within. Total focus on someone else—a child, a husband, a "patient," or an enemy[74]—prevents such self-centering.

For women, the distinction between selfishness and self-centering has been difficult to understand and to maintain. In part, this confusion comes from such male-defined ideas of self as "self-actualization"[75] in contrast to women's own more characteristic concern with relationships.[76] Among feminists, further confusion has been associated with the argument that paying attention to one's self wrongly detracts from political activism. Harriet Goldhor Lerner clarifies the matter by arguing that self-focus "does *not* mean that we view ourselves as the 'cause' of our problems, or that we view our struggles as being isolated from the broader context of family and culture." Feminist analysis of how personal experience derives from the cultural context permits the broad range of feminist political action, she says, only because we "recognized that if we did not clarify our own needs, define the terms of our own lives, and take action on our own behalf, no one else would do it for us."[77] Only when we shift our focus from men to ourselves are we capable of action on our own behalf. To bring this process down to the individual level, Lerner asserts that "as we become less of an expert on the other, we become more of an expert on the self. As we work toward greater self-focus, we become better able to give feedback, to share our perspective, to state clearly our values and beliefs and then stand firmly behind them."[78] Such communication permits reciprocity. It signals *recovery* from codependence. "We need a healthy sense of self so we can count on ourselves to take care of ourselves. The other person needs to know we'll leave his or her territory when that's appropriate. Both people need the reassurance that when we blend territories, no invasion, shaming, humiliation, trespassing, or overextended stays will occur."[79]

When disability is part of the relationship, communication toward reciprocity requires a clear understanding of exactly what the disability is and exactly how it affects the perspectives of the relationship participants. "Invasion, shaming, trespassing, or overextended stays" may indeed be temptations for the nondisabled partner if the disabled one cannot consistently present her own "values and beliefs," including her understanding of the exact boundary between the need for specific kinds of care and the ability to decide when, how, and by whom she prefers that the care be provided. To do so, the disabled woman must be not only self-centered and body aware, but also capable of "attentive love" toward the other person, that is, able to ask, "What are you going through?" and to attend to the answer.[80]

For the one who cares, besides attentive love, a clear distinction between responsibility *to* and responsibility *for* is required. If I tell you I will help you move from your wheelchair to your bed at 9:30, I assume a responsibility to do that (or arrange an appropriate alternative), but I am not responsible for your feelings, your happiness, or your decision about when you will go to sleep. To even attempt to be responsible for those aspects of your life intrudes on your privacy and your rights, and it may prevent your achieving a realistic understanding of your disability, of yourself, *and of me.* By being strong and indispensable, I avoid the risks associated with honesty (e.g., the possibility of conflict) and the possibility of your understanding me (and perhaps confronting me). In addition, I divert myself from attending to myself, to finding out what *I* am going through.[81]

## ACCEPTING HELP

People with disabilities often resent "help," rightly perceiving it as a one-sided social relationship in which the one who is helped is considered inferior. Fear of dependency or of never learning to be independent reinforces the resentment.[82] Rejection of help may be "both an expression of status anxieties and a realistic means for achieving self-reliance."[83] Women who reject symbolic help in the form of chivalrous gestures such as holding the door open for a "lady" are well aware of these status implications. Yet offering help appropriate to the particular situation is normal and not necessarily disability related. For example, a mother pushing a stroller may welcome a door-opening helper although a status-conscious male carrying two heavy briefcases may not if the helper is a woman. Still, help offered to a disabled person when it is needed may have the psychological effect of making the person feel "normal" because she is being "treated like anyone else" who needs situationally appropriate help.[84] It is not easy for the disabled person to achieve such psychological "normality," however, unless she has a clear understanding of what "situationally appropriate" might mean and has addressed the resentment that experience with the assumption of social inferiority has provoked.

Within the disability movement, where social discrimination is stressed, one barrier to clarification of situationally appropriate help is seldom discussed: misinterpretation by the disabled person of the offered help. Appropriate sensitivity to behaviors that reveal discriminatory beliefs of nondisabled people may be generalized to all situations, thus masking other possible interpretations. For example, Gliedman and Roth discuss the problems that characterize interactions between sighted and blind people that are caused by "the mechanics of interpersonal contact," that is, by behaviors that derive from individuals' habitual ways of expressing themselves in particular contexts but that are likely to be interpreted by blind people as behaviors caused by negative beliefs about disability. "Thus, when a sighted person behaves assertively toward a blind person so as to eliminate uncertainty, the blind man *[sic]* infers that the other's actions are caused by a belief that blindness makes him helpless."[85] Moreover, the disability itself may contribute to the misunderstanding. In extreme cases, the disabled person's brain may be incapable of processing information accurately. Jennifer, for example, is very sensitive to the emotional climate of those around her so that she knows when someone is upset or happy, but she always assumes that she is the cause of those feelings and cannot understand that the other person may be upset because the car broke down or happy because she got a promotion at work. Where mental disabilities are not involved, other disability may still prevent accurate interpretation: "It is very hard for me to distinguish friend from enemy, and to speak clearly and supportively to my friends, when I feel dizzy, or sick, or am in pain."[86] The friend who is being supportive may be seen as condescending—or merely irritating—in such circumstances, and the relationship misconstrued. Stephani Cook, a cancer survivor, understood this only when she was too sick to reciprocate care in any ordinary way, "too sick to do anything but lie here with my eyes closed." "My friends need to be supportive as I need to be sick," she says, "and when I stop interpreting our intercourse in a manner consistent with an ordinary-use model, I have stunningly powerful experiences of intimacy and sharing."[87] The key word here is *interpreting*. Misinterpretation prevents caring or distorts it.

Where the disease is progressive, disabilities multiply, and the need for help increases as the potential for reciprocity in the "ordinary-use model" decreases. To accept help requires acknowledging the progress of the disease; knowing that one kind of help is needed does not really prepare the individual for the next loss. Both the disabled person and the caregiver (or caregivers) are likely to feel anger or despair,[88] and both emotions block accurate interpretation. As long as an ordinary-use model of reciprocity is the only one available, resolution of these problems is unlikely.

The disability rights movement provides role models, a philosophic framework, and sometimes training in appropriate ways to ask for help. Generally this ability is preceded by rejection (or at least resentment) of *in*appropriate help. Finally, the person learns to distinguish between help that is needed and that which is intrusive or harmful. "As it became clear to me that some help was beneficial I was more capable of making choices and stating my preferences assertively."[89] The enormous difficulty many disabled people have in learning that some help is beneficial derives from the stigma on dependence and the overvaluation of independence that I have discussed above. Codependence increases the problem of making clear distinctions between beneficial and unnecessary help.

Necessary assistance allows the disabled person to be more independent. Arranging for needed help gives her a measure of control over her life and thus gives "some breadth to her concept of personal power."[90] As increasing numbers of people with disabilities acquire and pass on this insight, redefinition of in/dependence becomes possible. Movement activists directly teach a range of such beliefs. Children and newly disabled adults are encouraged to see that "caring for yourself means that you have to ask people to do certain things for you . . . to learn what your needs are and how to ask for them."[91] Needed assistance is defined as a responsibility of the public sector in the form of tax money or laws requiring ramps, braille labels, sheltered workshops, and other resources. Individuals are encouraged to rely on and demand such resources and to embrace the paradox "that handicapped people must rely on others' assistance in order to achieve their goal of independence from others."[92]

Because these issues, dependence, codependence, and independence, are central to the lives of women with disabilities and because the paradox of requiring dependence in order to be independent is integral to the disabilities themselves, disabled women are ideally situated to teach, by their examples, the rest of us how to incorporate the need for help with our yearning for relationship and our rightful fear of patriarchally defined dependence. "Every human being . . . is *dependent* on other people—for material things like food and roads, all the way up to intangibles like love and a sense of purpose in life. . . . Without help it takes me three hours to get dressed and out of bed in the morning. With the help of a paid attendant, I can be in my van and on my way to work in 45 minutes."[93] The connection between needing roads and needing a personal attendant simply does not occur to the rest of us until we learn to listen to women for whom both needs are a daily reality. Women with disabilities "confront issues of helplessness, autonomy and control daily and our struggle helps us grow."[94] The old, private resolutions (codependence, overreliance on a parent, lover, or single friend) are no longer acceptable in light of the redefinition of disability dependence as a civil rights issue. Purely public resolutions are incompatible with our need for relationships and with the resistance of public programs to individual needs and abilities. The resolution that distinguishes women with disabilities in feminist or other communities is self-definition in the context of a network of care. "At one point, I decided I would do everything myself. But suddenly I realized I was devoting my life to being blind. It would take me all day to do the shopping and the laundry, and it wasn't worth it. There are too many things I have to do in my life. . . . I'm fortunate that there are many women willing to help me live my life."[95] Willingness to accept help from "many women" differs powerfully from expecting it from one person. Insisting that no one but your lover can know that you are incontinent keeps both of you focused on the incontinence and keeps her focused on your attitude. To give and seek help without compromising the potential for intimacy requires willingness to do so outside the intimate relationship, and also to do it without a mechanistic belief in reciprocity.

> I may be simply too exhausted at the end of a day coping with architectural barriers and people's attitudes to "do my share," to keep and give and take "even Steven." I'm tired of keeping count. Of not asking one lesbian to help because she already did a "favor" for me today. Of reminding myself I can ask another lesbian because I did her two "favors" last week. I want to know within myself that I am a precious asset to this world and let go of ever needing to prove that to myself and others.[96]

To develop another model for accepting help in specific communities that assume that "keeping count" is necessary, women have adopted two closely related strategies: relying on a network of many helpers, and redefining reciprocity to include the "passing on" of care within an extended social group.

Developing a circle of caregivers so that no one person is responsible for meeting all of the needs of any one sick or disabled person has been an important strategy in some communities. Audre Lorde believes that black women "have a head start" in cancer survival strategies: "One secret is to ask as many people as possible for help, depending on all of them or on none of them at the same time. Some will help, others cannot. For the time being."[97] As Sarah Hoagland observes, "the need does not specify who is to meet it."[98] Primary caregivers often develop elaborate strategies for enlarging the circle of those who may be asked for help, making lists of several categories of needs and parallel lists of people who might meet them.[99] These may be efforts to control the uncontrollable, but they are also steps toward "depending on all of them or none of them at the same time." They may lead to an understanding that needing help encompasses both things the individual cannot do and things she can do but only at the cost of more important activities.[100]

Reciprocity can be redefined only when there is a clear understanding of exactly what help is needed and why and of the fact that the need does not specify who is to meet it. Then it is possible, first, to ask the helper to let the other woman know when she feels that she has reached her own limits. In the presence of such an agreement, the one who asks for help will not feel constrained to hold back her feelings.[101] Judy Katz, writing of her need for help in recovering from the trauma of rape, says that she discovered that "I would have to find ways to make it easier for [my friends] to help me."[102] Perhaps the hardest kind of help to accept is "simply to cry or talk with a friend, to be comforted."[103] To reach this point, as Katz did in agreeing with her friend that each could tell the other when she had heard enough, is to acknowledge that there is a reciprocity that cannot be documented on a scoreboard, that of sharing the human condition. "Everyone's troubles are everyone else's business. Not for gossip or curiosity or pity. Not to look and cluck. But to bear each other's difficulties, to learn compassion, to know the relief of speaking our own troubles, to know the satisfaction of hearing how all of us endure losses."[104] Whether the help takes the form of listening to feelings or of doing the laundry, transcending reciprocity (or simply walking around it) expands our awareness of what it is to be human, one who endures losses, who helps and can ask for help, who sometimes refuses to help or be helped. "Dependency is terrible only for those who live in the illusion of self-sufficiency and independence. We all need help at times, help of a kind neither money nor barter of services can repay. The only payment possible is to become the kind of person who can give such help to others."[105] In this view, the helper is not a rescuer,[106] but one who attends to her own needs and asks for appropriate help in turn, not because she is a victim (even of her own self-sacrifice) but because she lives outside the illusion of self-sufficiency.

The alternative to the dependence/independence dichotomy, then, is not interdependence in the sense of an exchange of dependencies, but an acknowledgment of "the way lives intertwine." "No one knows better than the hanging-in patient that no man or woman is an island, entire of itself. No one knows better than the patient whose life depends on extended, esoteric, at times debilitating treatment, that each of us is a piece of the continent, a part of the main. The bell signalling involvement in mankind tolls for the hanging-in patient with singular force and intensity."[107]


## RESOLUTION

The outcome of help-seeking, when it is "worked through" to a recognition of one's participation in the human community, may thus include a spiritual dimension like those advocated in various "recovery" programs, including programs for codependents. Whether the resolution is called "recovery," "undependence,"[108] "interdependence,"[109] "mutual dependence,"[110] or "cooperation,"[111] it requires attentive awareness of one's own abilities and disabilities; it requires "a woman's being effective on her own behalf, not needy and ineffective, not effective and altruistic, but *effective for herself*."[112] A community of women effective for themselves represents both a practical and a spiritual involvement in humankind. The way we move into such involvement is through a recovery or discovery process that women with disabilities are pressed by their disabilities to begin and that all of us can learn through our interactions with those women.

CHAPTER 12

# RECOVERY PROGRAMS

As the disability rights movement gathered strength in the 1980s, a parallel growth occurred in the so-called "recovery" movement. The interactions between these two developments have complex, interesting implications for each and for feminist theory as well. The movement for disability awareness is predominantly political, while the recovery movement is personal, intrapsychic, and, at least in its twelve step manifestations, determinedly apolitical. The same objections raised by feminists to this apolitical focus are at least implicit in the reactions of disability activists. In addition, the medical model on which most recovery programs are based is suspect to people with disabilities other than alcoholism and, indeed, the idea that alcoholism is a disease still evokes skepticism in some quarters. And the concept of "codependence" provokes anxiety about the already tenuous or conflicted relationships between caregivers and people with disabilities.

However, those same issues (medical self-help, personal and intrapsychic attentiveness, and recovery from codependence) reframe important aspects of disability experience. And the strong emphasis of most recovery programs on spirituality, acceptance of "things we cannot change," and living "one day at a time" parallels the positive philosophical impact of the disability experience for many people.

All of these are women's issues. The coincidence of codependent characteristics and feminine role requirements is the most obvious example. Among feminists, controversy over the value of twelve-step and other recovery programs has centered on their patriarchal Christian history, their adoption of a paternalistic medical model, and the intrapsychic, apolitical emphasis of their content. All of these are issues for people with disabilities as well. And both feminists and disability activists are appropriately concerned that such programs may reinforce patient-blaming (while ignoring societal responsibility), blur genuine differences among "diseases," and undermine caregiving relationships.

Still, large numbers of women, disabled and nondisabled, feminist or not, are attracted to these programs, "work" them, and believe that they provide support, awareness, and ideas not available or less directly and personally available through political movements. The uneasiness that this fact provokes among activists and scholars (perhaps especially women's studies scholars) suggests its relevance to women's understanding of the present conditions of activist and scholarly work.

## DISABILITY AND ADDICTIONS

The project of exploring connections and disconnections among these three movements is greatly complicated by the probability that most members of the disability and women's movements are themselves personally affected by drug and/or alcohol abuse. Chemical dependency is pervasive in all parts of American society. Among people with disabilities these problems are often compounded by heavy use of prescription drugs to address effects of the disability or illness. Street drugs (notably marijuana) too are often used for "medical" purposes, for example, to relieve nausea or pain. Moreover, families with disabled members often develop dynamics similar to those of alcoholic families, whether alcohol is present or not, as focus on or denial of the disability can become the dis-organizing principle of family life in the same way that alcoholism can. All generalizations about the relevance of recovery programs to those in political civil rights movements must therefore be read against a sobering background: the recognition that not all alcoholics get sober, not all women with disabilities sort out their dependence-independence issues, not all addicts or codependents want to "recover," and many women with disabilities are addicted to prescription or recreational drugs.

Resistance to and criticisms of recovery programs incorporate uncertainty about these facts. The critic may or may not be chemically dependent or in a close relationship with someone who is, and this may not be stated or even consciously known by the individual her- or himself. For this reason, some of the more persuasive arguments against such programs come from those who have participated as recovering addicts and then have proposed alternative programs during sobriety.[1]

The requirement of anonymity in twelve-step programs and many treatment groups further compounds the difficulty of evaluating such critiques, as participants' defenses or criticisms may remain unpublished or the experiences on which their comments are based, unspecified.

Finally, one primary symptom of chemical dependency is denial. The elaborate psychological and logical structures by which denial is protected profoundly influence the whole discussion. And the injunction in most recovery programs to refrain from "taking someone else's inventory" (listing their defects of character) sometimes inhibits challenges to arguments based on denial.

My own experience as I tried to write this chapter illustrates the problem. For over a year after I presented an abbreviated version at a professional meeting,[2] I was unable to write anything on the subject, despite ample leave time and comfortable personal space for writing. I used every device I knew for overcoming writer's block, consulted colleagues and counselors, and read large amounts of literature on related subjects. But I could not write until I realized that the underlying problem was my inability to be clear in the writing about the interaction of disability and recovery issues in my own personal experience. Here anonymity intersects other concerns about privacy with reference to alcoholism, codependence, and Jennifer's multiple disabilities. My preference for intellectualizing every experience and my training in scholarly "objectivity" further complicate the dilemma. And my feminist commitment to make clear my own biases contradicts most of the above.

Jennifer grew up in an alcoholic family. She exhibited many of the characteristics of a classic "lost child,"[3] and eventually sometimes of a scapegoat, but most of her serious emotional problems were caused by neurological impairment that interferes with her thinking and her ability to process what she sees and hears. Much of her anger was directed at her disabilities themselves; some, at family members. She has very little cognitive understanding of her disabilities and she routinely misinterprets sensory data about the people around her. Separating the effects of the alcoholic family on her chaotic interpretations of the world is impossible.

For me, the process of coming to terms with Jennifer's disabilities almost exactly recapitulates the teachings of twelve-step programs although I was not in a program at the time I first learned these things. When, years later, I did participate in twelve step programs, I recognized the connections and came to believe that having such a program would greatly have relieved the isolation and loneliness I experienced when I was confronted daily with my powerlessness over her disabilities and over the patriarchal and quasi-medical institutions on which she relies. It was only after some time in recovery programs that I acknowledged my own physical limitations and the extent to which comparison with Jennifer's more severe disabilities contributed to denial about my own body. At the time, I had been reading and writing about body awareness for several years.

As a feminist, I have always had serious reservations about certain aspects of recovery programs, which nevertheless have had a positive, transformative effect on my life. Indeed, they have reinforced and clarified my feminist beliefs. I write, therefore, from the perspective of one who is personally committed to all three movements and who is at least some of the time extremely uncomfortable in all three.

## STEPS TO RECOVERY

By far the most widespread and well-known recovery programs are the twelve-step programs derived from Alcoholics Anonymous (AA).[4] Most treatment programs use AA materials, incorporate the twelve steps (or at least the first three) into their activities, and plan AA, NA (Narcotics Anonymous), and Al-Anon (for family members and friends of alcoholics) into the aftercare plans of their clients. The twelve-step programs themselves differ from "treatment" in that they are groups of peers, not professionals, have "no dues or fees"; and "take no position on outside issues," including treatment modalities. The steps themselves structure individuals' processes toward recovery by encouraging them in the context of a supportive group to break their denial, recognize their spirituality, examine their lives, mend their relationships, and accept the diversity of their peers. Each of these activities has obvious relevance to the process by which people learn to live with disabilities.

## BREAKING DENIAL

The first step of Alcoholics Anonymous reads: "We admitted we were powerless over alcohol, that our lives had become unmanageable." Based on the premise that alcoholism is a progressive, fatal disease, this step describes a discovery relevant to those with other illnesses and disabilities. The word "powerless" has been problematic to many feminists and others who believe that powerlessness in the face of patriarchal power is socially constructed and designed to keep us subordinated. But people with intractable disabilities or with progressive fatal diseases learn that neither self-control nor manipulation of resources can change the basic nature of the problem, whether or not a changed environment mitigates its handicapping aspects. Without minimizing the positive effects of denial for some people at some times, we can see that admitting the unmanageability via willpower or self-control of a disability is the appropriate starting point for an understanding of how best to live *within* the situation. For example, when I admitted my powerlessness over Jennifer's disabilities and especially over the behaviors resulting from them, I could stop using my energies and hers to control these unmanageable aspects of her life and divert them instead to locating resources that permit her to be more comfortable in living with them. For her part, admitting that she cannot control her tremor enables her to give up her effort to be truly "normal" (unshaky), relieves the stress-related intensification of the tremor, and frees her time and energy to be who she *can* be—to be "normal" *for her*.

Awareness that the disability or some of its effects are unmanageable comes hard to me and is not acceptable to other people. There is considerable pressure on people with disabilities and on their families to manage "independently." If mothers, lovers, wives can be persuaded to manage, the larger community will not have to be responsible. Our own desires to control the uncontrollable are thus constantly reinforced from outside. Accepting powerlessness and unmanageability can thus lead to increased pressure on others to accept responsibility hitherto assigned to the individual.

In connection with the first step, twelve step groups commonly use the "serenity prayer," which asks for "the serenity to accept the things I cannot change." In the case of disability, this might mean, for example, accepting that no amount of exercise will improve one's ability to walk. However, using a wheelchair might improve one's mobility. The prayer continues to ask for "the courage to change the things I can." The process of learning that the disability is indeed intractable may be accompanied by considerable anger before anything resembling serenity or courage can be attained. The process does not suggest that the individual should give up and die (or become wholly dependent on others) because she has a disability or disease, but that she invest her physical and psychological resources in what she can change instead of denying the real limits the disability imposes. This involves humility, which Sara Ruddick (in another context) defines as "a selfless respect for reality," "a metaphysical attitude one takes toward a world beyond one's control."[5]

None of this suggests surrender to oppression. Sarah Lucia Hoagland's discussion of the relationship of powerlessness to moral agency is, I think, the best feminist discussion of this point. Moral agency, she says, "involves resisting the belief that if we can't control a situation, our actions make no difference and we are powerless."[6] The misconception, she suggests, comes from "regarding power as an ability to control things," which leads either to denial that there is a problem or to assuming blame for the whole situation, thus undermining our moral agency. The fact that we are powerless, as defined by masculinist thought, leads to the assumption that "nothing we do makes any difference."[7] Hoagland is not speaking of twelve step programs here, but what she says about moral agency as the ability "to go on under oppression . . . to create meaning through our living,"[8] provides a feminist analysis of the ways in which admitting powerlessness need not mean surrendering to patriarchal domination.

Where disability is an issue, such an analysis may help an individual distinguish between the disability as a locus of powerlessness and the hospital or doctor's office as the locus of patriarchal authority. The distinction applies whether the doctor is suggesting childlike dependence or compulsory self-help. One of Bernie Siegel's correspondents, protesting against excessive reliance on self-healing for people with illnesses, writes,

> I am in charge of my attitude and what I give to my life and how I treat my body. But I am not in control of the outcome of my illness. It has been a very long time growing to this understanding, and letting go of my sense of failure. I kept turning back on myself, thinking that I must be doing something wrong, or I wasn't trying hard enough or maybe I was somehow sabotaging myself. Because after all, if I was doing it right I wouldn't be sick, be in pain . . . it is so important to work for goals that are attainable.[9]

Ending denial permits a realistic assessment of what goals might be attainable, and a shift of focus from an unattainable future, in which, for example, an alcoholic drinks moderately, to a workable present, in which she or he does not drink today. Al-Anon advocates "emotional sobriety" one day at a time, following the AA model. Autobiographical literature about living with chronic illness repeatedly uses the same phrase. Breaking through denial makes the temporal philosophy accessible. "Our acceptance of life's unpredictability frees us of our preoccupation with *more* time and allows us to use *this* time—today."[10]

To give up denial requires giving up the irrational belief in self-control ("If I eat right I won't have cancer"; "If I grit my teeth I can walk upstairs"). To rely on something beyond self-control is an extraordinarily difficult step.

## SPIRITUALITY

By far the most controversial aspect of twelve-step programs among women is their spiritual basis. The twelfth tradition of AA begins, "Anonymity is the spiritual foundation of all our traditions," certainly a problematic concept for women challenging our historic anonymity, having been silenced. Still more problematic is the use of masculine god-talk. The second step reads, "Came to believe that a power greater than ourselves could restore us to sanity," and the third refers to "God as we understood Him." Although participants in these programs consistently assure newcomers that "God" can be interpreted any way the individual chooses and the word is frequently translated as "the group," "the program," or even "the goddess," there is a strong history of Christian emphasis on God the Father. Most meetings end with the Lord's Prayer. Given the bias of American culture, the emphasis is certainly on a patriarchal Christian god.

The editors of *With the Power of Each Breath*, a feminist disability anthology, say that they planned to include a chapter on spirituality because "many women with disabilities seek spiritual assistance for strength and solace as we face the things that cannot be fixed," but "the articles we received did not represent a broad enough spectrum of what spirituality can mean for us."[11] Part of the problem here, too, I suspect, is the cultural definition of spirituality as tied to Christian religion. There is also some debate in feminist circles about New Age spirituality and Wicca (feminist witchcraft) as well as other feminist spiritual practices. The twelve step "higher" power, "as we understand her," encompasses these to different degrees in different groups, but with at least tolerance in most and respect in many. Most groups also support looking for the site of spirituality in the woman's self.

The ease or difficulty with which women can accept twelve-step god-talk depends on their individual histories/herstories. Christians and post-christian feminists, witches and pagans, people from fundamentalist and "high church" backgrounds, Jewish women and atheists, Black Baptists and Southern Baptists, goddess worshippers and therapy seekers, women from Muslim families and Confucian scholars—we bring our whole and divided selves to the subject of spirituality. One remarkable characteristic of twelve-step programs is their acceptance in principle, despite the founding fathers' masculine, Christian, capitalist bias, that each individual's own possibly eccentric "higher power" or spiritual belief is what she or he needs to get and stay sober, to be well. In light of this, the program emphasizes a spiritual, not a religious, "solution." Indeed, many supporters of twelve-step programs explicitly reject religion. For example, Anne Wilson Schaef and Diane Fassel state that "whenever we confuse religion with spirituality, we are opting for the structure, control, and rules of an addictive system. This reliance on religion may remove us from the inner search only we can do from the depths of our own being."[12]

My purpose in this chapter is not to defend twelve-step programs against charges of Christian bias or to present a full account of how women fit goddess beliefs or other feminist spiritual beliefs into the programs but to give a general idea of how disability experience is related to the basic twelve-step process. I will return later to feminist objections to twelve-step programs, but here I propose to look at three issues in twelve step spirituality for their relevance to women's experience with disability. They are surrender, humility, and "letting go." All three derive from the acknowledgment of powerlessness over the "disease."

The third and seventh steps encourage members to "turn our will and our lives over to the care of God as we underst[and] Him," and to "humbly ask God to remove our shortcomings." Even if we alter the pronouns and resist the hierarchical implications of "higher" power, the concepts of surrender and humility are difficult. The clearest feminist discussion of humility that I have found is Sara Ruddick's in "Maternal Thinking." Ruddick distinguishes between obedience, which "respects the actual control and preferences of dominant people," and humility, "which respects indifferent nature, the incomprehensible supernatural, and human fallibility."[13] This formulation can be applied to experience of disability in which body awareness, consciousness of one's limitations, interrupts grandiosity and forces (or permits) the individual not only to recognize human fallibility but to stop "taking personally" the fact of having been apparently singled out for accident or illness. Thus the woman is not the victim of hostile forces but of "indifferent nature" and is limited not because she or her mother did something wrong but because she is one of the humans. (Political implications of this philosophy are discussed below.)

Surrender, then, is based on this attitude of humility. It means letting go of the need to control everything and to defend ourselves at every turn.[14] Surrender is the action that follows admission of powerlessness. If a woman has a physical disability over which she admits that she is powerless, accepts the fact that she did not cause it and cannot control the fact that she has it (though she may be able to alleviate some of its symptoms), she may have the humility to "respect" indifferent nature and to take her place among other limited humans. Instead of a position of abnegation before a "higher" power conceptualized as a golden idol or a punishing dictator, the power greater than oneself, then, is "that voice within, the intuitive self, your gut instinct. The essential thing is that the isolation that occurs around the addiction is broken down."[15] Carol Pearson suggests that the effect of relying on someone outside oneself moves the individual beyond the dualism of dependence/independence because with support one can gradually learn to take charge of one's life while accepting and learning how to get appropriate help.[16] Surrender, then, is not relinquishing self but relinquishing the belief that in isolation, help-less, one can control every aspect of one's life.

This sense of the meanings of humility and surrender is closely affiliated with the perception of believers in the pagan and goddess movements that human life is part of a larger web of life that includes all of nature,[17] "a spiritual acceptance of the human presence on earth, a respect for and 'inspiration in the movements of the sun, moon, and stars, the flight of birds, the slow growth of trees, and the cycles of the seasons.' "[18] We become aware of these connections when "we choose to surrender to [things], to meet them on their own terms, to accept them for what they are. It is impossible to experience the essence of things when preoccupied with the thought of making them conform to our expectations."[19]

Essentially the twelve steps encourage the individual to acknowledge and try to deepen her or his spiritual awareness. The eleventh step says "to improve our conscious contact." The process comes from bonding among people who have suffered, grieved, admitted powerlessness. A similar process takes place among women who live with disabilities. As a woman moves out of denial of her limitations into recognition that more resources are needed than can be obtained alone and that efforts to be totally independent are indeed crazy-making, she begins also to accept that she is not, as AA members say, "terminally unique." Instead she is "just part of the universe, not in charge of it."[20] She comes to a "spiritual acceptance of the human presence on earth."[21] She is connected with other human beings whose limitations may be quite different from her own and with the rest of nature and is thus less inclined to judge herself or other people.[22] Carol Pearson, who observes a parallel between feminist consciousness-raising groups and twelve-step groups in the development of this awareness, names it a process of "letting go": "Beyond the dualism that sees 'life as suffering' or 'life in Eden' is an awareness of pain and suffering as part of the flow of life."[23] But of course it is *only* part. The point of breaking through denial is to see the pain or sorrow or limitation in the context of a whole life, and of a larger world that incorporates others' whole lives.

## THE EXAMINED LIFE

Knowing that one is powerless lessens denial and begins a process toward self-knowledge: knowledge of one's human limitations and connection with other limited people. But that knowledge is only partial. A more holistic self-knowledge means knowing from within the *self* what one's specific assets and limitations may be and having a conscious awareness of the whole range of possibilities. It means knowing the implications of one's attitudes, addictions, and unawareness. To reach this insight requires an integration of contact with the spiritual aspect of oneself; willingness to recognize, name, and feel emotions; and intellectual processing of factual information. The device by which twelve-step programs facilitate this integration is the personal inventory. AA calls it "a searching and fearless moral inventory," emphasizing that it should provide an honest evaluation of the individual's attributes and limitations. As twelve-step programs have proliferated, so have guidelines for the inventory, gradually moving away from the original emphasis on "resentments" and "defects of character" to the whole range of attributes and, especially in "adult children" groups, on how even dysfunctional behaviors were originally survival strategies. Except in unusual circumstances (such as illiteracy or inability to use writing devices), the inventory is supposed to be written.

Writing encourages clarity. The emphasis on autobiography, surveying the whole of one's life, develops contextual thinking so that one sees the obsession or crisis or relationship of the present moment as part of one or several lifelong patterns. It is "reduced to size." The "searching and fearless" qualities of the inventory, when it is carefully done, are believed to prevent relapse into denial and self-destructive behaviors. It is harder to forget what you have written despite fear.

The written inventory is a private document. It clarifies the individual's experience. The fifth step then calls for its content to be spoken "to God, to ourselves, and to another human being." The twelve steps are derived from a number of religious traditions, all of which incorporate some form of private or public confession. In a study of psychological "therapies" in several cultures, E. Fuller Torrey notes that all incorporate confession, either private or public. "Confession, solidifies the bond between client and therapist, and through ventilation of the problems, often provides the client with a greater sense of mastery of them. . . . In addition to sharing the guilt and obtaining emotional catharsis, confession often produces a re-living of painful experiences (abreaction) that may be therapeutic."[24] In twelve-step groups confession is private in the formal fifth step, with a continuous public component as members are encouraged to go to meetings and tell the truth about their lives. To be honest with oneself, to put that honesty into words, to tell another person, and to be heard or at least listened to attentively encourages the individual to take her- or himself seriously and to be willing to give up unrealistic expectations.

One of my experiences with this dynamic showed me its effectiveness in breaking denial about disability issues. I was participating as the nondisabled member of a panel on hidden disabilities at a women's studies conference.[25] As one panelist after another told her personal story about how her disability impacted her life, I felt overwhelmed by the recognition of how my own life has been limited by my superwomanly effort to live out the full productivity and political responsibility of two lives, my own and Jennifer's. I spoke, then, about my own physical limitations, about how dis-abled I have become through the stress of this unrealistic overcommitment. Although I had a dull background awareness of this situation before,

I "forgot" it most of the time. Having confessed publicly, I now remember, and have taken steps to change, to integrate my limitations into my work-style.

Nancy Mairs, writing about fear, describes the process by which inventory and confession work, though she is not discussing twelve-step programs.

> Fear and anger and grief feel so unpleasant to us that we're eager to transform them into confidence and affection and joy. But you can't transform what you haven't grasped. The first step toward transformation is to locate your feelings, recognize them, admit them out loud to yourself and, when necessary, to others. . . . By naming your 'shameful' feelings, you take possession over them instead of letting them possess you. This is the beginning of transformative power.[26]

Mairs's essays themselves exemplify this process, and because their content is often the impact of disability on her life, they encourage other women with disabilities to articulate similar self-knowledge. Susan Griffin expands on the idea that self-knowledge liberates by allowing a woman to own her shameful feelings instead of letting them own her by pointing out that denying emotions usually results in projecting them onto another person, thus turning the other person into an enemy. To own them instead is empowering.[27]

Janice Raymond, writing of female friendship, suggests that the "habit of reflection" enables a woman to be loyal to herself, to have faith in her own insight. Raymond associates this loyalty with the "rigors of discernment" necessary to honest evaluation of relationships with others.[28] And bell hooks, probing resistance among black women to being "open," says that "it has been a political struggle for me to hold to the belief that there is much which we— black people—must speak about, much that is private that must be openly shared, if we are to heal our wounds (hurts caused by domination and exploitation and oppression), if we are to recover and heal ourselves." The openness, she says, "is about how to be well and telling the truth is about how to put the broken bits and pieces of the heart back together again."[29]

These are steps toward accepting responsibility for one's own life and toward a self-knowledge that comes from thoughtful intro-spection. Through them, one cultivates the ability to see what has really happened, neither taking on the whole responsibility nor blam-ing it all on the other person. The knowledge of self leads toward the ability to distinguish between one's own part in a situation and that of the other people involved. Obviously this skill is important in sort-ing out relationships in political as well as personal situations.

## BOUNDARIES AND RELATIONSHIPS

Participants in AA initially focus only on not drinking. But the twelve steps are based on a belief that to continue not drinking, the alco-holic must mend relationships, first with one's self and one's spiri-tual nature and then with other people. The eighth and ninth steps constitute the vehicle for attending to relationships:

(8) Made a list of all persons we had harmed and became willing to make amends to them all.

(9) Made direct amends to such people whenever possible, except when to do so would injure them or others.

In practice, members are advised to proceed very cautiously with these steps, taking care not to injure *themselves* or others, and to be sure they understand the complexity of the situation before rushing into apologies that might make matters worse. Al-Anon, the second twelve-step program, addresses itself to relationships rather than drugs; it is primarily a women's organization in its history, although "the only requirement for membership is alcoholism in a relative or friend." Many members of other twelve-step programs enter Al-Anon when they are ready to work on relationship issues. Here the impor-tance of maintaining boundaries while making amends and the con-cept of detachment are central issues.

The process of working the eighth step, thinking through a particular situation and becoming willing first to acknowledge one's own part in it and then to make amends, is similar to what Janice Raymond calls the "power of scrutiny in our interactions with others." Such careful discernment, she says, provides "insight—

even insight into our mistakes."[30] The power of scrutiny derives from our willingness to explore the complexity of our interactions, without resorting to praise or blame of either the other person or oneself. Sarah Hoagland, discussing the way praise and blame interfere with our understanding of moral agency, stresses the fact that focusing on who is to blame diverts our attention from "the interactive nature of the situation," and "keeps us justifying our behavior and hence focused away from [its] full complexity."[31]

Recognizing the boundaries and overlaps between one's own part in an interaction and the other person's in order to make appropriate amends frequently requires an attitude of detachment. To make amends for boundary violations involves attentive respect for boundaries thereafter. Somehow individuals must learn to be engaged without being enmeshed, to be "participatory and involved without losing themselves."[32] The notion of "loving detachment" is one of the most difficult for newcomers or outsiders to Al-Anon to understand, because it evokes fears of abandonment and is easily confused with hostile withdrawal. The concept is rather one of respect for the other person's difference, her or his distinct separateness. Sara Ruddick provides a useful example in the detachment of mothers from their children. It is, she says, "a giving up, a letting grow. To love a child without seizing or using it, to see the child with the patient, loving eye of attention." It involves "looking, self-restraining, and empathy."[33] Detachment means accepting difference, attentively hearing the other perspective. "When we are urged to practice *detachment,* it never means *disinterest.* The latter would express only despair and hopelessness, while loving detachment gives us every hope."[34]

In addition to the eighth and ninth steps, twelve-step programs encourage detachment and attentiveness through the group process of meetings. Conventional wisdom in the programs holds that members learn most from listening to newcomers, not only because they remind others of what it was like when they were new, but also because of their intrinsic wisdom. Members are frequently reminded that they never know who will say what they need to hear, so they should listen carefully to everyone. The general practice in meetings is to allow each person (or as many as time permits) to speak without interruption or commentary. Carol Pearson links Alcoholics Anonymous with feminist consciousness-raising, suggesting not that they are interchangeable, but that both provide love, "an opportunity for individuals to tell and retell their story in a way that overcomes denial," an analysis that avoids blaming the speaker, and "encouragement to begin to talk about taking responsibility for their own lives."[35] This last point is essential. If anyone else offers to take responsibility, even to the extent of offering advice, dependency—or resistance to change—is reinforced. Mary Ambo makes a similar point about disability movement groups: "We provide a place where we all have permission and freedom to express our feelings . . . 'without the fear of being perceived as pathetic, and without creating the assumption that we are asking someone else to "fix" us and make us better.' "[36] Starhawk, who advocates twelve-step groups especially for women who see themselves as victims, describes a number of other groups that stay with a woman "to be there for her and yet to let her have her own fears, her own journey, her own battle . . . without taking them [her fear, pain, etc.] over or trying to cure them, so that what she encounters will not isolate her, but will draw her closer to other human beings."[37] These include consciousness-raising groups, women's circles, Quaker dialogue, and Native American rounds, each of which incorporates uninterrupted talking, attentive listening, and restraint from questioning or advice-giving.[38] For the speaker, they emphasize honesty.[39] The noncritical, nonjudgmental listeners are essential to the speaker's ability to be honest.

In addition, confidentiality is important; hence the twelve-step requirement of anonymity, which protects not only the addict whose disease is subject to social stigma, but everyone who attempts to speak honestly about anything that has been hidden from someone outside the group. Anonymity prevents the development of "stars" as well as the revelation of embarrassing facts. It also prevents the fear of appearing less than perfect from inhibiting honest expression of whatever a member has to say. Anonymity in this case does not "protect" a woman's speech from ever being heard; instead it protects her right to speak without being misquoted or judged: where all speakers are equal, each is responsible for finding her own way; in the absence of advice, there is no pressure to be other than herself.[40] The nonverbal message to participants is like that attributed by Suzanne Pharr to consciousness-raising groups: that "we are capable of presenting and analyzing our own lives, that we are not alone in our experiences, and that we hold within ourselves our own answers and capacity for being in charge of our lives."[41]

None of this is to say that these various kinds of groups are equivalents. Consciousness-raising and twelve-step groups, for example, differ in that the former end with a political analysis and the latter scrupulously avoid such analysis. They agree, however, in respecting the speaker's time and individual voice. One result is that when many and varied voices are respected, speakers and listeners learn not to try to coerce others into matching them. Thus the twelfth step, a proselytizing step, is commonly interpreted to mean that the experienced member explains the program by telling her or his own story and not by telling the other person what to do. The step reads, "Having had a spiritual awakening as a result of these steps, we tried to carry this message to others, and to practice these principles in all our affairs." The emphasis on spirituality and the stress on living by the principles of the preceding steps result in a belief that it is by practicing the program that a member attracts others.

## FEMINIST REACTIONS

Among feminists there has been considerable personal discomfort and public disagreement about twelve-step programs, all of it relevant to disability issues as well. The discussion has centered on three characteristics of recovery programs: their basis in patriarchal, Christian religion; their focus on personal intrapsychic "recovery"; and their apolitical nature. Each of these is seen by many as leading the participant away from feminist political analysis and action.[42] By others, the criticism is labeled a misunderstanding of how the program works.

Bill Wilson and Dr. Bob Smith, the founders of Alcoholics Anonymous, got sober under the influence of the Oxford groups, a Christian movement. From them, they derived the emphasis on surrender to a higher power (clearly God the Father), the moral inventory, making amends, and helping others to believe. Wilson was a stockbroker and most of the early AA members were, or aspired to be, businessmen. Their language (the anonymous AA "Big Book" was written mainly by Bill Wilson) is sexist, with heavy use of financial and business language. On those rare occasions when imagery is drawn from what could be seen as women's experience, it is inaccurate (e.g., the supposed effectiveness of sweeping only one side of the street). Since the Big Book and *Twelve Steps and Twelve Traditions* (also written by Wilson)[43] are still the texts on which the AA program is based, most meetings are still strongly influenced by this sexist, heterosexist, Christian, capitalist bias. Furthermore, the emphasis on confession of character defects and submissiveness to a higher power reinforce subordination and internalized self-blame.

Even Anne Wilson Schaef, who strongly advocates twelve-step programs, stresses that women must overcome the feeling of power-lessness and claim our own personal power, which comes from in-side us.[44] Other women who state that they need AA as a support group in which their alcoholism is addressed express shock at the white, middle-class, Christian, male perspective and discomfort at what they experience as pressure not to name their lesbianism or even to proclaim their feminism.[45] Some of these women stay and eventually even affirm their AA experience because, as Sharon Stone-key says, it is "the only support group in town," but the acceptance comes only after "gradually I found ways to redesign and interpret [AA] so that it was compatible with me and my feminist values."[46]

As we have seen, twelve-step spirituality can indeed be inter-preted in ways that are meaningful to feminists, and the format of meetings, stressing acceptance of what people say about their indi-vidual spiritual experience, makes such interpretation possible. Nev-ertheless, it is a reinterpretation that requires vigilance and some risk. Especially frustrating for most women is the relentless barrage of masculine generic pronouns, used of alcoholics and, especially, of God. In the context of a long-term practice of other steps toward self-knowledge, a woman's experience nevertheless tends toward an increasing conceptualization of the internal awareness of her spiritu-ality as womanly because it is her *own* spirituality and she is a woman. Even when a woman describes her spirituality as feminine qualities (for example, nurturing) in God the Father, she is articulat-ing a woman's experience derived from her embodied self. Disability experience, centered as it is on the woman's own body and how she uses it in the presence of her disability, is self-centering and de-centers the spiritual priorities of external guides.

Not surprisingly, many women have chosen to attend separatist twelve-step groups, especially women's and lesbian or lesbian/
gay groups. Initially resistant to such separations, AA now accepts
these groups and refers people to them, though most women and gay
men also attend "mixed" groups. Such separations reflect the problems inherent in twelve-step programs as patriarchal institutions.
They also challenge feminist theory in several complex ways.

An important part of the twelve-step message is that no individual participant is unique, that simply attending meetings and
listening to many, diverse stories will help the individual feel
connected to the others, as just one among many alcoholics, for
example. Separatist groups may to some extent interfere with this
message, which helps to weaken denial and forge a spiritual connection. However, the importance of women's separate space is an article of faith for many feminists, and the experience of homophobia,
antisemitism, or racism in meetings may represent a more powerful
alienation than the separatist group could. For feminist theorists
it is also a critical challenge that AA or Al-Anon is indeed often
"the only group in town." When a significant number of (or even one
or two) outspoken, politically oriented feminists attend twelve-step
meetings, the dynamic of the group is altered as they, like everyone
else, are listened to, uninterrupted, and others are influenced. For
example, I have met several men who began to use feminine pronouns to refer to God after they heard this usage in meetings.

In addition to separate women's AA groups, and the usually
female-dominated Al-Anon and CODA (Codependents Anonymous)
groups, there are two programs that I know of developed by women
as alternatives to twelve-step programs. Both have thirteen steps or
principles and both omit the focus on character defects and a
"higher" power. The thirteen steps of Women for Sobriety, founded
by Jean Kirkpatrick in 1976, are a series of affirmations based on the
premise that "guilt, depression, low (or no) self-esteem are the problems of today's woman and dependence upon alcohol temporarily
masks her real needs, which are for a feeling of self-realization and
self-worth."[47] The thirteen affirmations are designed to reinforce self-
esteem. Bonita Swan's thirteen steps are a feminist attempt to structure women's groups along spiritual lines without reference to God.
They are not called "steps" except in the title of Swan's book, and are
supposed to be used in a circular or spiral way and not as a hierarchi-

cal ladder. In contrast to the twelve-step higher power, these guide-lines say, "My higher self is within me and is the power I use to control my life." Nurturing the bond with this power creates energy that is used in generating an ethical inventory. Willingness to change is the responsibility of the woman herself; it is not turned over to a higher power. And the "amends" steps are more clearly about choosing relationships: "I will call to memory those people who have touched my life and name our true relationship. With 'ill will toward none,' I affirm, reclaim, amend or dismiss past relationships." The series ends with an affirmation: "All women are beautiful, intelligent, strong and powerful, and that includes me."[48] Both of these alternatives counter women's self-defeating or self-deprecating thoughts with a strong, affirming concept of woman. Both take an intrapsychic or psychological approach though both acknowledge social role constriction as the source of women's damaged self-concept.

The self-centering approach is another aspect of recovery programs that has been criticized by some feminists. There are two reasons for this objection: first, that it prevents the woman from seeing the societal causes for her dilemma, and second, that it diverts women's energy from important political work. In twelve step groups, the responsibility for recovery rests entirely on the individual, even though addiction is called a disease. The larger social context is not addressed. Such subjects as economic inequality, sexual abuse, and racial bigotry are not addressed.[49] The fact that some individuals sometimes discuss these issues in meetings in no way compensates for their systematic exclusion. Indeed, the AA tenth tradition states that AA has "no opinion on outside issues," a rule that is rigorously enforced.

The response of AA members—including many who found AA inhospitable to their feminism—to the criticism that AA is apolitical is that it is *alcohol,* not *recovery,* that interferes with our ability to see and deal with other oppressions. "If [our oppressors] are going to get us," says Celinda Cantu, "let them get us sober, we will leave a much more visible trail."[50] And Margot Oliver points out that we cannot wait to deal with addictions until the social causes are corrected. In the long run we must do that, she says, but in the short term women are dying. Only if they are alive in body and spirit can they work to change destructive social conditions.[51]

The concept of powerlessness is not contradictory to assuming responsibility for one's own life but, rather, is a prerequisite. Only when we accept powerlessness over things we cannot change, such as human mortality or the effect of allergens on our bodies, can we distinguish between situations where it is realistic to take action and those where it is not. As Carol Pearson observes, AA and con-sciousness-raising encourage women to move out of denial and self-involvement and to help others *by asserting their own truth.*[52] In twelve-step programs the inventory and the exploration of bound-aries in relationships provide the self-knowledge necessary to know-ing truth in order to act on it. A woman whose energy is absorbed in trying to avoid using a wheelchair has no resources with which to work toward better wheelchair access.

One insight from twelve-step programs that is often missed in political groups is that change must start where each women is and not in others' ideas of where she should be. Someone who goes into herself to recover from being hurt (by chemicals, by a relation-ship, by illness, by society) does so initially because she is in great pain. To require her to ignore that pain or to avoid others with sim-ilar difficulties advances no political causes.

This is in no way to suggest that political analysis is unnec-essary. bell hooks's discussion of women's self-help literature is a clear exposition of this need. Focusing her negative criticism espe-cially on Robin Norwood's *Women Who Love Too Much* (which strongly advocates twelve-step programs), hooks recognizes that Norwood "speaks to the pain and anguish many women feel in per-sonal relationships, particularly the pain heterosexual women feel in relationships with men," but hooks says that is by no means enough, because Norwood "in no way acknowledges political realities, the oppression and domination of women." In the absence of political analysis, the personal work of women reinforces rather than chal-lenges their subordination. Far from therefore dismissing Norwood's and other self-help literature, which "is read by masses of women across race, class, and sexual preference lines," hooks suggests that feminists should both ask why women are so attracted "to narratives that suggest we are responsible for male domination" and "acknowl-edge our failure to create adequate models for radical change in everyday life that would have meaning and significance for masses of women."[53] In short, several valid feminist criticisms of recovery pro-grams indicate not only the absence of feminist analysis within those programs but also the absence of effective psychological or spiritual components in feminist organizations.

## A DISABILITY PERSPECTIVE

The disability movement has not engaged in much discussion of recovery programs, but the feminist critique has obvious relevance to the movement. Two areas of particular concern for women with disabilities are the concept of powerlessness and the apolitical nature of recovery groups. In addition, the use of a medical model for recovery is an especially conflicted idea in light of many disability experiences in the United States.

If powerlessness is a common experience for women in our society, confronted as we are with institutionalized sexism, it is doubly a problem for women with disabilities, who experience institutionalized ableism as well as physical or mental powerlessness in the face of genuine biological or biochemical disabilities. Breaking through denial about these limitations, including the societal ones, is essential to understanding one's own situation including one's abilities. Still, recognizing that the disabilities are real and often intractable, and deciding not to struggle to control what cannot be controlled, must not, if the individual is to survive, be converted into passive, fatalistic submission. If it is, the individual will not be able to distinguish between "accepting" muscle atrophy, for example, and "accepting" the necessity of staying home for the rest of her life, to say nothing of estimating what political changes are feasible within the constraints of this year's legislature.

For a woman to know that she is powerless over alcohol does not mean that she cannot act in the world. It means that she has to acknowledge her limitations and work on living a balanced life within those limitations. Similarly, overcoming relationship addiction does not mean giving up relationships. For a woman with disabilities, seeking political solutions is very important, but it is much more difficult and less effective if she has not acknowledged her real limitations. "Normalization" based on denial does not work. A woman with asthma cannot do effective political work in unventilated smoke-filled rooms. Placing someone in a job she cannot do defeats her and the cause of job placement for disabled people. Placing a retarded woman alone in a neighborhood where she has no peers increases her isolation. None of us is likely to achieve a realistic awareness of herself and others if we are in an environment in which denial is institutionalized in policies, theories, and language that are not realistic about individual limitations.

Ironically, such politically institutionalized denial is at least as characteristic of disability as of feminist organizations. Where this is true, the twelve-step process may be useful in addressing denial and thus may contribute, albeit indirectly, to increased political effectiveness. The eighth- and ninth-step examination of boundaries and relationships can contribute to the individual's ability to decide what aspects of her or his problems are susceptible to political change and which changes will help rather than hurt the balance in that individual's life. For example, as Jennifer's guardian I may decide against the advice of some advocates for retarded people to respect her need for a community of her peers in preference to their belief that she needs mainstreaming. Instead of isolating her to demonstrate that she can survive "independently," and then spending my own energies trying to mitigate her loneliness, I may use my resources to change policies that force such all-or-nothing decisions. Such difficult decisions are likely to be selfish or misinformed if the decision maker has not made a searching and fearless examination of her own characteristic behaviors, addressed her own denial, and examined the boundaries between herself and the several institutions involved, including the disability rights movement, as well as between herself and the person with the disability. The same is true of relationships of women with disabilities and their attendants or caregivers.

From a disability perspective, a more complex political/personal problem with recovery programs is their use of a medical model. Twelve step and other recovery programs are based on a disease model of alcoholism and drug addiction. In the case of alcoholism, the model makes sense not only for its original purpose of removing the blame from the victim, but, today, for medical reasons, as we now know that genetic and biochemical factors are involved in alcoholism as in diabetes and other chronic illnesses. The disease concept makes it possible to transfer some of the insights of recovery programs to other illnesses and disabilities. There are problems, however, first with extending the disease model to "relationship addiction" and some other compulsions that appear to have no bio-logical component (though there may be body chemicals involved [e.g., adrenaline] and stress-related or stress-exacerbated physical problems); second, with assuming that medical "treatment" is necessary for nonmedical problems; and third, with encouraging dependency on institutionalized medicine (or, for that matter, on institutionalized religion). The very notion that "recovery" is neces-sary is offensive to some people with disabilities, because "there is no reason to assume that medical conditions are disabilities or that they should necessarily be stigmatizing."[54]

When the disease concept is extended to other problems that are not demonstrably diseases, the dilution of the meaning of dis-ease may lead to a lack of respect for *real* diseases, as well as for societal causes. The recovery model, which suggests that a woman can recover from acute alcoholism by not drinking and by working to mend her relationships, has very limited application to a woman who is not going to recover from having had polio. Indeed, people who have made the most dramatic polio "recoveries" are those most sus-ceptible to post-polio syndrome. A woman with environmental illness cannot recover from living in a world full of chemicals. Her being in a recovery program, acknowledging that she cannot prevent her body's negative reactions to chemicals does not—cannot—mean *accept-ing* the chemicals. It may not mean that she can eliminate them from her environment, either. Feminist groups are beginning to ask that participants in their activities refrain from wearing perfumes, for example, but the effort has not been especially successful. Being in a feminist community does not make us automatically willing to clean up the environment.[55] AA meetings are notorious for excessive tobacco smoke.

Changing what I can, then, may mean arranging for a few smoke-free meetings. It may mean telling a woman face to face that I cannot spend time with her perfume. It may mean supporting the antinuclear movement with money or by wearing a button but not by living in a tent at a peace camp. It may mean writing a letter but not walking the marble halls of the legislature. These are acknowledg-ments of my powerlessness over my limitations but assertions of my ability within those limitations.

Labeling codependence, which is basically feminine role conditioning, a disease becomes victim-blaming when it is combined with the current emphasis in popular psychology on self-help in chronic illness. To say the codependent spouse is "as sick as" or "sicker than" the alcoholic (or the person with Alzheimer's disease or diabetes or ulcerative colitis) can be extremely annoying to the one with the chronic illness—even alcoholism if the person is struggling with recovery. It encourages denial of the seriousness of the physical illness and blurs consciousness of real differences in what can be changed. In contrast, a recovery program based on respect for the illness can be very effective. For example, Robin Norwood reports of her support group for women with clinical depression, "It was a condition we had to respect before we could expect others to take it seriously." When, therefore, they "came to regard it as a disease," they were able to develop "tools for coping more realistically with the outer environment and with our inner thought processes."[56] And Lily Collet suggests that even in Al-Anon, where disease is clearly a metaphor, not a medical diagnosis, it facilitates recovery: "In a culture with an exaggerated sense of human perfectibility and the efficacy of human will, we had a metaphor—'disease'—that allowed us to face our problems and get help from each other without blaming ourselves, or others, for our limitations."[57]

When I began to examine the recovery group process from a disability perspective, I saw the feminist reactions somewhat differently. First, the spiritual awareness that often follows disability experiences links people who have suffered with each other in the face of "indifferent nature"; the connections among people and the planet are experienced from each individual's spiritual center. This as much as feminist spirituality has formed my concept of a power greater than myself and made it possible for me to participate in the spiritual aspect of twelve-step programs. Second, the acceptance of my limitations as a human being was grounded in my understanding of Jennifer's limitations as a woman with disabilities and my powerlessness over those limits. This helped to lessen the denial that feminist organizations had nurtured in me with their models of the competent dyke and the professional superwoman. Third, the efficacy of disability support groups as distinct from political or consciousness-raising groups had made me aware of the need for grass-roots peer groups to address the emotional impact of mixed personal/political powerlessness. The presence in my life of both feminist and disability small groups provided a context in which I could see how twelve-step groups differed from the others in the emphasis on boundaries and amends, in integrating physical and medical with emotional and spiritual components, and in the concept of "recovery" as spiritual healing rather than therapy or political reform.

Finally, twelve-step programs seem to me to do better than either the feminist or the disability groups I know well in encouraging acceptance of diversity, from which I conclude not that the twelve step groups are better, but that those of us in the other movements can learn from them something about what is missing from our present organizations.


## DIVERSITY

In a summary of the impact of AA groups on newcomers, the Big Book says, "The very practical approach to his *[sic]* problems, *the absence of intolerance of any kind,* the informality, the genuine democracy, the uncanny understanding which these people had were irresistible" (italics added).[58] The format of meetings, which stresses the importance of attentive listening without criticism or advice and provides as many individuals as possible with the opportunity to talk, reinforces the goal of tolerance, acceptance of each individual exactly as she or he is at the time. Acknowledging the many experiences of recovery that are likely to be present in any given group, twelve-step programs usually encourage participants to accept and express their own present feelings and beliefs. Starhawk, who advocates twelve-step meetings for many women, describes the importance of such a process in feminist groups: "Honoring ourselves, our feelings, our human imperfections, allows us to start where we are, and let others start where they are."[59] Developing this skill is not easy, especially in political groups, which tend to be driven by their action agendas. Practice in a recovery group is an effective starting point. Sarah Hoagland's discussion of lesbians' criticism of each other's work closely follows the twelve-step concept of detachment and even uses characteristic Al-Anon language:

> Thus, we regard the one who critiques our work as making a statement as much about herself as about our work: her critique becomes as much a reflection of her interests, de-

fenses, focus, ability and limits. It is a statement from where she stands, from her own center and connected to her own needs; and we can use the information we gain from it to further consider what we are doing from where we stand, from our center. We can take what we find useful and, if we're not dependent on her approval, leave the rest.[60]

"I am suggesting," Hoagland says, "we can start with where each one is—rather than trying to force some idea of where we should be." Changes, she adds, "come in each lesbian's own time—as she is able and ready—and not on someone else's schedule."[61]

The problem, as Hoagland acknowledges, is that most lesbian groups—and I would add feminist and disability groups—are resistant to such detachment. To provide the daily repetitive practice that such an attitude requires is outside the scope of most such groups as they are constituted today. It is exactly this practice that twelve-step programs provide. Their acceptance is surely one reason they have been so attractive to many women.

There is considerable rhetorical support in feminist and disability groups of the necessity for grass-roots organizing. I would suggest that twelve-step programs probably *are* our grass roots if "our" means *women* (not already converted, politically correct, feminist disability activists). If we are to start where women are, we will find a great many of them in twelve-step programs.

CHAPTER

# THINKING ABOUT JENNIFER
# AND ME, 1992

When I began the process that was to become this book, I wanted a feminist theory that would answer my questions about Jennifer. What I found was a deeper understanding of my own life as a woman, a limited, thinking, feeling, politically imperfect woman. In the process, I have been able to find connections between other women's writings about disability and about feminism and my own experience of living with Jennifer's disabilities and my limitations. I have gained a better understanding of feminist theory, especially as it addresses women's vulnerability and our difficulties in working together through our differences and our fears. I began by thinking about Jennifer and about other women with disabilities like hers and I now end, for the moment, by thinking about women with limitations like Jennifer's and those with limitations like mine.

As I write this chapter, Jennifer is probably as happy as she has been since her early, relatively nondisabled childhood. She lives with nine other women who have varying degrees of mental retardation and with a series of house managers and trainers in a large modern house in a small Oklahoma town. She attends classes on such subjects as personal hygiene and laundry sorting in a nearby intermediate care facility and for an hour or two each afternoon she works in a sheltered workshop. She can walk unsupervised a couple of blocks to a convenience store to buy a soft drink, a miraculous new freedom for someone who needed twenty-four-hour-a-day supervision during all of the past eleven years.

My concerns about the reinforcement of traditional sex roles proved well grounded. After twelve years of training (and the invention of a submersible electric razor) Jennifer has learned to shave her legs, but not yet to apply nail polish and makeup; those lessons continue. On a daily basis a more important issue is whether she needs supervision while she showers and washes her hair. Still, the nail polishing lessons go on. Because her appearance now is deviant (she looks and acts "retarded"), the gestures toward conventional feminine appearance may smooth her experience in small town life, but won't make her "blend in."

Jennifer's greatest anxieties during the past ten years have been about boyfriends, marriage, and childbearing, concerns appropriate to her chronological age but invariably provoked by pressures from the workers in her various agencies and from her peers. Her own anxieties of choice have been about why no T-shirts or toys are available in honor of the Beverly Hillbillies and the Dukes of Hazzard. Her present houseparent and trainer are more interested in her getting through the day's routine than in her dating, and so her distress about boys and babies has abated.

Because normalization is the official policy of the state agency that administers her welfare benefits, Jennifer is not allowed to have toys, though the toys marketed on TV are her passionate interest, so she has "collections," which are officially considered age appropriate. Her present collections are of GI Joe figures and Ninja Turtles; Jennifer dreams of being a macho hero.

Each year when asked her career goals, she says she wants to be a TV star and resists her trainers' pressures to consider cleaning TV studios instead. Their pressures make her anxious, though, because she wants to please them, or at least not to make them angry. In fact, Jennifer spends a lot of time being upset by what she fears is her inability to meet others' expectations, an anxiety that comes to a crisis when she perceives (rightly) that I don't want her to get married and have children and (perhaps wrongly) that other significant adults (her supervisors and her peers) believe that she should.

I no longer believe that I can persuade all of her teachers and trainers to agree with my view of Jennifer's abilities or to see me as a good mother, nor do I believe I can convince Jennifer that her peers' interpretations of her life are less accurate than those of people without mental disabilities. I no longer expect to persuade women with other disabilities to agree with me or to understand my point of view. I no longer believe that I can be superwoman enough to meet Jennifer's productivity quotas in addition to my own.

What I do know is how to be humanly present with Jennifer as she is, a woman with very serious limitations, intense anxieties, simple pleasures. One by one, and with enormous difficulty, I have given up the roles of interpreter, teacher, trainer, and therapist, until now what I give Jennifer is my physical presence, and access to what she loves best, pizza and "action figures." I still protect her by choosing her placement, attempting to cooperate with her case workers, managing her legal guardianship, and reminding her to wear her glasses. But Jennifer is not the central figure in my life and I am not the focus of hers.

I wanted to know how a girl with such severe limitations could become a woman, a whole person. Jennifer simply grew up. She was always a whole person, one whose disabilities and the behaviors they entail are basic to her personality, are her predominant traits. Now she is a woman with those traits, those behaviors. I believed that my job as her mother was to nurture her independence so that she could be a whole and responsible adult; she became a dependent adult, who needs protection so that she can survive and be responsible for the limited self-care that is within her abilities. She is a survivor, but she is not strong. Both of us know that. What has been harder for both of us to learn is that I too am not strong.

Jennifer's disabilities have handicapped me—socially, of course, because of stigma, but also physically because of stress, and emotionally because of grief. As I have come to terms with these facts, I have learned to live outside the illusion of self-sufficiency and to accept help. I no longer expect reciprocity, nor do I train Jennifer for it. Real acceptance of her particular disabilities includes acceptance of an unequal, uneven relationship. What I have, instead, is the multidirectional reciprocity of a women's community, the reciprocity of sharing the human condition. Like Jennifer, I am one who endures losses, who sometimes refuses to help or be helped, and yet who sometimes helps and sometimes can ask for help.

None of this was true before I began exploring my feminist questions about Jennifer. I did not even know and feel and act as if I were in a bad situation. I did not know that her losses and mine were appropriate occasions for grief, that I could live with such grief and not die of it. I did not yet know that I could not keep her safe. Exploring the meanings of her womanhood, my motherhood, our lives together as women, enabled me to see that, like her, I am capable of suffering, fragile, human.

I had passed as less limited than I am. I believed women in general to be less limited than we are. Sometimes as I have worked on this book I have wanted to sound more optimistic, cheerful, and competent than I am, but I have learned that disguising the pain, denying the sorrow, even "managing" too well denies the human connection. What Jennifer has given me is that connection. Jennifer taught me the limits of her life—and mine.

# NOTES

## CHAPTER 2: NOTES TOWARD A NEW THEORY

1. It is no coincidence that one of the more challenging probes of problems in feminist relationships was written by a woman who has experienced a serious disability or that her essay addresses issues of dependency. Russ, "Power and Helplessness in the Women's Movement."

2. Lorde, *The Cancer Journals*.

3. Evelyn West Ayrault, for example, warns that the mother of a handicapped adolescent must not let the child perceive her own grief or anger. Ayrault, *Helping the Handicapped Teenager Mature*.

4. Weil, "Learning in a Partnership," 63–64.

5. Voysey, *A Constant Burden*, 161.

6. Susan Contratto, personal communication, 1982.

7. Ayrault roundly condemns the mothers of handicapped adolescents for considering their own convenience in performing domestic chores if this involves making decisions about where the child should be while those tasks are being performed. *Helping the Handicapped Teenager Mature*, 102.

8. Cited by Chodorow, *The Reproduction of Mothering*, 87. See also Benjamin, *The Bonds of Love*, 18–24.

9. Daly, *Beyond God the Father*.

10. There are a few institutions where the values of women have had a positive impact on policy. Shelters for victims of domestic violence and some parts of the hospice movement are hopeful examples.

11. Daly, *Gyn/Ecology*, and Griffin, *Woman and Nature*.

12. Rich, *Of Woman Born*, 152, 166.

13. I am indebted to Dorothy Dinnerstein for the idea that lacking a feeling of safety may be a positive condition. *The Mermaid and the Minotaur*, 136.

14. Miller, *Toward a New Psychology of Women*, 31–32.

15. Beatrice Wright, in *Physical Disability—A Psychological Approach*, makes this point more clearly than any of her successors. In many ways Wright's book, published before the contemporary women's movement, is a pioneering model for a feminist approach to disability.

16. Pauline Bart has pointed out that this model is that of an adolescent, working-class, Gentile male, an image that is inappropriate for many—perhaps most—women. Cited in Letty Cottin Pogrebin, "Anti-semitism in the Women's Movement," *Ms.*, 10(12): 66.

17. Joan Nestle uses the term "decorum of illness" to explain why certain subjects are unmentionable between a woman who is ill and her lover. "N.Y. Lesbian Illness Support Group," 8.

18. Wright, *Physical Disability*, 15, 242.

19. Voysey, *A Constant Burden*, 168–91.

20. Daly, *Beyond God the Father*, 23ff.

21. Gilligan, *In a Different Voice*.

22. Cited in Robinault, *Sex, Society and the Disabled*, 189.

23. Miller, *Toward a New Psychology of Women*, 7.

24. Thompson, "Comment on Rich's 'Compulsory Heterosexuality.'"

25. This idea does not mean a "support" group, but rather a group of colleagues who have thought through the same issues. The phrase "a community of like-minded people" comes from Miller, *Toward a New Psychology of Women*, 132.

26. Ibid., 13.

## CHAPTER 3: LANGUAGE AND BIOGRAPHY

1. Mairs, "On Being a Cripple," 118.

2. Women and Disability Awareness Project, *Building Community*.

3. Graham, *In the Company of Others*, 24, 134.

4. Frick, "Keynote Address," 8.

5. Finger, *Past Due*, 37.

6. Zola, "Does It Matter What You Call Us?" 12.

7. Penelope, *Speaking Freely*, 140.

8. Ibid., 145–46.

9. Hearn, "A Woman's Right to Cruise," 49. Notice that Hearn calls herself "a blind lesbian," not "a lesbian with visual impairment."

10. Ibid., 49. Hearn is speaking specifically of "the lesbian movement."

11. Bowe, *Comeback*, 6–7.

12. Fine and Asch, "Introduction," 6–7.

13. Ibid., 7.

14. "Merry," in Campling, *Images of Ourselves*, 33.

15. Bowe, *Comeback*, 165. But the World Health Organization defines disability as the limitations resulting from the impairment.

16. "Merry," in Campling, *Images of Ourselves,* 33.

17. Gliedman and Roth, *The Unexpected Minority,* 9.

18. Connors, "Disability, Sexism and the Social Order," 93.

19. Finger, "Claiming All of Our Bodies," 293.

20. Mitchell, *See Me More Clearly,* 107.

21. Ibid., 107.

22. Dixon, "Interview with Marj Schneider," 22.

23. Davies, "Lame," 43.

24. Ibid., 44.

25. Atatimur, "Women Defy the Boxes," 13.

26. Henley, "A Time to Dance," 13.

27. Duffy, *All Things are Possible.*

28. Ambo, "Speaking Out," 230.

29. Mairs, "On Being a Cripple," 119.

30. Cross, "A Letter to Neil Marcus," 23.

31. Dixon, "Interview," 22, quoting Marj Schneider.

32. Thompson, "Anger," 79–80.

33. Rooney, "The Issue Is Ability," 67.

34. Connors, "Disability, Sexism, and the Social Order," 92–93.

35. Clausen, "Political Morality of Fiction," 18.

36. Dejanikus, "Genetic Screening," 3.

37. Finger, *Past Due,* 186; Deford, *Alex,* 57–58.

38. Golden, "Physical Difference Workshop," 28. Dixon, "Interview" 22. Penelope, *Speaking Freely,* 207.

39. Penelope, *Speaking Freely,* 208. Penelope credits Anne Leighton with leading her to this insight.

40. Hoagland, *Lesbian Ethics,* 17. Penelope, *Speaking Freely,* 208–209.

41. Allen, *Lesbian Philosophy,* 70–71.

42. Meyerdine, "Visual Impairment Politics," 16.

43. Mushroom, "The Weight of Words," 35.

44. Clausen, "Political Morality of Fiction," 18.

45. Penelope, *Speaking Freely,* 207–208.

46. Henley, "A Time to Dance," 13.

47. Snowden, "The Education of a Blind Woman" (interview with JoAnn Giudicessi), 7.

48. Bronston, "Concepts and Theory of Normalization," 506.

49. Lyon, *Playing God in the Nursery,* 118.

50. Jennett, "Disability After Head Injury," 12.

51. Shilts, *And the Band Played On,* 315.

52. Ibid., 542.

53. Ibid., 320.

54. Kenneth Clark, *Dark Ghetto,* quoted in Bernard, "Reviewing the Impact of Women's Studies on Sociology," 209.

55. Gliedman and Roth, *The Unexpected Minority,* 302–303.

56. Demetrakopoulos, *Listening to Our Bodies,* 49.

57. See, for example, Penelope, *Speaking Freely;* Spender, *Man Made Language;* Daly, *Gyn/Ecology.*

58. Christ, "Remapping Development," 54–55.

59. Lyon, *Playing God in the Nursery,* 137.

60. French, *Beyond Power.*

61. Personal communication cited by Luepnitz, *The Family Interpreted,* 178.

62. Cited by Meyers, *Like Normal People*, 121.
63. Chodorow, *Feminism and Psychoanalytic Theory*, 179.
64. Starhawk, *Dreaming the Dark*, 13.
65. Siegel, *Peace, Love and Healing*, 34–35. Siegel is reporting the research of Janice Kiedt Glaser.
66. Rosenblatt, *Bitter, Bitter Tears*, 107.
67. Killilea, *Karen; With Love from Karen*.
68. Stinson and Stinson, *The Long Dying of Baby Andrew*.
69. Rabin, *Six Parts Love*.
70. Malcolm, *This Far and No More*.
71. David Rabin was an M.D.; Emily Bauer a Ph.D. psychologist.
72. Sager, "Just Stories," 191, 198.
73. Gaettens, "The Hard Work of Remembering," 76–77, 80, 85, 88–89.
74. Zola, "Depictions of Disability," 9. Zola cites Harlan Hahn, Adrienne Asch and Lawrence Sacks, Susan Sontag, Joseph Turow and Lisa Coe.
75. Phillips, "Disability and Ethnicity in Conflict," 196.
76. Wilson, with Weir, *Hidden Agendas*.
77. Jelinek, *The Tradition of Women's Autobiography*, xii.
78. Goffman, *Stigma*, 62–63.
79. Jelinek, *The Tradition of Women's Autobiography*, 187–88.
80. Goffman, *Stigma*, 62–63.
81. Phillips, "Disability and Ethnicity in Conflict," 213.
82. Hancock, *The Girl Within*, 198–200.
83. Finger, *Past Due*.
84. McKay, "Black Women's Autobiographies," 8–9.
85. Seligman and Darling, *Ordinary Families, Special Children*, 84.
86. Patton, *Inventing AIDS*, 51.
87. Ibid., 53, 57.
88. Quoted in Arpad, review of *Tapestries of Life*, 311–12.
89. Minnich, "Friendship Between Women," 287–88.
90. Frigga Haug, ed., *Female Sexualization: A Collective Work of Memory* (London: Verso, 1987), cited in hooks, *Talking Back*, 33. This is similar to hooks's view of her own autobiography, 157, and hooks, "Telling the Story," 64–65.
91. Hancock's *The Girl Within* is a good example of such qualitative analysis.
92. My training in the humanities is evident here, another indication of academic bias, in this case, toward texts.
93. Finger, *Past Due*, 171–72.
94. Hoagland, *Lesbian Ethics*, 181.
95. Lyon, *Playing God in the Nursery*, 312.
96. Ferguson, "Is There a Lesbian Culture?" 82.
97. Strong, *Mainstay*, 114.
98. Sarton, *Recovering*, 196.
99. Blackwell-Stratton, et al., "Smashing Icons," 313.
100. Weiss, "Disabled Women," 6.
101. Swallow, "Both Feet in Life," 202. (Reprinted in McEwan and Sullivan, *Out the Other Side*, 47.)
102. Thompson, "Anger," 83.
103. Bowe, *Comeback*, 8.
104. Galloway, "I'm Listening as Hard as I Can," 5.
105. Thompson, "Anger," 81–82.

106. For a clear summary of subjective reasons different people have for committing themselves to disability organizations, see Henderson and Bryan, *Psychological Aspects of Disability,* 262–65.
107. Russell, "Letter from the Editor," 5.
108. Brown, "Power, Responsibilities, Boundaries," 39–40.
109. Fine and Asch, "Disabled Women," 11–12.
110. Dixon, "Interview with Marj Schneider," 22, citing Schneider.
111. Matthews, *Voices from the Shadows,* 128, 130.
112. Mushroom, "The Weight of Words," 35.
113. Lanser, "Who *Are* the 'We'?" 18–20.
114. Penelope, *Speaking Freely,* 213.
115. Hoagland, "Dear Julie," 73.
116. Bronston, "Concepts and Theory of Normalization," 506.
117. Gordon, "In Defense of Big Words," 20.
118. Penelope, *Speaking Freely,* 235.
119. Zimmerman, "The Politics of Transliteration," 682.

## CHAPTER 4: PRODUCTIVITY AND PACE

1. Lewis and Weigert, "Structures and Meanings of Social Time," 432–59.
2. Daly, *Beyond God the Father.*
3. Hall, *The Dance of Life.*
4. Blumberg, *Headstrong,* 60.
5. Smith, *Free Fall,* 72.
6. Mairs, *Plaintext,* 12.
7. Conway, "Living with Limitations," 8.
8. Featherstone, *A Difference in the Family,* 100.
9. Voysey, *A Constant Burden.*
10. Mary Winfrey Trautmann comments on pressures to remain politically active in feminist organizations and on her friends' belief that in accepting a circumscribed life because of her daughter's illness, she is "being a martyr," neglecting herself. *The Absence of the Dead Is Their Way of Appearing,* 88–89.
11. Gliedman and Roth, *The Unexpected Minority.*
12. Hall, *The Dance of Life,* 35. See also Levine, with Ellen Wolff, "Social Time," 35.
13. Bowe, *Comeback,* 77.
14. Rubin, *Caring,* 43.
15. Ibid., 34.
16. Mace and Rabins, *The 36-Hour Day,* 22, 162, 175.
17. Squire, *The Slender Balance,* 216.
18. Ottenberg, *Pursuit of Hope,* 137.
19. Mitchell, *See Me More Clearly,* 37.
20. Mace and Rabins, *The 36-Hour Day,* 27, 49, 74.
21. Killilea, *Karen,* 130–32.
22. Simonton, *The Healing Family,* 195.
23. Quoted in Donnelly, *Recovering from the Loss of a Child,* 141.
24. Cantor, *And a Time to Live,* 94.
25. Hall, *The Dance of Life,* 126.
26. Melton, *When Children Need Help,* 32.
27. Lund, *Eric,* 86. Patricia J. Mills, using patient Penelope's weaving and unweaving as her example, suggests that "the rhythm and tedium of women's domesticated

life" represents a "trauma of eventlessness," a woman's pain in contrast to men's pain of alienation. Mills, "Memory and Myth." See also Donovan, *Feminist Theory*, 126, on waiting as women's time in contrast to men's mode of questing.

28. Mace and Rabins, *The 36-Hour Day*, 216.

29. Lewis, *A Grief Observed*, 38–39.

30. Sourkes, *The Deepening Shade*, 56.

31. Hall, *The Dance of Life*, 40.

32. Forman and Sowton describe such pauses in women's narratives: "when silence is allowed its place . . . moments of great peace and serenity, when the writer creates fluently and abundantly in a manner that enables her to become aware of her inner world." *Taking Our Time*, xiv.

33. Dorros, *Parkinson's*, 6, 21.

34. Ibid., 108–109. See also Pitzele, *One More Day*, Jan. 11 entry: "The true measure of knowing ourselves, regardless of how capable we seem to be, is to stop the activity before we get too exhausted, before we have too much pain, before we cause an accident."

35. Ottenberg, *Pursuit of Hope*, 103.

36. Kleiman and Dody, *No Time to Lose*. Carol Schmidt describes "working [her] schedule around the timing for [heavy doses of] tetracycline, which I could only take when I had not eaten or had any milk for many hours, nor planned any food intake." "Do Something About Your Weight," 250.

37. Hall, *The Dance of Life*, 91.

38. Glaser, *Theoretical Sensitivity*, 19.

39. Carillo, Corbett, and Lewis, *No More Stares*, 103.

40. Daly, *Beyond God the Father*, 43.

41. Chernin, *The Obsession;* Millman, *Such a Pretty Face;* Rich, *Of Woman Born*.

42. Lerner, *A Death of One's Own*, 189–90.

43. Sarton, *A World of Light*, 245.

44. Sarton, *Recovering*, 120.

45. Sarton, *The House by the Sea*, 264. Sarton also describes how her disabilities from a stroke disrupt the ability to do daily tasks and how resumption of the simplest of these gradually gives structure to her days. *After the Stroke.*

46. Dorros, *Parkinson's*, 131–32. Karen Thompson, in the role of caregiver, expressed frustration at being unable to work on rehabilitation with her disabled lover, Sharon, at the times of day when Sharon was at her best. Thompson and Andrezejewski, *Why Can't Sharon Kowalski Come Home?* 119.

47. Dorros, *Parkinson's*, 182.

48. Rubin, *Caring*, 129–30.

49. Hall, *The Dance of Life*, 49. Nel Noddings suggests "that women have been especially fortunate in their opportunities to celebrate the repetition of ordinary life and thus achieve a balance of being and doing." *Caring*, 130.

50. The "timelessness" of housework and child rearing is culture bound, however, since the household is organized around the "working day"; the woman socializes her children for entry into the work force. Haunani-Kay Trask, *Eros and Power*, 90.

51. Rossi, *From This Day Forward*, 247–48.

52. Mace and Rabins, *The 36-Hour Day*, 23.

53. Leach, *Letter to a Younger Son*, 79–80.

54. Hall, *The Dance of Life*, 37–38.

55. Stephanie Demetrakopoulos reports that men's and women's images of time differ in that men see the weaver and women see the cloth. *Listening to Our Bodies*, 61–62.

56. Featherstone, *A Difference in the Family,* 122.
57. Jacobs, *The Search for Help,* 100.
58. Ottenberg, *Pursuit of Hope,* 136.
59. Massie and Massie, *Journey,* 148.
60. Cook, "Chronic Illness," 21.
61. T. Bell, quoted in Sourkes, *The Deepening Shade,* 16.
62. Sourkes, *The Deepending Shade,* 55.
63. Meryman, *Hope,* 19.
64. Graham, *In the Company of Others,* 24.
65. Wilson, *This Stranger, My Son,* 15.
66. Junker, *The Child in the Glass Ball,* 142.
67. Rubin, *Caring,* 80.
68. Butler, *Why Survive?* 409.
69. Simonton, *The Healing Family,* 31.
70. Weisman, *Intensive Care,* 64–65.
71. Rosenfeld, *The Time of Their Dying,* 149.
72. Sarton, *Recovering,* 27.
73. Simonton, *The Healing Family,* 31.
74. Lund, *Eric,* 343.
75. Meryman, *Hope,* 80–81.
76. Massarani and Massarani, *Our Life with Caleb,* 60–61, 108, 111–12.
77. Quoted in Donnelly, *Recovering from the Loss of a Child,* 128.
78. Quoted in Spingarn, *Hanging in There,* 12.
79. Ottenberg, *Pursuit of Hope,* 94.
80. Ibid., 92–93.
81. Spingarn, *Hanging in There,* 15.
82. Cited in Taylor, "Adjustment to Threatening Events," 1163.
83. Smith, *Free Fall,* 81. My italics.
84. Simonton, *The Healing Family,* 190.
85. Ibid., 189.
86. Ibid., 110.
87. Smith, *Free Fall,* 87.
88. Cited by Hall, *The Dance of Life,* 78.
89. Lewis and Weigert, "Structures and Meanings of Social Time," 444–45.
90. Hall, *The Dance of Life,* 5.
91. Bowe, *Comeback,* 77.
92. Ottenberg, *Pursuit of Hope,* 94, 139.
93. Dorros, *Parkinson's,* 6, 21. See Levine and Wolff on the Type-A chronic sense of urgency in relation to other illnesses and dysfunctions. "Social Time," 35.
94. Cf. "Declaration of Principles," 1.
95. Fine and Asch, "Disabled Women," 12.
96. Gliedman and Roth, *The Unexpected Minority,* 28.
97. Marc Gold, cited by Meyers, *Like Normal People,* 148.
98. Jones, "Lights of My Life," 65.
99. Hall, *The Dance of Life,* 78–79.
100. Melton, *When Children Need Help,* 207.
101. "Three Cheers for Work Center" (editorial), *Daily Oklahoman,* July 15, 1983.
102. E.g., among many others, Buck, *The Child Who Never Grew;* Buck and Zarfoss, *The Gifts They Bring.*
103. E.g., among others, Rich, *Of Woman Born;* Daly, *Gyn/Ecology;* Griffin, *Woman and Nature.*

104. Lerner, *A Death of One's Own*, 269.
105. Massie and Massie, *Journey*, 111.
106. Rich, *Of Woman Born*, 21.

## CHAPTER 5: GRIEF

1. Olshansky, "Chronic Sorrow," 49–54; Wikler, Wasow, and Hatfield, "Chronic Sorrow Revisited," 63–70. Chronic sorrow is also characteristic of grief over other losses, including death, at least in some cultures. See, for example, Rosenblatt, *Bitter, Bitter Tears*.
2. Solnit and Stark, "Mourning and the Birth of a Defective Child," 523–37.
3. Mitchell, *See Me More Clearly*, 22.
4. Featherstone, *A Difference in the Family*, 234.
5. D'Arcy (1968) cited in Irvin, Kennell, and Klaus, "Caring for Parents of an Infant with a Congenital Malformation," 175.
6. Featherstone, *A Difference in the Family*, 233.
7. Roskies, *Abnormality and Normality*, 20.
8. Stewart, *Counseling Parents of Exceptional Children*, 103.
9. Roskies, *Abnormality and Normality*, 93–94. Buscaglia, *The Disabled and Their Parents*, 92.
10. Wright, "The Period of Mourning in Chronic Illness," 58.
11. For application of a wholistic model to disability, see Martha Wingerd Bristor, "The Birth of a Handicapped Child," 25–32.
12. Wikler, Wasow, and Hatfield, "Chronic Sorrow Revisited," 64. See also Burgraff, "Consulting with Parents of Handicapped Children," 214–21. Hollingsworth and Pasnau, *The Family in Mourning*, 97–98.
13. Wikler, Wasow, and Hatfield, "Chronic Sorrow Revisited," 68.
14. Disability rights activists may have some difficulty with the idea of chronic sorrow because of the implication that disability is a continuous, tragic loss deserving of continuous grief, a notion that contradicts the ideology of "physical difference." The fact that "recurrent sorrow" accurately names parents' own description of their experience is only a partial answer to this objection because mistrust of parents' views of disability also characterizes some members of the independent living movement. I believe that some of these difficulties can be resolved by careful attention to individual differences among disabilities and among parents. See Buscaglia, *The Disabled and Their Parents*, 118–19, and Irvin, Kennel, and Klaus, "Caring for Parents of an Infant with a Congenital Malformation," 174, for losses to family caused by chronic grief of parents.
15. Bowlby, *Making and Breaking of Affectional Bonds*, 49.
16. Ibid., 98.
17. Silverman, *Helping Women Cope with Grief*, 32–33.
18. Weisman, "Is Mourning Necessary?" 14.
19. Roskies, *Abnormality and Normality*, 55, 65–66.
20. Grief after a death often recurs on anniversaries and when significant objects are encountered. Hendin, *Death as a Fact of Life*, 183. Rosenblatt, *Bitter, Bitter Tears*, 30–40, 154–60.
21. Wikler, Wasow, and Hatfield, "Chronic Sorrow Revisited," 63–70.
22. Rosenblatt, *Bitter, Bitter Tears*, 27–28.
23. Dickens, *Miracles of Courage*, 132.
24. Fortier and Wanlass, "Family Crisis Following the Diagnosis," 20.
25. Wikler, Wasow, and Hatfield, "Chronic Sorrow Revisited," 69–70.
26. Rosenblatt, *Bitter, Bitter Tears*, 153–54.

27. Buck, *The Child Who Never Grew*, 35–36.

28. Sarton, *Recovering*, 214.

29. Frick, "Keynote Address," 6.

30. Mairs, "On Being a Cripple," 126.

31. Mairs, *Plaintext*, 17.

32. Mace and Rabins, *The 36-Hour Day*, 164.

33. Seidenberg and DeCrow, *Women Who Marry Houses*, 70.

34. Zaiger, "Women and Bereavement," 36. Miller, *Toward a New Psychology of Women*, 83.

35. Goffman, *Stigma*, 120. Wright, *Physical Disability*, 15, 17, 242.

36. Simonton, *The Healing Family*, 225. Voysey, *A Constant Burden*, 144. Caroff and Dobrof, "Social Work," 257–58.

37. Simonton, *The Healing Family*, 100–101.

38. DeFrain, Taylor, and Ernst, *Coping with Sudden Infant Death*, 24–25. Donnelly, *Recovering from the Loss of a Child*, 93. Stearns, *Living Through Personal Crisis*, 159.

39. Reed, "Anticipatory Grief Work," 346–47. Dobihal and Stewart, *When a Friend Is Dying*, 180–81. Caroff and Dobrof, "Social Work," 260–61.

40. Silverman, *Helping Women Cope with Grief*, 31.

41. Falvo, Allen, and Maki, "Psychological Aspects of Invisible Disability," 6. Roskies, *Abnormality and Normality*, 181.

42. Kennedy, "Maternal Reactions to the Birth," 410–16.

43. Voysey, *A Constant Burden*, 177.

44. Bowlby, *Making and Breaking of Affectional Bonds*, 101–102. Dobihal and Stewart, *When a Friend Is Dying*, 180–81. Simonton, *The Healing Family*, 224–25. Schild, "Social Work Services," 281. Fortier and Wanlass, "Family Crisis Following the Diagnosis," 20. Hendin, *Death as a Fact of Life*, 110, 169. Wright, "The Period of Mourning," 59.

45. Notably Mormons and Christian Scientists. Hollingsworth and Pasnau, *The Family in Mourning*, 123.

46. Wolfe, "Surviving Your Children," 5c.

47. Stearns, *Living Through Personal Crisis*, 88. Burst, "Split Decision," 14.

48. Irvin, Kennel, and Klaus, "Caring for Parents of an Infant with a Congenital Malformation," 176. Olshansky, "Chronic Sorrow," 50.

49. Donnelly, *Recovering from the Loss of a Child*, 63.

50. Yalom, *Love's Executioner*, 142.

51. Nighswonder, "Vectors and Vital Signs in Grief Synchronization," 273. As the term implies, "morbid grief reaction" is a grief considered by external observers to be excessive to the point of morbidity.

52. Butler, *Why Survive?* 383.

53. Hollingsworth and Pasnau, *The Family in Mourning*, 148. Cantor, *And a Time to Live*, 57.

54. Colman, *Hanging On*, 78–79. Taves, *The Widow's Guide*, 5. Stinson and Stinson, *The Long Dying of Baby Andrew*, 156.

55. Geoffrey Gorer, quoted in Parkes, *Bereavement*, 9, and in Butler, *Why Survive?* 383. See also Zaiger, "Women and Bereavement," 35.

56. Black American culture and Jewish American culture provide much more support for mourning over death, but black culture particularly encourages heroic coping with other losses. Scott, *The Habit of Surviving*.

57. Kushner, *When Bad Things Happen to Good People*, 139.

58. Campbell, *The Hero with a Thousand Faces*.

59. Whitfield, *Healing the Child Within*, 96–97.
60. Ibid., 97–99.
61. Roskies, *Abnormality and Normality*, 49.
62. Stearns, *Living Through Personal Crisis*, 6. Cantor, *And a Time to Live*, 54.
63. The concept "legitimation of suffering" is developed fully by Voysey, *A Constant Burden*.
64. Simonton, *The Healing Family*, 224–25.
65. Noddings, *Caring*, 37–38.
66. Kiley, *The Wendy Dilemma*, 141–42.
67. Miller, *Toward a New Psychology of Women*, 31–32.
68. Silverman, *Helping Women Cope with Grief*, 67–68.
69. Leach, *Letter to a Younger Son*, 21–22.
70. David M. Kaplan, quoted by Bordow, *The Ultimate Loss*, 54.
71. Wagner, "A Four-Wheeled Journey," 58.
72. Buscaglia, *The Disabled and Their Parents*, 268.
73. Sherry Zitter makes this same point about a mother's mourning over her daughter's coming out as a lesbian. "Coming Out to Mom," 184.
74. Silverman, *Helping Women Cope with Grief*, 27–28.
75. Kolbenschlag, *Kiss Sleeping Beauty Good-bye*, 127–28.
76. Verda Heisler, quoted in Buscaglia, *The Disabled and their Families*, 179.
77. Johnson, *Hidden Victims*, 14.
78. Rollin, *First, You Cry*, 143.
79. This is by no means the same as coming out as disabled or as concerned about a particular disability.
80. Buck, *The Child Who Never Grew*, 30.
81. Buscaglia, *The Disabled and Their Families*, 88.
82. Massie and Massie, *Journey*, 166.
83. Buck, *The Child Who Never Grew*, 23.
84. Stearns, *Living Through Personal Crisis*, 127. Featherstone, *A Difference in the Family*, 238. DeFrain, Taylor, and Ernst, *Coping with Sudden Infant Death*, 91.
85. Featherstone, *A Difference in the Family*, 238.
86. Stearns, *Living Through Personal Crisis*, 11–14.
87. Mairs, "On Being a Cripple," 127.
88. Schiff, "Learning the Lessons of Survival," 10. Massie and Massie, *Journey*, 167. Featherstone, *A Difference in the Family*, 238.
89. Quoted by Buscaglia, *The Disabled and Their Families*, 186. Schweitzer says *man* is fully human when *he* sees the other's suffering as *his* own.
90. Stearns, *Living Through Personal Crisis*, 49.
91. Featherstone, *A Difference in the Family*, 229.
92. Mairs, *Plaintext*, 23.
93. Yalom, *Love's Executioner*, 129.

## CHAPTER 6: MOTHER-BLAMING

1. Other factors include communication problems with physicians and problems in accepting the diagnosis.
2. Osmond, Franks, and Burtle, "Changing Views of Women and Therapeutic Approaches," 18.
3. Park and Shapiro, *You Are Not Alone*, 122–23.
4. Walsh, *Schizophrenia*, 159–60.
5. DeMyer, *Parents and Children in Autism*, 121. Notice how autism becomes the mother's label as well as the child's.

6. Sturdivant, *Therapy with Women,* 58.

7. Rimland, letter to the editor, *Newsweek,* Oct. 8, 1990, 14.

8. DeMyer, *Parents and Children in Autism,* 158.

9. Harris, "The Family and the Autistic Child," 129.

10. Mannoni, *The Retarded Child and the Mother.*

11. Kirman, *The Mentally Handicapped Child,* 76.

12. Tavris, "How Psychology Shortchanges Mothers," 74–75.

13. Caplan, *Don't Blame Mother,* 47. Judith Arcana adds to the list asthma, ulcerative colitis, coeliac disease, and ulcers. *Every Mother's Son,* 76.

14. Caplan, "Take the Blame Off Mother," 70.

15. Footnoting such references would require many pages of citations. I have drawn this list from two dozen heavily overlapping articles. One good summary of literature on attitudes of parents toward retarded children is Appel, et al., "Changes in Attitudes of Parents of Retarded Children Effected Through Group Counseling."

16. Walsh, *Schizophrenia,* 165–67; Weisskopf, "Maternal Guilt and Mental Health Professionals," 5.

17. Abraham Fineman cited in Lyon, *Playing God in the Nursery,* 305.

18. Henderson and Bryan, *Psychosocial Aspects of Disability,* 174–75.

19. Hubbard, "Caring for Baby Doe," 86.

20. For a detailed description of these cases, see Lyon, *Playing God in the Nursery,* 47–49, 142–76, and John Parker, "Infant 'Death Row' Image at HSC Denied," 2.

21. Hubbard develops this point, "Caring for Baby Doe," 8. My own view is that parents of children with Down's syndrome and spina bifida (or the specific disability in question) as well as individuals with those disabilities should be consulted in the parent's decision-making process.

22. Rich, *Of Woman Born,* 1976.

23. Friday, *My Mother, My Self.*

24. Chodorow, *The Reproduction of Mothering;* Dinnerstein, *The Mermaid and the Minotaur.*

25. Copper, *Over the Hill,* 53. See also MacDonald, with Rich, *Look Me in the Eye;* Allen, "Indian Summer," 184.

26. Nelson, "Flowersong," 123.

27. Ibid., 126–27.

28. MacDonald, with Rich, *Look Me in the Eye.*

29. Wilson, *This Stranger, My Son,* 205; Kleiman and Dody, *No Time to Lose,* 94.

30. Cepko, "On Oxfords and Plaster Casts," 58.

31. Chernin, *Reinventing Eve,* 127, 130, 133. See also Benjamin, *The Bonds of Love,* 23–24.

32. Lerner, *Women in Therapy,* 230.

33. Ibid., 248.

34. Chodorow, *Feminism and Psychoanalytic Theory,* 82–90.

35. Featherstone, *A Difference in the Family,* 80.

36. Erikson, *Identity, Youth and Crisis,* 28.

37. Weisskopf, "Maternal Guilt and Mental Health Professionals," 8.

38. Hancock, *The Girl Within,* 153.

39. Lugones, "Playfulness, 'World'-Travelling, and Loving Perception," 162.

40. Arcana, *Every Mother's Son,* x.

41. Konanc and Warren, "Graduation," 138.

42. Sylvia Schild, "Social Work Services," 460–61.

43. Samuelson, "A Letter to My Daughter/Myself," 163.

44. Cepko, "On Oxfords and Plaster Casts," 58.
45. Featherstone's *A Difference in the Family* is a fine book on disability by a mother/professional.
46. Walsh, *Schizophrenia*, 165.
47. Demeter, *Legal Kidnapping*, 69.
48. Deford, *Alex*, 41.
49. Lund, *Eric*, 192.
50. Lorenz, *Our Son, Ken*, 105.
51. Lyon, *Playing God in the Nursery*, 68, 239–40.
52. Mantle, "A Truly Formidable Challenge," 15.
53. Remington, "Particles of Silence," 4.
54. Featherstone, *A Difference in the Family*, 97.
55. Schopler and Reichler, cited in DeMyer, *Parents and Children in Autism*, 256.
56. Roskies, *Abnormality and Normality*, 288.
57. Ibid., 117.
58. Ibid., 132–33.
59. Arcana, "Blaming the Mother," 23.
60. Ibid.
61. Rich, *On Lies, Secrets and Silence*, 264.
62. Hancock, *The Girl Within*, 151.
63. Witkin-Lanoil, *The Female Stress Syndrome*, 91.
64. French, *Beyond Power*, 375.
65. Samuelson, "A Letter to My Daughter/Myself," 155–56.
66. Browning, "Justice Department Intervenes," 7.
67. Anna Luepnitz, *The Family Interpreted*, 145–46.
68. Ibid., 145; Seidenberg and DeCrow, *Women Who Marry Houses*, 91–96.
69. Hancock, *The Girl Within*, 152. See also Miller, *Toward a New Psychology of Women*.
70. Wooley, "Consuming Emotion," 3.
71. Sanford and Donovan, *Women and Self-Esteem*, 75.
72. Henderson and Bryan, *Psychosocial Aspects of Disability*, 175–76.
73. Caplan, *Don't Blame Mother*, 48.
74. Arcana, "Blaming the Mother," 22.
75. Bulkin, in Gardiner et al., "An Interchange on Feminist Criticism," 644–45.
76. Chinn, Drew, and Logan, *Mental Retardation*, 470–71.
77. Clausen, "On the Political Morality," 18.
78. Frye, "The Meaning of Difference," 7.
79. Audre Lorde's explication of the importance of difference in *Sister Outsider* is a basic resource for most subsequent feminist discussions of difference.
80. Rich, *Of Woman Born*, 16.

## CHAPTER 7: DENIAL AND NORMALIZATION

1. Hereafter I use *normalization* without the quotation marks that denote the problematic nature of this concept, but my intention is to explore that problem, not to adopt the word uncritically.
2. Lessing, "Denial and Disability," 21.
3. Dobihal and Stewart, *When a Friend Is Dying*, 26–27.
4. Simonton, *The Healing Family*, 87–89.
5. "Anxiety Part of Cope," *Oklahoma Daily*, Aug. 29, 1984, 18. This is an Associated Press report on a paper given at a meeting of the American Psychological Asso-

ciation (Toronto, Aug. 18, 1984) by Madelon Visintainer of Yale University Medical School.

6. Levy, "How the Rhino Got Its Flaky Skin," 32.

7. Rabin, *Six Parts Love*, 95–96.

8. Deford, *Alex*, 149–50.

9. Siegel, *Peace, Love and Healing*, 33.

10. Versluys, "Physical Rehabilitation and Family Dynamics," 58–65.

11. Wright, *Physical Disability*, 211. McGriff, *Learning to Live with Neuromuscular Disease*, 46.

12. Ottenberg, *Pursuit of Hope*, 46.

13. Chinn, Drew, and Logan, *Mental Retardation*, 356. Chinn, Drew and Logan also acknowledge that denial may be the only defense available to parents under extreme emotional stress, 357.

14. Fortier and Wanlass, "Family Crisis Following the Diagnosis," 19.

15. Branden, *Honoring the Self*, 6.

16. Lerner, *A Death of One's Own*, 57–58.

17. Ambo, "Speaking Out," 224.

18. Ungerecht, "Age and Image," 262.

19. Roskies, *Abnormality and Normality*, 181.

20. Strong, *Mainstay*, 81.

21. Rabin, *Six Parts Love*, 154. David's own view was that these people were refusing to accept him as he was, namely, unwilling to talk about it.

22. Sourkes, *The Deepening Shade*, 36–37.

23. Mason, "Dear Harvey," 21.

24. House, "A Radical Feminist Model," 34.

25. Among the many illustrations of the last point is Dashu, "Seizures," 204.

26. "Merry," quoted in Campling, *Images of Ourselves*, 29–30.

27. Ruddick, "Maternal Thinking," 218.

28. Seligman and Darling, *Ordinary Families, Special Children*, 126.

29. The most famous of these are the work of O. Carl Simonton and Stephanie Matthews Simonton. S. M. Simonton, *The Healing Family*; O. C. Simonton, S. M. Simonton, and J. L. Creighton, *Getting Well Again*.

30. It is believed that the therapies imply an unrealistic degree of control over the cancer and suggest that life-style and personality traits cause it.

31. Taylor, "Adjustment to Threatening Events," 1170–71.

32. Meyerowitz, "The Impact of Mastectomy," 123–124.

33. Cantor, *And a Time to Live*, 88.

34. Sourkes, *The Deepening Shade*, 15.

35. Ibid., 49.

36. Irvin, Kennell, and Klaus, "Caring for Parents of an Infant with a Congenital Malformation," 179.

37. Barsch, *The Parent of the Handicapped Child*, 96–97. See also Olshansky, "Chronic Sorrow," 50–51.

38. Featherstone, *A Difference in the Family*, 14.

39. Parkes, *Bereavement*, 72. See also Hendin, *Death as a Fact of Life*, 175, and Stearns, *Living Through Personal Crisis*, 62–63.

40. Buscaglia, *The Disabled and Their Parents*, 93.

41. Thompson and Andrzejewski, *Why Can't Sharon Kowalski Come Home?*, 42.

42. Patterson, "Chronic Illness in Children," 69–107.

43. Roskies, *Abnormality and Normality*, 244, 284–86. Voysey, *A Constant Burden*, 131.

44. Ernst and Goodison, *In Our Own Hands,* 157. See chapter 8 for a discussion of movement beyond passing.

45. Dorros, *Parkinson's,* 15–16.

46. Meyers, *Like Normal People,* 22–23. Frank Bowe, *Rehabilitating America,* 99–100, makes essentially the same point about Roger Meyers.

47. Taylor, "Adjustment to Threatening Events," 1168.

48. Kubie, "Chronic Illness and Hidden Neurotic Difficulties," 43: "Physical handicaps have multiple idiosyncratic meanings to each individual on conscious, preconscious and unconscious levels."

49. Frick, "Keynote Address," 8. See also Wright, *Physical Disability,* 108.

50. Mairs, "On Being a Cripple," 120.

51. Mairs, "I'm Afraid. I'm Afraid. I'm Afraid," 86–87.

52. Seligman and Darling, *Ordinary Families, Special Children,* 141, citing P. F. Vadasy, R. R. Fewell, D. J. Meyer, and M. T. Greenberg, "Supporting Fathers of Handicapped Young Children: Preliminary Findings of Program Effects, Analysis and Intervention," *Developmental Disabilities* 5:125–37.

53. Cox-Gedmark, *Coping with Physical Disability,* 17.

54. Pearson, *The Hero Within,* 158–59.

55. Goffman, *Stigma,* 115–16.

56. Ibid., 119–30.

57. Buscaglia, *The Disabled and Their Parents,* 18.

58. Ibid., 121.

59. Wright, *Physical Disability,* 338.

60. Frick, "Keynote Address," 6. Frick is describing resistance to this change.

61. Schiff, "Learning the Lessons of Survival," 10. Smith, *Free Fall,* 94.

62. Taylor, "Adjustment to Threatening Events," 1165.

63. Gliedman and Roth, *The Unexpected Minority,* 111.

64. Chinn, Drew, and Logan, *Mental Retardation,* 366.

65. Delcampo, Chase and Delcampo, "Growth Disorders in Children," 83.

66. Barsch, *The Parent of the Handicapped Child,* 338–39.

67. Voysey, *A Constant Burden,* 197–211.

68. Fortier and Wanlass, "Family Crisis Following the Diagnosis," 21.

69. Featherstone, *A Difference in the Family,* 245–46.

70. Brown, *Yesterday's Child,* 208.

71. Ibid., 50–51.

72. Nighswonder, "Vectors and Vital Signs in Grief Synchronization," 274.

73. I credit a statement by Eleanor Roosevelt for bringing me consciously to this insight. Quoted in Robinault, *Sex, Society and the Disabled,* 189.

74. Featherstone, *A Difference in the Family,* 215, 220, 229.

75. Although such mental illnesses as schizophrenia and paranoia are also "mental disabilities," I will not address them here as their dynamics differ from those of mental retardation and dementia. I would emphasize, however, that our experience with deinstitutionalization of mental patients demonstrates societal denial at a dysfunctional extreme.

76. Brown, *Between Health and Illness,* 167–68.

77. Mace and Rabins, *The 36-Hour Day,* 33.

78. Ibid., 34–35.

79. Ibid., 38, 116–17.

80. Ibid., 208.

81. Jennett, "Disability After Head Injury," 11–12.

82. Ibid., 1. Oliver Sacks emphasizes the loss of judgment and identity that

accompanies many neuropsychological disorders but is rarely addressed by neuro-psychologists. Sacks, *The Man Who Mistook His Wife for a Hat,* 18.

83. Menolascino, "Psychiatric Aspects of Retardation in Young Children," 417. Affect hunger is an effect of being deprived of close emotional relationships (in some institutions) and therefore being "hungry" for them.

84. Edgerton, *The Cloak of Competence,* 162–72, 197–99, 205–209.

85. Branden, *Honoring the Self,* 91. See also Robbins, "Stroke," 22: "More than my arms or my legs, my mind was 'me.' "

86. "University Moves to Aid Disabled Student," *OSU* [Oklahoma State University] *Today,* Feb. 1985, 8.

87. House, "A Radical Feminist Model," 34.

88. And of schizophrenia as well. See Walsh, *Schizophrenia,* 32, 39–41, 49–50.

89. Fischer, *Linked Lives,* 161, makes a similar point about the confusion experienced by old people as a result of their health problems. In that case the parents do not acknowledge their confusion and their children are the ones whose task is acceptance.

90. Sarton, *The House by the Sea,* 223. See also 235, 239, 282–83. Powell, "Alzheimer's Disease," 54. Like Sarton, Powell emphasizes the extent to which both patient and caregiver "feel alone, abandoned and afraid."

91. Juul, "European Approaches and Innovations," 326.

92. Meyers, *Like Normal People,* 108.

93. Ibid., 326.

94. Chinn, Drew, and Logan, *Mental Retardation,* 315–16, 320–21.

95. Roskies, *Abnormality and Normality,* 21.

96. Ibid., 240.

97. Bronston, "Concepts and Theory of Normalization," 495–96.

98. Ibid., 513.

99. Seligman and Darling, *Ordinary Families, Special Children,* 65.

100. Luterman, *Counseling Parents of Hearing-Impaired Children,* 176.

101. Ibid., 177.

102. Stewart, *Counseling Parents of Exceptional Children,* 7–8.

103. Bowe, *Comeback,* 49.

104. Alice Crespo, quoted in Rousso, *Disabled, Female, and Proud!* 100.

105. Luterman, *Counseling Parents of Hearing-Impaired Children,* 175.

106. Chinn, Drew, and Logan, *Mental Retardation,* 227.

107. Share, "Educational Services," 255–56.

108. Sacks, *The Man Who Mistook His Wife for a Hat,* 199.

109. Ibid., 200.

110. Collier and Horowitz, *The Kennedys,* 115.

111. Ibid., 116.

112. Beaucher, "My Last Legs," 115.

113. Women and Disability Awareness Project, *Building Community.*

114. Weinberg, "Autonomy as a Different Voice," 276–77.

115. Raymond, "We're a Family Now," 152. Raymond is quoting Kathy Schwaninger.

116. Dorris, *The Broken Cord,* 166–67 and *passim.*

117. Menolascino, "Psychiatric Aspects of Retardation," 406.

118. VanGelder, "Elaine Brody," 100.

119. Kirman, *The Mentally Handicapped Child,* 94.

120. Bader, "Respite Care," 42–43.

121. Dickman, with Gordon, *One Miracle at a Time,* 127.

122. Strauss, *Chronic Illness,* 5–6.

123. DeMyer, *Parents and Children in Autism*, 194, 203–204.
124. Kirman, *The Mentally Handicapped Child*, 77.
125. DeMyer, *Parents and Children in Autism* 195.
126. Walsh, *Schizophrenia*, 140.
127. Finch and Groves, "By Women for Women," 427–38.
128. Wilke, "The Wholeness of the Family of God," 58.
129. Briar and Ryan, "The Anti-Institution Movement," 21–23.
130. Ibid., 27.

## CHAPTER 8: PASSING

1. Henderson and Bryan, *Psychosocial Aspects of Disability*, 96–97. Bickelhaupt, "The Health History," 34. Boswell, *Christianity, Social Tolerance, and Homosexuality*, 16.
2. Wright, *Physical Disability*, 19.
3. Buscaglia, *The Disabled and Their Parents*, 101. Wright, *Physical Disability*, 18–19.
4. See, for example, Sherry Zitter, "Coming Out to Mom," 185. Zitter includes discussion of the double coming out of "differently abled" lesbians, 187. Cutter, "Dear Mom and Dad," 216. See Klaich, *Woman Plus Woman*, 197, for the political impact of this reasoning.
5. Henderson and Bryan, *Psychosocial Aspects of Disability*, 96–97. Gliedman and Roth, *The Unexpected Minority*, 24.
6. Goffman, *Stigma*, 97.
7. See Copper, "The View from Over the Hill," 59, for a discussion of ascribed asexuality in old women. See also a revised version of the same essay in Allen, *Lesbian Philosophies and Cultures*, 232–34.
8. Such fears generate a "benign paranoia," a heightened sensitivity to signs of homophobia. Kus, "Coming Out: Its Nature, Stages, and Health Concerns," 36.
9. Klaich, *Woman Plus Woman*, 5.
10. Klepfisz, "Resisting and Surviving in America," 101.
11. Cliff, *The Land of Look Behind*, 23.
12. Stonekey, "Reminders" 46–49. See also Piasecki, "The Day After Tomorrow Show," 200. Piasecki describes coming out as an alcoholic as being parallel to coming out as a lesbian "so far as the similarity in the fear, misunderstanding, and ignorance surrounding the two words." Smith, "Alcoholism," 131, makes the same point.
13. Dublin Lesbian and Gay Men's Collectives, *Out for Ourselves*, 177.
14. Klaich, *Woman Plus Woman*, 229. On military passing, see Humphrey, *My Country, My Right to Serve*.
15. Sontag, *AIDS and Its Metaphors*, 32–33.
16. Lorde, *The Cancer Journals*, 66.
17. A woman who is unable (or unwilling) to conceal her difference may still engage in passing. Passing, in this case, refers to the woman's efforts to conform to the body code in order to deemphasize her difference and assert membership in the majority culture. For a discussion of how the white body code affects black people, even when they do not pass, see Pettigrew, *A Profile of the Negro American*, 53.
18. Reinharz, "Friends or Foes," 512. See also Freedman, *Beauty Bound*, and Chapkis, *Beauty Secrets*.
19. Henderson and Bryan, *Psychosocial Aspects of Disability*, 155.
20. Ibid., 149.
21. Goffman, *Stigma*, 74.

22. Crawford, "Family Building Process," 202, 197–98.

23. Strong, *Mainstay*, 53. Strong describes family members' self-protective lies about the seriousness of a partner's chronic illness to avoid the spread of the partner's vulnerability to the well spouse.

24. Walsh, *Schizophrenia*, 25–26. Ardis Burst believed that her competence as a worker would be questioned if she were known to be the parent of a handicapped child. Burst, "Split Decision," 12, 14.

25. "Beth" and "Catherine," personal communications, 1989. Significantly, neither of these two informants chooses to be identified.

26. The coming out process for mothers of lesbians is a central theme of the personal stories in Rafkin, *Different Daughters*. For parental passing where the child has disabilities, see Seligman and Darling, *Ordinary Families, Special Children*, 90.

27. Ironically, one benefit to the family member may be reinforcement of her denial. Samuelson, "A Letter to My Daughter/Myself," 160–61.

28. Goffman, *Stigma*, 49–50. See also Gliedman and Roth, *The Unexpected Minority*, 28.

29. And lesbian/gay researchers. Plummer, *Making of the Modern Homosexual*, 228.

30. Denneny, "Chasing the Crossover Audience," 16–21.

31. Klaich, *Woman Plus Woman*, 37.

32. Finger, *Past Due*, 180–81.

33. Klaich, *Woman Plus Woman*, 37.

34. See, for example, on a mother's experience, Burst, "Split Decision," 12, 14.

35. Klaich, *Woman Plus Woman*, 214–15.

36. Rule, *Lesbian Images*, 9. Rule discusses her experience of hostility from closeted lesbians, fearful of being "outed" by association with her. See also Brown, "Take a Lesbian to Lunch," 185–95. Ponse, *Identities in the Lesbian World*, 79–80.

37. Audre Lorde discusses the constant drain of energy caused by being out and therefore expected to educate the oppressor, suggesting that this energy "might better be used in redefining and constructing the future." Lorde, *Sister Outsider*, 114–15.

38. Klaich, *Woman Plus Woman*, 24–25.

39. Siegel, *Peace, Love and Healing*, 160–61.

40. Personal observation in women's studies session at the Western Social Science Association meeting, Albuquerque, April 26–29, 1989.

41. Margolies, Becker, and Jackson-Brewer, "Internalized Homophobia," 229–41. See also Pharr, *Homophobia*.

42. Thompson, "Anger," 81–85.

43. See, for example, Rose, "Psychiatric Torture," 27; and Thompson; "Anger," 83.

44. Copper, *Over the Hill*. MacDonald, with Rich, *Look Me in the Eye*.

45. Bechdol, "*With Wings*—A Review," 22.

46. "Declaration of Principles," 1.

47. See the chapters on passing in Myrdal, *An American Dilemma*, and Pettigrew, *A Profile of the Negro American*. For discussion of literary portrayals of light-skinned black women and effects of their option to pass, see Cliff, "The Black Woman as Mulatto."

48. See Klaich, *Woman Plus Woman*, 110, on the lesbian population invisible to research.

49. Chapkis, *Beauty Secrets*, 109. Chapkis is talking about token female employees who pass as believers in corporate culture.

50. Grahn, *Another Mother Tongue*, 26. See also Ponse, *Identities in the Lesbian*

*World*, 61, on the belief that passing requires accepting "casual slanders."

51. "Amy," personal communication, March 11, 1985.

52. Cliff, *The Land of Look Behind*, 71.

53. Daly, *Gyn/Ecology*, 91, 332–33.

54. Healey, "Growing to Be an Old Woman," 60–61.

55. Lewis, *Sunday's Women*, 95.

56. Pharr, *Homophobia*, 73.

57. Grahn, *Another Mother Tongue*, 27.

58. Simon, "Never-Married Women as Caregivers," 34. Simon is discussing the emotive dissonance of long term caregivers. She in turn, cites A. R. Hochschild, *The Managed Heart*, 90. See also Clark, *The New Loving Someone Gay*, 133.

59. Henderson and Bryan, *Psychosocial Aspects of Disability*, 74–75. Joan Patterson describes the difficulties of getting children with invisible illnesses to comply with treatment regimens. Patterson, "Chronic Illness in Children and the Impact on Families," 69–107.

60. Falvo, Allen, and Maki, "Psychological Aspects of Invisible Disability," 2–6.

61. Fisher and Galler, "Friendship and Fairness," 81.

62. Brown, "From Alienation to Connection," 15.

63. In PTSD that results from incest, the violence is often covert. Rape and war are among the other causes of PTSD.

64. Browne, Connors, and Stern, *With the Power of Each Breath*, 173–74.

65. Norwood, *Letters from Women Who Love Too Much*, 266, 263.

66. Zevy and Cavallero, "Invisibility, Fantasy, and Intimacy," 93.

67. James Sawry and Charles W. Telford, *Psychology of Adjustment*, 71–72, quoted in Henderson and Bryan, *Psychosocial Aspects of Disability*, 136–37.

68. Chapkis, *Beauty Secrets*, 159.

69. Goffman, *Stigma*, 99.

70. Kolbenschlag, *Kiss Sleeping Beauty Good-bye*, 47.

71. Copper, *Over the Hill*, 73–74.

72. Klaich, *Woman Plus Woman*, 28–29.

73. Lewis, *Sunday's Women*, 63.

74. Grahn, *Another Mother Tongue*, 28. Kus, *Keys to Caring*, 35, discusses the danger of a passing person's becoming an anti-gay crusader.

75. Grier, "The Garden Variety Lesbian," 240.

76. Pharr, *Homophobia*, 73.

77. Buscaglia, *The Disabled and Their Parents*, 165. See also Rabin, *Six Parts Love*, 84–86.

78. Thompson and Andrzejewski, *Why Can't Sharon Kowalski Come Home?* 126.

79. Goffman, *Stigma*, 97. This behavior is also called "counterfeit secrecy," Ponse, *Identities in the Lesbian World*, 73; "fictional acceptance," and, of course, "active denial," Seligman and Darling, *Ordinary Families, Special Children*, 71, 90. See also Hall, "Stereotypes and Stigma," 232. For discussion of counterfeit secrecy between fat women and their friends, see Millman, *Such a Pretty Face*, 14.

80. See, among others, Featherstone, *A Difference in the Family*, 11; Hauch, "Depression in the Life of a Lesbian," 53; and Grahn, *Another Mother Tongue*, 24.

81. Lewis, *Sunday's Women*, 90–91.

82. Ibid., 101. Polly Kellogg's "Breaking Up" is about overreliance on a relationship because of passing. She emphasizes the importance of being out at least far enough to have a lesbian community for support.

83. Raven, "Reaching Across the Void," 117–18.

84. Saxton and Howe, *With Wings*, xi.

85. Grahn, *Another Mother Tongue,* 105.
86. Ibid., 23.
87. Ibid., 103.
88. Yates, "Tools for Change," 18.
89. Pharr, *Homophobia,* 86.
90. Goffman, *Stigma,* 101–102.
91. On unconscious passing, see hooks, *Feminist Theory,* 64.
92. "Annelis" in Chapkis, *Beauty Secrets,* 189.
93. Goffman, *Stigma,* 50–51.
94. On powerlessness and control, see Hoagland, *Lesbian Ethics,* 114–56. This is also a central concern in twelve-step programs.
95. Espin, "Issues of Identity in the Psychology of Latina Lesbians," 39.
96. Kus, *Keys to Caring,* 37.
97. Participating in demonstrations (especially in far away cities) is another self-affirming survival strategy, Sturgis, "New Age Fills a Need," 17.
98. Wainwright, *Stage V,* 78.
99. Irena Klepfisz says that she is not out as a lesbian in Jewish circles, but she says that people who read her poems must know; they pretend not to know. Klepfisz, "Resisting and Surviving in America," 106.
100. Bonnie Zimmerman, "The Politics of Transliteration," 671.
101. Writers on disability also stress the liberating power of naming. See, for example, Klugman, "Meditations on Cancer," 10. Fisher and Galler, "Conversation Between Two Friends," 185.
102. Nancy Toder suggests seeing such women not as "in the closet" but as "on their way out." Toder, "Sexual problems of Lesbians," 30.
103. hooks, *Feminist Theory,* 161–62.
104. Alice Miller, *For Your Own Good,* 85.
105. Pharr, *Homophobia,* 84–85.

## CHAPTER 9: NATURE AND TECHNOLOGY

1. Rich, *Of Woman Born,* 39.
2. Ortner, "Is Female to Male as Nature Is to Culture?" This is the germinal feminist essay on the subject.
3. Beverly Brown and Parveen Adams, "The Feminine Body and Feminine Politics," *m/f* (1979):51–58, cited in Swartz, "Is Thin a Feminist Issue?" 435.
4. DuBois, et al., *Feminist Scholarship.* Chapter 3 provides a good summary of feminist literature responding to this tradition.
5. Rich, *Of Woman Born.* Bandarage, "Spirituality, Politics and Feminism Are One," 81. Allen, *Lesbian Philosophy,* 62–88.
6. Griffin, *Pornography and Silence.*
7. Chernin, *The Obsession,* 129–30.
8. Harding, "The Instability of the Analytical Categories," 662.
9. Brown, "Thinking About Food Prohibitions," 13.
10. Clausen, "Political Morality of Fiction," 19.
11. Kolodny, *The Lay of the Land; The Land Before Her.*
12. Lerner, *A Death of One's Own,* 188.
13. Massie and Massie, *Journey,* 111.
14. Raymond, *A Passion for Friends,* 230.
15. Rapp, "A Womb of One's Own," 10.
16. Gordon, "Baby M," 7.
17. Zimmerman, "The Politics of Transliteration," 674.

18. Bunch, "Food, Politics and Power," 93–94.

19. Linda Pasta, "Notes from a Delivery Room," quoted in Poston, "Childbirth in Literature," 30.

20. Caputi, "In Review: *Pure Lust: Elemental Feminist Philosophy*, by Mary Daly," 87–88.

21. Poston, "Childbirth in Literature," 20. Petchesky, "Fetal Images," 273, 277, 287.

22. Rapp, "A Womb of One's Own," 10.

23. Allen, *Lesbian Philosophy*, 72–73.

24. Squire, *The Slender Balance*, 101–102.

25. Wolf, *The Beauty Myth*. McBridge, "The Slender Imbalance," includes a good survey of the literature on women's negative body image.

26. Chapkis, *Beauty Secrets*. This was the most political of recent books on body image, before the publication of Wolf's *The Beauty Myth*.

27. Fisher, *Body-Consciousness*, 13–14. Fisher states that body depersonalization is more extreme for men, but his examples are drawn from the impact of fashion on women.

28. Chernin, *The Obsession*, 35.

29. This point is widely discussed in feminist literature. See, especially, Schoenfielder and Wieser, *Shadow on a Tightrope*.

30. Freedman, *Beauty Bound*, 45.

31. Sanford and Donovan, *Women and Self-Esteem*, 370.

32. Freedman, *Beauty Bound*, 18–19.

33. Erikson, *Identity, Youth and Crisis*, 60–61.

34. Sanford and Donovan, *Women and Self-Esteem*, 370–71.

35. Fisher, *Body-Consciousness*, 15–16, 83.

36. Ibid., 73–74. Fisher sees our reaction to this body anxiety of childhood as a direct cause of racism.

37. Ibid., 6–7. McCoy, *Coping with Teenage Depression*, 164.

38. Fisher, *Body-Consciousness*, 31.

39. Bergner, Remer, and Whetsell, "Transforming Women's Body Image," 34.

40. Browne, Connors, and Stern, *With the Power of Each Breath*, 246. Robbins, "Stroke," 18.

41. Fisher, *Body-Consciousness*, 137–38.

42. MacDonald, "Ageism in the Women's Movement," 35.

43. Trask, *Eros and Power*, 144.

44. MacDonald, "Ageism in the Women's Movement," 20.

45. Sugars, "Journal Piece," 266.

46. Simonton, Simonton, and Creighton, *Getting Well Again*, 196. Simonton, *The Healing Family*, 226.

47. Wallis, "Diabetes' New Gospel of Control," 75.

48. Whillans, "Adjusting to Chronic Pain," 52.

49. Brown, *Between Health and Illness*, 36–37, 59–60, 71–72.

50. Perls, *Gestalt Therapy Verbatim*, 17.

51. Trask, *Eros and Power*, 131.

52. Davis, "Time, Productivity and Disability," Chapter 4 of this volume is an expanded version of this paper.

53. Broder, "'Space Program' to Benefit Disabled," 6.

54. Lyon, *Playing God in the Nursery*, 114.

55. McDonnell, *Not an Easy Choice*, 102.

56. Ibid., 110.

57. Roskies, *Abnormality and Normality,* 172–74. Just one of these mothers said that her child was so severely injured that "his protheses are part of him; without prostheses he would not be a human being," 273–74.

58. Summary of work in progress by Caroline Kaufmann, "Disabled People and Enabling Technologies," 8–9.

59. Griffin, "Split Culture," 5.

60. Ibid., 4.

61. Diamond and Quinby, "American Feminism in the Age of the Body," 121.

62. Lyon, *Playing God in the Nursery,* 69.

63. Daniel Callahan quoted in McDonnell, *Not an Easy Choice,* 103.

64. Henderson and Bryan, *Psychosocial Aspects of Disability,* 101, 107.

## CHAPTER 10: CAREGIVERS AND DIFFERENCE

1. See, for example, Schaef, *Co-dependence;* Subby, *Lost in the Shuffle;* Beattie, *Codependent No More.* Chapter 11 of this volume deals specifically with codependence as related to feminism and disability.

2. Raymond, *A Passion for Friends,* 187.

3. Trask, *Eros and Power,* 61; see also 76. Bernardez, "Prevalent Disorders of Women," 21–22. Of course men sometimes provide care, but "for women, caregiving is an expected duty; for men it is an unexpected expression of compassion." Sommers and Shields, *Women Take Care,* 16.

4. O'Donnell, "Alcoholism and Co-alcoholism," 67.

5. Fischer, *Linked Lives,* 194.

6. The mother-infant relationship becomes more reciprocal as the child moves toward (adult) equality with the parent. The caregiver-adult relationship is initially equal. As the disease progresses, the appropriate developmental task is to maintain the adult-to-adult relationship, not to encourage growth toward potential adulthood.

7. MacDonald, "Ageism in the Women's Movement," 8.

8. Gilligan, *In a Different Voice.*

9. Noddings, *Caring.*

10. Cohen, "The Feminist Sexuality Debate," 80.

11. Branden, *Honoring the Self,* 254. See also Paul Monette, *Borrowed Time,* 263.

12. Branden, *Honoring the Self,* 228.

13. Simon, "Never-Married Women as Caregivers," 33.

14. Miller, *Toward a New Psychology of Women,* 52, 61.

15. Ruddick, "Preservative Love and Military Destruction," 238. Fisher and Tronto, "Toward a Feminist Theory of Caring," 57.

16. Russ, "Power and Helplessness in the Women's Movement," 49–56. MacDonald, "Ageism in the Women's Movement," 7.

17. Russianoff, *Women in Crisis,* 19.

18. Prince, "Women and Love Ideology," 8–11.

19. Raymond, *A Passion for Friends,* 220.

20. Abel, "Adult Daughters and Care," 484.

21. Bader, "Respite Care," 39.

22. Fisher and Tronto, "Toward a Feminist Theory of Caring," 42.

23. Fisher, "Alice in the Human Services," 126.

24. Abel and Nelson, "Circles of Care," 7.

25. Indeed, the pay scale for nurses' aids falls below the actual cost of subsistence. Diamond, "Nursing Homes as Trouble," 175.

26. Abel and Nelson, " Circles of Care," 16.

27. Reinharz, "Friends or Foes," 509–10.

28. Abel, "Adult Daughters and Care," 9–10. De Graves, "Women Caring for Women," 212–13.

29. Lewis, "Older Women and Health," 13.

30. Kutner and Gray, "Women in Chronic Renal Failure," 115.

31. Finch and Groves, "By Women for Women," 434–36.

32. Reinharz, "Friends or Foes," 504.

33. Clarke, "Family Caregivers," 13.

34. Nancy Eustis, Kay Greenberg, and Sharon Patten, *Long Term Care for Older Persons: A Policy Perspective,* cited by Abel "Family Care for the Frail Elderly," 74. Hispanics and Blacks are also less likely to place family members in nursing homes, so that family caregivers experience still more stress, Sommers and Shields, *Women Take Care,* 117–18.

35. Wood, "Labors of Love," 29. Shields, "Who Will Need Me . . . ," 12.

36. Simon, "Never-Married Women as Caregivers," 35. Shields, "Who Will Need Me . . . ," 13. Sommers and Shields, *Women Take Care,* 22, 48, 53. Briar and Ryan, "The Anti-Institution Movement," 20. Ironically, people who *volunteer* to assist disabled people may exhibit improved physical health. Katz and Liu, *The Codependency Conspiracy,* 203.

37. Lorde, *Sister Outsider,* 122.

38. The agendas of different disability groups and those of different social movements often conflict with each other. Their priorities almost certainly do. Unfortunately, it is common when faced with such differences to consider others' views politically incorrect.

39. Frye, "The Meaning of Difference." Raymond, *A Passion for Friends,* 207ff.

40. hooks, *Feminist Theory,* ix–x. Josette Mondanaro says that she (an M.D.) has to be aware that those "beneath" her in a hierarchial work situation think more hierarchically than she does and thus are more easily hurt by her behavior than the behavior itself would justify (e.g. not saying "hello" when preoccupied). Whether her perception is correct or not, the workplace dynamic reflects the impact of class on interpretation by both parties. Perrone, Stockel, and Krueger, *Medicine Women, Curanderas and Women Doctors,* 164.

41. Sturgis, "Is This the New Thing," 26.

42. Lorde, *Sister Outsider,* 111–12. Frye, "The Meaning of Difference," 7.

43. Raymond, *A Passion for Friends,* chapter 5. See also Ferguson, "Motherhood and Sexuality," 22. Fisher and Tronto point out that friendship based on autonomy and choice excludes those aspects of caring that involve inequality on those measures, "Toward a Feminist Theory of Caring," 52–53. Sarah Lucia Hoagland stresses that peer relationships do not require having equal abilities but, rather, having different ones. *Lesbian Ethics,* 282. Thus any hierarchical analysis, including class analysis, may inhibit the development of friendship.

44. Ernst and Goodison, *In Our Hands,* 94.

45. Professionals in particular are often judged unworthy of such sensitive understanding because of their higher status, but they too experience grief, guilt, and vulnerability and need support. Seligman and Darling, *Ordinary Families, Special Children,* 179–80.

46. Ernst and Goodison, *In Our Hands,* 70.

47. Gilligan, *In a Different Voice,* 19, 62, 173.

48. Noddings, *Caring,* 8, 96. Groups, in contrast, shift from caring awareness of relationship to abstract problem solving. 25, 61.

49. Hackman and Raymond, "Caring for Bobbi," 23.

50. Boucher, "Last Year This Time," 88.

51. Butler and Rosenblum, "Cancer in Two Voices," 96–97. Abel and Nelson point out that privatized caregiving networks obscure the need for concern in the wider community. "Circles of Care," 7. Janet Farrell Smith demonstrates how the white middle-class value on privacy inhibits formation of social support networks. "Parenting and Property," 209–10.

52. Kornblatt, "Aging, Disability and Long-Term Care," 10.

53. Bailey, "More Different Than Others?" 4.

54. Hoagland provides a feminist analysis of this crucial distinction. *Lesbian Ethics*, 288.

55. Shields, "Parenting and Property," 13.

56. Sommers and Shields, *Women Take Care*.

57. For an excellent feminist analysis of the policy implications of respite care, transfer payments, and so on, see Abel, "Adult Daughters and Care," 479–95.

58. Lorde, *Sister Outsider*, 129.

59. Sandra Harding, "The Instability of the Analytical Categories," 648.


CHAPTER 11: CODEPENDENCE AND IN/DEPENDENCE

1. Robinault, *Sex, Society and the Disabled*, 141.

2. Connors, "Disability, Sexism and the Social Order," 98.

3. Debra Connors interview quoted in Carrie Dearborn, "Learning to Ask for Help," 8–9.

4. Cliff, "Notes on Speechlessness," 5.

5. Saviola, "Personal Reflections on Physically Disabled Women," 113.

6. Berry, "Woman Stresses Blindness' Advantages."

7. Witherow, "Hello Walls," 2.

8. Goodman, "The Right to Die," 16.

9. Hevey, "We Have Come to Understand," 13. Hevey writes about his daughter, Merle, who has Parkinson's.

10. Gliedman and Roth, *The Unexpected Minority*, 85–86.

11. Witkin-Lanoil, *The Female Stress Syndrome*, 93.

12. Quoted in Susanna Sturgis, "Is This the New Thing," 20–21. See also Hoagland, *Lesbian Ethics*, 100–11.

13. Chinn, Drew, and Logan, *Mental Retardation*, 237.

14. Ryan and Ryan, *A Private Battle*, 420.

15. Roskies, *Abnormality and Normality*, 235.

16. Wright, *Physical Disability, A Psychological Approach*, 185–86. The second edition of this volume, heavily revised, is subtitled *A Psychosocial Approach*.

17. Lifchez and Davis, "Living Upstairs, Leaving Home, and at the Moscow Circus," 69.

18. Kopp, *An End to Innocence*, 120.

19. Smith, *Free Fall*, 84, 117.

20. Kushner, *When Bad Things Happen to Good People*, 87.

21. Massie and Massie, *Journey*, 87.

22. See Joanna Russ on a similar phenomenon in feminist groups where "trembling sisters" depend on "magic mommas." "Power and Helplessness in the Women's Movement," 50.

23. Ayrault, *Helping the Handicapped Teenager Mature*, 111.

24. Ibid., 109.

25. See, for example, Robinault, *Sex, Society, and the Disabled*, 108.

26. In the case of people with mental retardation, this argument is fully presented in Pratt, "The Fallacy in the Concept of Deinstitutionalization," 1–3.

27. Greenspan, *A New Approach to Women and Therapy*, 259.

28. See Butler, *Why Survive?* 166; Meadow, " 'True Womanhood' and Women's Victimization," 121–22.

29. Raymond, "Medicine as Patriarchal Religion," 185–86.

30. Massie and Massie, *Journey*, 56 (Robert Massie).

31. Saviola, "Personal Reflections on Physically Disabled Women," 115.

32. "Summary Report of Conference on Disabled Women," in City of New York Commission on the Status of Women, *Exploring Attitudes Toward Women with Disabilities*, 20–21.

33. Miller, *Toward a New Psychology of Women*, 4–7.

34. Marsh, *The Emerging Rights of Children*, 9–15.

35. Ibid., 53–55.

36. Delcampo, Chase, and Delcampo, "Growth Disorders in Children," 82.

37. Register, "Letting the Angel Die," 3. Register has Caroli's Disease.

38. Wright, "Devaluation in Chronic Illness," 44–45.

39. I have noticed during the past ten years a slippage in the language of my daughter's educators, who used to be called "teachers" and now are called "trainers." The development is ironic in a period when "normalizing" is the purported goal.

40. Dowling, *The Cinderella Complex*, 107–108, 113.

41. Ibid., 133.

42. Ernst and Goodison, *In Our Own Hands*, 258.

43. See MacDonald, "Old Lesbians," 58–59, for a description of this dynamic as imposed by young women on old women.

44. Robinault, *Sex, Society and the Disabled*, 111, note a.

45. Seidenberg and DeCrow, *Women Who Marry Houses*, 12.

46. Chinn, Drew, and Logan, *Mental Retardation*, 292.

47. Roskies, *Abnormality and Normality*, 165.

48. Bowe, *Rehabilitating America*, 133.

49. Ibid., 173.

50. Spingarn, *Hanging in There*, 53–54.

51. Connors, "Disability, Sexism and the Social Order," 105–106.

52. Williams, "Special Concerns in Counseling the Intellectually Limited," 320.

53. Wright, *Physical Disability*, 308. Although either parent may focus on autonomy as the overriding goal, it is usually the mother whose job is to reinforce the goal on a daily basis.

54. Greenspan, *A New Approach to Women and Therapy*, 298–99.

55. Ibid., 297.

56. Miller, *Toward a New Psychology of Women*, 103.

57. Ibid., 94.

58. Lessing, "Denial and Disability," 21.

59. Connors, "Disability, Sexism and the Social Order," 98.

60. Grothaus, "Abuse of Women With Disabilities," 126.

61. Beattie, *Codependent No More*, 27.

62. For brief summaries of these definitions, see Schaef, *Co-dependence*, 13–19; Beattie, *Codependent No More*, 27–28.

63. Subby, *Lost in the Shuffle*, 84.

64. Subby, more than most writers on codependence, emphasizes the societal aspects of these rules. Ibid., 16–17 and *passim*.

65. Ibid., 29, items 1, 2, 4, 5.
66. Treadway, "Codependency," 40.
67. Fisher and Galler, "Friendship and Fairness," 176–77.
68. Beattie, *Beyond Codependency*, 166–67.
69. Hoagland, *Lesbian Ethics*, 90.
70. Ibid., 99–100.
71. See Ibid., 73, for the historical context of this dichotomy.
72. Siegel, *Peace, Love and Healing*, 162.
73. Quoted in Collet, "After the Anger, What Then?" 28.
74. See Griffin, *Made from This Earth*, 177, on the subject of codependence with an enemy. Griffin does not use the word *codependence*. See also Dowling, *The Cinderella Complex*, 151, 161; Miller, *Toward a New Psychology of Women*, 84–85; Kiley, *The Wendy Dilemma*, 66.
75. Lerner, *The Dance of Intimacy*, 68–69.
76. Gilligan, *In a Different Voice*.
77. Lerner, *The Dance of Intimacy*, 207–208.
78. Ibid., 209.
79. Beattie, *Beyond Codependency*, 185.
80. Ruddick, "Maternal Thinking," 224.
81. Schaef and Fassel, *The Addictive Organization*, 105.
82. Wright, *Physical Disability*, 224–25.
83. Ibid., 229.
84. Ibid., 240.
85. Gliedman and Roth, *The Unexpected Minority*, 382–83.
86. Spencer, "The Politics of Disability," 10.
87. Cook, *Second Life*, 287–88. For another example of the positive intimacy in such care, see Sommers and Shields, *Women Take Care*, 197.
88. Malcolm, *This Far and No More*, 63. Malcolm is writing about ALS, using the letters and diaries of "Emily Bauer," a pseudonym.
89. Wagner, "A Four-Wheeled Journey," 62. See also Woronov, "A See-by-Logic Life," 172.
90. Kolb, "Assertiveness Training for Women with Visual Impairments," 92.
91. Dearborn, "Learning to Ask for Help," 8.
92. Weinberg, "Autonomy as a Different Voice," 271. Weinberg is quoting R. Burt, "Constitutional Law and the Teaching of Parables," *Yale Law Journal*, 93:455.
93. "Paula," quoted in Carillo, Corbett, and Lewis, *No More Stares*, 75.
94. Wagner, "A Four-Wheeled Journey," 59.
95. Baetz, *Lesbian Crossroads*, 257.
96. Lambert, "Disability and Intimacy," 14.
97. Lorde, *A Burst of Light*, 124. See also hooks, *Talking Back*, 30–31.
98. Hoagland, *Lesbian Ethics*, 152.
99. See, for example, Lerner, *A Death of One's Own*, 106; Snow, "Living at Home," 26; Simonton, *The Healing Family*, 58.
100. Fisher and Galler, "Conversation Between Two Friends," 15.
101. Katz, *No Fairy Godmothers, No Magic Wands*, 30.
102. Ibid., 36.
103. Bloch, *Lifetime Guarantee*, 129.
104. Ibid., 129.
105. Lerner, *A Death of One's Own*, 116.
106. For the distinction between helping and rescuing, see Simonton, *The Healing Family*, 158–59.

107. Spingarn, *Hanging in There*, 81.
108. Russianoff, *Why Do I Think I Am Nothing Without a Man?* 7.
109. See, among many others, Lessing, "Denial and Disability," 21; Bardwick, *In Transition*, 129; Chodorow, *Feminism and Psychoanalytic Theory*, 162.
110. Kaplan, with Cunningham, "Fallacies of 'The Cinderella Complex,' " 87.
111. Golden, "A Good Place to Live," 29.
112. Russ, "Power and Helplessness in the Women's Movement," 56.

## CHAPTER 12: RECOVERY PROGRAMS

1. Jack Trimpey, *Rational Recovery from Alcoholism*. Kirkpatrick, *Turnabout*. Kirkpatrick, *A Fresh Start*. Swan, *Thirteen Steps*.
2. "Twelve Step Programs: Transforming Women's Lives or Not?" Presented at the National Women's Studies Assn. meeting, Towson, Md., June 18, 1989, "Relationships, Disability, Codependence, Recovery Programs and the Examined Life," Presented at the National Women's Studies Assn. meeting, Akron, Ohio, June 23, 1990.
3. Wegscheider, *Another Chance*, 89–149 presents a summary of the family roles usually discussed together in alcoholism treatment.
4. My quotations from the twelve steps and twelve traditions are taken from the literature of Alcoholics Anonymous and Al-Anon. *Alcoholics Anonymous* (popularly called "The Big Book"), *One Day at a Time in Al-Anon*.
5. Ruddick, "Maternal Thinking," 217.
6. Hoagland, *Lesbian Ethics*, 13.
7. Ibid., 122–23.
8. Ibid., 13.
9. Siegel, *Peace, Love and Healing*, 172–73.
10. Pitzele, *One More Day*, Jan. 2 entry.
11. Browne, Connors, and Stern, *With the Power of Each Breath*, 11.
12. Schaef and Fassel, *The Addictive Organization*, 67.
13. Ruddick, "Maternal Thinking," 221.
14. Kaptchuk and Croucher, *The Healing Arts*, 98. Kaptchuk and Croucher are citing Hans Selye.
15. Connell, "New Alcoholic Support Group," 4.
16. Pearson, *The Hero Within*, 40–41.
17. Goldenberg, *Returning Words to Flesh*, 201–202.
18. Arcana, *Every Mother's Son*, 185. Arcana is quoting Starhawk, *The Spiral Dance*, 2–3.
19. Rifkin, *Time Wars*, 209.
20. Loulan, "It's a Wonder We Have Sex at All," 95.
21. Arcana, *Every Mother's Son*, 185. Arcana is describing the Goddess.
22. Siegel, *Peace, Love and Healing*, 212, 198.
23. Pearson, *The Hero Within*, 46.
24. Torrey, *Witchdoctors and Psychiatrists*, 88.
25. "The Question That Never Gets Raised: A Question of Survival," Presented at the National Women's Studies Assn. meeting, Akron, Ohio, June 22, 1990.
26. Mairs, "I'm Afraid. I'm Afraid. I'm Afraid," 86.
27. Griffin, *Made from This Earth*, 176.
28. Raymond, *A Passion for Friends*, 172–73.
29. hooks, *Talking Back*, 2–3.
30. Raymond, *A Passion for Friends*, 173.
31. Hoagland, *Lesbian Ethics*, 218.

32. Schaef and Fassel, *The Addictive Organization,* 218–19.

33. Ruddick, "Maternal Thinking," 224.

34. Al-Anon Family Group Headquarters, *One Day at a Time in Al-Anon,* 308.

35. Pearson, *The Hero Within,* 41.

36. Ambo, "Speaking Out," 330.

37. Starhawk, *Dreaming the Dark,* 47.

38. Ibid., 101–105.

39. Ibid., 28.

40. Norwood, *Letters from Women Who Love Too Much,* 237–38.

41. Pharr, *Homophobia,* 86.

42. My generalizations about feminist responses to twelve step programs are based on many private discussions both in and outside of meetings. Some of the published critiques are Tallen, "Twelve Step Programs"; Johnson, "Twelve Steps into the Fog" and "We Are Not Sick!" in *Wildfire,* 129–145, 147–59. Freeman, "Twelve Steps Anonymous."

43. Alcoholics Anonymous World Services, *Twelve Steps and Twelve Traditions.*

44. Schaef, *When Society Becomes an Addict,* 144–45.

45. Aldridge, "Sobering Thoughts," 158–59. Cantu, "In Sobriety, You Get Life," 88–89.

46. Stonekey, "Reminders," 47.

47. Women for Sobriety, "Are You a Woman Who Drinks to Cope?"

48. Swan, *Thirteen Steps.*

49. Margit K. Epstein and E. K. Epstein, "Codependency as Social Narrative." Presented at the Conference of American Association for Marriage and Family Therapy, Oct. 27, 1989.

50. Cantu, "In Sobriety, You Get Life," 88–89.

51. Oliver, "Killing Us Softly," 140.

52. Pearson, *The Hero Within,* 40–43.

53. hooks, *Talking Back,* 33–34.

54. Connors, "Disability, Sexism and the Social Order," 93.

55. The National Women's Studies Association routinely prints such a request, but women with environmental illness report continued problems. When the National Lesbian Conference printed the request in their early publicity, some lesbians charged the organizers with being insensitive as the request would exclude some women (presumably perfume wearers).

56. Norwood, *Letters from Women Who Love Too Much,* 263–64.

57. Collet, "After the Anger, What Then?" 28.

58. Alcoholics Anonymous World Services, *Alcoholics Anonymous,* 160.

59. Starhawk, *Dreaming the Dark,* 42.

60. Hoagland, *Lesbian Ethics,* 149.

61. Ibid., 286.

# WORKS CITED

Abel, Emily K. "Adult Daughters and Care for the Elderly." *Feminist Studies* 12, no. 3 (Fall 1986): 479–97.

———. "Family Care for the Frail Elderly." In *Circles of Care,* edited by Emily K. Abel and Margaret K. Nelson. Albany: State University of New York Press, 1990.

Abel, Emily, and Margaret K. Nelson. "Circles of Care: An Introductory Essay." In *Circles of Care,* edited by Emily K. Abel and Margaret K. Nelson. Albany: State University of New York Press, 1990.

Al-Anon Family Group Headquarters. *One Day at a Time in Al-Anon.* New York: Al-Anon Family Group Headquarters, 1973.

Alcoholics Anonymous World Services. *Alcoholics Anonymous.* 3d ed. New York: Alcoholics Anonymous World Services, 1976.

———. *Twelve Steps and Twelve Traditions.* New York: Alcoholics Anonymous World Services, 1981. (Originally published 1953.)

Aldridge, Alice. "Sobering Thoughts." In *Out from Under: Sober Dykes and Our Friends,* edited by Jean Swallow. San Francisco: Spinsters/Aunt Lute, 1983.

Allen, Jeffner. *Lesbian Philosophy: Explorations.* Palo Alto, Calif.: Institute of Lesbian Studies, 1986.

———, ed. *Lesbian Philosophies and Cultures.* Albany: State University of New York Press, 1990.

Allen, Paula Gunn. "Indian Summer." In *Long Time Passing,* edited by Marcy Adelman. Boston: Alyson, 1986.

Ambo, Mary. "Speaking Out." In *With the Power of Each Breath: A Disabled Women's Anthology,* edited by Susan Browne, Debra Connors, and Nanci Stern. San Francisco: Cleis, 1985.

Appel, Melville J., Clarence M. Williams, and Kenneth N. Fishell. "Changes in Attitudes of Parents of Retarded Children Effected Through Group Counseling." In *Counseling Parents of the Mentally Retarded,* edited by Robert L. Noland. Springfield, Ill.: Charles C Thomas, 1970.

Arcana, Judith. *Every Mother's Son: The Role of Mothers in the Making of Men.* Seattle: Seal Press, 1986.

———. "Blaming the Mother." *Sojourner* 12, no. 12 (Aug. 1987): 22–23.

Arpad, Susan S. Review of *Tapestries of Life: Women's Work, Women's Consciousness, and the Meaning of Daily Experience,* by Bettina Aptheker. *NWSA Journal* 2, no. 2 (Spring 1990): 311–14.

Atatimur, Sara. "Women Defy the Boxes that Silence Us," *New Women's Times* 7, no. 2 (Feb. 1982): 12–13.

Ayrault, Evelyn West. *Helping the Handicapped Teenager Mature.* New York: Association Press, 1971.

Bader, Jeanne E. "Respite Care: Temporary Relief for Caregivers." *Women and Health* 10, no. 2/3 (Summer/Fall 1985): 39–52.

Baetz, Ruth. *Lesbian Crossroads.* Tallahassee: Naiad, 1988. (Originally published 1980.)

Bailey, Susan McGee. "More Different Than Others? Mothering a Child with Special Needs." *Working Paper no. 171,* Wellesley College Center for Research on Women, 1987.

Bandarage, Asoka. "Spirituality, Politics and Feminism Are One." *Women of Power,* no. 3 (Winter/Spring 1986): 80–81, 88.

Bardwick, Judith M. *In Transition: How Feminism, Sexual Liberation, and the Search for Self-Fulfillment Have Altered America.* New York: Holt, Rinehart & Winston, 1979.

Barsch, Ray H. *The Parent of the Handicapped Child: The Study of Child-Rearing Practices.* Springfield, Ill.: Charles C Thomas, 1968.

Beattie, Melody. *Codependent No More.* New York: Harper/Hazelden, 1987.

———. *Beyond Codependency and Getting Better All the Time.* San Francisco: Harper/Hazelden, 1989.

Beaucher, Suzanne. "My Last Legs." In *With the Power of Each Breath: A Disabled Women's Anthology,* edited by Susan Browne, Debra Connors, and Nanci Stern. San Francisco: Cleis, 1985.

Bechdol, Barbara. "*With Wings*—A Review." *Off Our Backs* 17, no. 11 (Dec. 1978): 22.

Benjamin, Jessica. *The Bonds of Love: Psychoanalysis, Feminism and the Problem of Domination.* New York: Pantheon, 1988.

Bergner, Mary, Pam Remer, and Charles Whetsell, "Transforming Women's Body Image: A Feminist Counseling Approach." *Women and Therapy.* 4, no. 3 (Fall 1985): 25–38.

Bernard, Jessie. "Reviewing the Impact of Women's Studies on Sociology." In *The Impact of Feminist Research in the Academy,* edited by Christine Farnham. Bloomington: Indiana University Press, 1987.

Bernardez, Teresa. "Prevalent Disorders of Women: Attempts Toward a Different Understanding and Treatment." *Women and Therapy* 3, no. 3/4 (1984): 17–27.

Berry, Jane. "Woman Stresses Blindness' Advantages." *Daily Oklahoman,* Oct. 26, 1982.

Bickelhaupt, Ethan. "The Health History: What to Look for and How to Ask." In *Keys to Caring: Assisting Your Gay and Lesbian Clients,* edited by Robert J. Kus. Boston: Alyson, 1990.

Blackwell-Stratton, Marian, Mary Lou Breslin, Arlene Meyerson, and Susan Bailey. "Smashing Icons: Disabled Women and the Disability and Women's Movements." In *Women with Disabilities,* edited by Michelle Fine and Adrienne Asch. Philadelphia: Temple University Press, 1989.

Bloch, Alice. *Lifetime Guarantee: A Journey Through Loss and Survival.* Boston: Alyson, 1981.

Blumberg, Rena. *Headstrong.* New York: Crown, 1982.

Bordow, Joan. *The Ultimate Loss: Coping with the Death of a Child.* New York: Beaufort Books, 1982.

Boswell, John. *Christianity, Social Tolerance, and Homosexuality.* Chicago: University of Chicago Press, 1980.

Boucher, Sandy. "Last Year This Time." *Sinister Wisdom* 32 (Summer 1987): 84–89.

Bowe, Frank. *Rehabilitating America: Toward Independence for Disabled and Elderly People.* New York: Harper & Row, 1980.

―――. *Comeback: Six Remarkable People Who Triumphed Over Disability.* New York: Harper & Row, 1981.

Bowlby, John. *The Making and Breaking of Affectional Bonds.* New York: Methuen/Tavistock, 1979.

Branden, Nathaniel. *Honoring the Self: Personal Integrity and the Heroic Potentials of Human Nature.* Los Angeles: Jeremy P. Tarcher, 1983.

Briar, Katherine Hooper, and Rosemary Ryan. "The Anti-Institution Movement and Women Caregivers." *Affilia: Journal of Women and Social Work* 1, no. 1 (Spring 1986): 20–31.

Bristor, Martha Wingerd. "The Birth of a Handicapped Child—a Holistic Model for Grieving." *Family Relations* 33, no. 1 (Jan. 1984): 25–32.

Broder, David S. " 'Space Program' to Benefit Disabled." *Norman [Oklahoma] Transcript,* July 13, 1985, 6.

Bronston, William G. "Concepts and Theory of Normalization." In *The Mentally Retarded Child and His Family,* edited by Richard Koch and James C. Dobson. New York: Bruner/Mazel, 1976.

Brown, Barbara B. *Between Health and Illness: New Notions on Stress and the Nature of Well Being.* Boston: Houghton Mifflin, 1984.

Brown, Helene. *Yesterday's Child.* New York: Signet, 1977.

Brown, Kathie. "Thinking About Food Prohibitions." *Heresies* 21 (1987): 10–15.

Brown, Laura. "Power, Responsibilities, Boundaries: Ethical Concerns for the Lesbian Feminist Therapist." *Lesbian Ethics* 1, no. 3 (Fall 1985): 39–40.

Brown, Laura S. "From Alienation to Connection: Feminist Therapy with Post-Traumatic Stress Disorder." *Women and Therapy* 5, no. 1 (Spring 1986): 13–26.

Brown, Rita Mae. "Take a Lesbian to Lunch." In *Out of the Closets: Voices of Gay Liberation,* edited by Karla Jay and Allen Young. New York: Douglas/Links, 1972.

Browne, Susan, Debra Connors, and Nanci Stern, eds. *With the Power of Each Breath: A Disabled Women's Anthology.* San Francisco: Cleis, 1985.

Browning, Beth. "Justice Department Intervenes in Baby Jane Doe Case." *Off Our Backs* 13, no. 11 (Dec 1983): 7.

Buck, Pearl. *The Child Who Never Grew.* New York: John Day, 1950.

Buck, Pearl S., and Gweneth Zarfoss. *The Gifts They Bring: Our Debt to the Mentally Retarded.* New York: John Day, 1965.

Bunch, Charlotte. "Food, Politics and Power: A Feminist Perspective." *Heresies* 21 (1987): 92–94.

Burgraff, M. Z. "Consulting with Parents of Handicapped Children." *Elementary School Guidance and Counseling* 13 (Feb. 1979): 214–21.

Burst, Ardis. "Split Decision." *Savvy* 6, no. 5 (May 1985): 12, 14.

Buscaglia, Leo. *The Disabled and Their Parents.* New York: Holt, Rinehart & Winston, 1983.

Butler, Robert N. *Why Survive? Being Older in America.* New York: Harper & Row, 1975.

Butler, Sandra, and Barbara Rosenblum. "Cancer in Two Voices (Chapter One)." *Sinister Wisdom* 32 (Summer 1987): 90–97.

Campbell, Joseph. *The Hero with a Thousand Faces.* Princeton: Princeton University Press, 1949.

Campling, Jo, ed. *Images of Ourselves: Women with Disabilities Talking.* Boston: Routledge, 1981.

Cantor, Robert Chernin. *And a Time to Live: Toward Emotional Well-Being During the Crisis of Cancer.* New York: Harper & Row, 1978.

Cantu, Celinda. "In Sobriety, You Get Life." In *Out from Under: Sober Dykes and Our Friends,* edited by Jean Swallow. San Francisco: Spinsters/Aunt Lute, 1983.

Caplan, Paula J. "Take the Blame Off Mother." *Psychology Today* 20, no. 10 (Oct. 1986): 70–71.

————. *Don't Blame Mother: Mending the Mother-Daughter Relationship.* New York: Harper & Row, 1989.

Caputi, Jane. "In Review: *Pure Lust: Elemental Feminist Philosophy,* by Mary Daly." *Trivia: A Journal of Ideas,* no. 5 (Fall 1984): 80–89.

Carillo, Ann Cupola, Katherine Corbett, and Victoria Lewis. *No More Stares.* Berkeley: Disability Rights Education and Defense Fund, 1982.

Caroff, Phyllis, and Rose Dobrof. "Social Work: Its Institutional Role." In *Anticipatory Grief,* edited by Bernard Schoenberg, Arthur C. Carr, Austin H. Kutscher, David Peretz, and Evan K. Goldberg. New York: Columbia University Press, 1974.

Cepko, Roberta. "On Oxfords and Plaster Casts." In *With Wings: An Anthology of Literature by and About Women with Disabilities,* edited by Marsha Saxton and Florence Howe. New York: Feminist Press, 1987.

Chapkis, Wendy. *Beauty Secrets: Women and the Politics of Appearance.* Boston: South End Press, 1986.

Chernin, Kim. *The Obsession: Reflections on the Tyranny of Slimness.* New York: Harper & Row, 1981.

————. *Reinventing Eve: Modern Woman in Search of Herself.* New York: Harper & Row, 1987.

Chinn, Philip C., Clifford J. Drew, and Don R. Logan. *Mental Retardation: A Life Cycle Approach.* St. Louis: C. V. Mosby, 1979.

Chodorow, Nancy. *The Reproduction of Mothering: Psychoanalysis and the Sociology of Gender.* Berkeley: University of California Press, 1978.

————. *Feminism and Psychoanalytic Theory.* New Haven: Yale University Press, 1989.

Christ, Carol P. "Remapping Development: The Power of Divergent Data." In *The Impact of Feminist Research in the Academy,* edited by Christine Farnham. Bloomington: Indiana University Press, 1987.

City of New York Commission on the Status of Women. *Exploring Attitudes Toward Women with Disabilities: A Curriculum Guide for Employers and Educators.* New York: Commission on the Status of Women, 1979.

Clark, Don. *The New Loving Someone Gay.* Berkeley: Celestial Arts, 1987.

Clarke, Elizabeth. "Family Caregivers." *OWL Observer* 5, no. 5 (Sept./Oct. 1985): 1, 13.

Clausen, Jan. "On the Political Morality of Fiction (Part One)." *Off Our Backs* 15, no. 6 (June 1985): 17–20.

Cliff, Michelle. "Notes on Speechlessness." *Sinister Wisdom* 5 (1978): 5–10.

————. *The Land of Look Behind.* Ithaca: Firebrand, 1987.

————. "The Black Woman as Mulatto: A Personal Response to Margaret Walker's Vyrey, Among Others." *American Voice,* no. 17 (Winter 1989): 10–19.

Cohen, Cheryl H. "The Feminist Sexuality Debate: Ethics and Politics." *Hyaptia* 1, no. 2 (Fall 1986): 71–86.

Collet, Lily. "After the Anger, What Then? ACOA, Self-Help or Self-Pity." *Family Therapy Networker* 14, no. 1 (Jan./Feb. 1990): 22–31.

Collier, Peter, and David Horowitz. *The Kennedys.* New York: Summit, 1984.

Colman, Hilda. *Hanging On.* New York: Atheneum, 1977.

Connell, Joan. "New Alcoholic Support Group Offers an Alternative to AA." *Norman [Oklahoma] Transcript,* Aug. 11, 1990, 4.

Connors, Debra. "Disability, Sexism, and the Social Order." In *With the Power of Each Breath: A Disabled Women's Anthology,* edited by Susan Browne, Debra Connors, and Nanci Stern. San Francisco: Cleis, 1985.

Conway, Karin. "Living with Limitations." *Savvy* 5, no. 9 (Sept. 1984): 8.

Cook, Loree. "Chronic Illness." *Off Our Backs* 13, no. 9 (Oct. 1983): 21.

Cook, Stephani. *Second Life.* New York: Ballantine, 1981.

Copper, Baba. "The View from Over the Hill: Notes on Ageism Between Lesbians." *Trivia,* no. 7 (Summer 1985): 48–63.

————. *Over the Hill: Reflections on Ageism Between Women.* Freedom, Calif.: Crossing Press, 1988.

Cox-Gedmark, Jan. *Coping with Physical Disability.* Philadelphia: Westminster Press, 1980.

Crawford, Sally. "Family Building Process." In *Lesbian Psychologies,* edited by Boston Lesbian Psychologies Collective. Urbana: University of Illinois Press, 1987.

Cross, Merry. "A Letter to Neil Marcus." *Complete Elegance,* no. 6: 23.

Cutter, Wendy Judith. "Dear Mom and Dad." In *The Coming Out Stories,* edited by Julia Penelope Stanley and Susan J. Wolfe. Watertown, Mass.: Persephone, 1980.

Daly, Mary. *Beyond God the Father: Toward a Philosophy of Women's Liberation.* Boston: Beacon, 1973.

_____. *Gyn/Ecology: The Metaethics of Radical Feminism.* Boston: Beacon, 1978.

Dashu, Max. "Seizures." In *With the Power of Each Breath: A Disabled Women's Anthology,* edited by Susan Browne, Debra Connors, and Nanci Stern. San Francisco: Cleis, 1985.

Davies, Joyce. "Lame." In *With Wings: An Anthology of Literature by and About Women with Disabilities,* edited by Marsha Saxton and Florence Howe. New York: Feminist Press, 1987.

Davis, Barbara Hillyer. "Time, Productivity and Disability." *Midwest Feminist Papers V.* Midwest Sociologists for Women in Society, 1985: 30–34.

Dearborn, Carrie. "Learning to Ask for Help." *Gay Community News,* Sept. 28–Oct. 24, 1986, 8–9.

"Declaration of Principles." *Independent Living Advocate,* no. 5 (Aug. 1983): 1.

Deford, Frank. *Alex: The Life of a Child.* New York: Viking, 1983.

DeFrain, John, Jacque Taylor, and Linda Ernst. *Coping with Sudden Infant Death.* Lexington, Ky.: Lexington Books, 1982.

de Graves, Diane. "Women Caring for Women." *RFR/DRF* 11, no. 2 (July 1982): 212–13.

Dejanikus, Tacie. "Genetic Screening." *Off Our Backs* 13, no. 5 (May 1983): 3.

Delcampo, Robert L., Teresa Chase, and Diane S. Delcampo. "Growth Disorders in Children: The Impact on the Family System." *Family Relations* 33 (Jan. 1984): 79–84.

Demeter, Anna. *Legal Kidnapping.* Boston: Beacon, 1977.

Demetrakopoulos, Stephanie. *Listening to Our Bodies: The Rebirth of Feminine Wisdom.* Boston: Beacon, 1983.

DeMyer, Marian K. *Parents and Children in Autism.* Washington, D.C.: V. H. Winston & Sons, 1979.

Denneny, Michael. "Chasing the Crossover Audience and Other Self-Defeating Strategies." *Out/Look* 1, no. 4 (Winter 1989): 16–21.

Diamond, Irene, and Lee Quinby, "American Feminism in the Age of the Body." *Signs* 10, no. 1 (Autumn 1984): 119–25.

Diamond, Timothy. "Nursing Homes as Trouble." In *Circles of Care,* edited by Emily K. Abel and Margaret K. Nelson. Albany: State University of New York Press, 1990.

Dickens, Monica. *Miracles of Courage.* New York: Dodd Mead, 1975.

Dickman, Irving R., with Sol Gordon. *One Miracle at a Time.* New York: Simon & Schuster, 1985.

Dinnerstein, Dorothy. *The Mermaid and the Minotaur.* New York: Harper, 1976.

Dixon, Edi. "Interview with Marj Schneider: Womyn's Braille Press." *Off Our Backs* 13, no. 1 (Feb. 1988): 22.

Dobihal, Edward F., Jr., and Charles William Stewart. *When a Friend Is Dying.* Nashville: Abingdon Press, 1984.

Donnelly, Katherine Fair. *Recovering from the Loss of a Child.* New York: Macmillan, 1982.

Donovan, Josephine. *Feminist Theory: The Intellectual Traditions of American Feminism.* New York: Ungar, 1987.

Dorris, Michael. *The Broken Cord.* New York: Harper, 1989.

Dorros, Sidney. *Parkinson's: A Patient's View.* Washington, D.C.: Seven Locks Press, 1981.

Dowling, Collette. *The Cinderella Complex: Women's Hidden Fear of Independence.* New York: Summit, 1981.

Dublin Lesbian and Gay Men's Collectives. *Out for Ourselves.* Dublin: Women's Community Press, 1987.

DuBois, Ellen Carol, Gail Paradise Kelly, Elizabeth Lapovsky Kennedy, Carolyn W. Korsmeyer, and Lillian S. Robinson. *Feminist Scholarship: Kindling in the Groves of Academe.* Urbana: University of Illinois Press, 1985.

Duffy, Yvonne. *All Things Are Possible.* Ann Arbor: A. J. Garvin, 1981.

Edgerton, Robert B. *The Cloak of Competence: Stigma in the Lives of the Mentally Retarded.* Berkeley: University of California Press, 1967.

Epstein, Margit K., and E. K. Epstein. "Codependency as Social Narrative." Paper presented at the Conference of American Association for Marriage and Family Therapy, October 27, 1989.

Erikson, Erik H. *Identity, Youth and Crisis.* New York: Norton, 1968.

Ernst, Sheila, and Lucy Goodison. *In Our Own Hands: A Women's Book of Self-Help Therapy.* Los Angeles: Jeremy P. Tarcher, 1981.

Espin, Olivia M. "Issues of Identity in the Psychology of Latina Lesbians." In *Lesbian Psychologies,* edited by Boston Lesbian Psychologies Collective. Urbana: University of Illinois Press, 1987.

Eustis, Nancy, Kay Greenberg, and Sharon Patten. *Long Term Care for Older Persons: A Policy Perspective.* Monterey, Calif.: Brooks/Cole, 1984.

Falvo, Donna R., Harry Allen, and Dennis R. Maki. "Psychological Aspects of Invisible Disability." *Rehabilitation Literature* 43, no. 1 (Jan./Feb. 1982): 2–6.

Featherstone, Helen. *A Difference in the Family.* New York: Basic Books, 1980.

Ferguson, Ann. "Motherhood and Sexuality: Some Feminist Questions." *Hypatia* 1, no. 2 (Fall 1985): 3–22.

———. "Is There a Lesbian Culture?" In *Lesbian Philosophies and Cultures,* edited by Jeffner Allen. Albany: State University of New York Press, 1990.

Finch, Janet, and Dulcie Groves. "By Women for Women: Caring for the Frail Elderly." *Women's Studies International Forum* 5, no. 5 (1982): 427–38.

Fine, Michelle, and Asch, Adrienne. "Introduction: Beyond Pedestals." In *Women with Disabilities,* edited by Michelle Fine and Adrienne Asch. Philadelphia: Temple University Press, 1989.

———. "Disabled Women: Sexism Without the Pedestal." In *Women and Disability: The Double Handicap,* edited by Mary Jo Deegan and Nancy A. Brooks. New Brunswick, N.J.: Transaction Books, 1985.

Finger, Anne. "Claiming All of Our Bodies: Reproductive Rights and Disability." In *With the Power of Each Breath: A Disabled Women's Anthology,* edited by Susan Browne, Debra Connors, and Nanci Stern. San Francisco: Cleis, 1985.

———. *Past Due: A Story of Disability, Pregnancy and Birth.* Seattle: Seal Press, 1990.

Fischer, Lucy Rose. *Linked Lives: Adult Daughters and Their Mothers.* New York: Harper & Row, 1987.

Fisher, Berenice. "Alice in the Human Services: A Feminist Analysis of Women's Work in the Caring Professions." In *Circles of Care,* edited by Emily K. Abel and Margaret K. Nelson. Albany: State University of New York Press, 1990.

Fisher, Berenice, and Roberta Galler. "Conversation Between Two Friends about Feminism and Disability." *Off Our Backs* 11, no. 5 (May 1981): 14–15.

———. "Friendship and Fairness: How Disability Affects Friendship Between Women." In *Women with Disabilities,* edited by Michelle Fine and Adrienne Asch. Philadelphia: Temple University Press, 1989.

Fisher, Berenice, and Joan Tronto. "Toward a Feminist Theory of Caring." In *Circles of Care,* edited by Emily K. Abel and Margaret K. Nelson. Albany: State University of New York Press, 1990.

Fisher, Seymour. *Body-Consciousness: You Are What You Feel.* Englewood Cliffs, N.J.: Prentice-Hall, 1973.

Fortier, Laurie M., and Richard Wanlass. "Family Crisis Following the Diagnosis of a Handicapped Child." *Family Relations* 33, no. 1 (Jan. 1984): 13–24.

Freedman, Rita. *Beauty Bound.* Lexington, Mass.: D. C. Heath, 1985.

Freeman, Beth. "Twelve Steps Anonymous." *Off Our Backs* 19, no. 3 (March 1989): 20–21.

French, Marilyn. *Beyond Power: On Women, Men and Morals.* New York: Ballantine, 1985.

Frick, Nancy M. "Keynote Address: Some Suggested Solutions to Very Real Problems." In *Proceedings from Polio Update 1984.* New York: Easter Seal Society, 1984.

Friday, Nancy. *My Mother, My Self.* New York: Delacorte Press, 1977.

Frye, Marilyn. "The Meaning of Difference." *Working Paper* no. 16. Eugene, OR: University of Oregon Center for the Study of Women in Society, 1985.

Gaettens, Marie-Luise. "The Hard Work of Remembering: Two German Women Reexamine National Socialism." In *Taking Our Time: Feminist Perspectives on Temporality,* edited by Frieda Johles Forman and Caoran Sowton. New York: Pergamon, 1989.

Galloway, Terry. "I'm Listening as Hard as I Can." In *With Wings: An Anthology of Literature by and About Women with Disabilities,* edited by Marsha Saxton and Florence Howe. New York: Feminist Press 1987.

Gardiner, Judith Kegan, Elly Bulkin, Rena Patterson, and Annette Kolodny. "An Interchange on Feminist Criticism: On 'Dancing Through the Minefield.' " *Feminist Studies* 8, no. 3 (1982): 629–75.

Gilligan, Carol. *In a Different Voice: Psychological Theory and Women's Development.* Cambridge: Harvard University Press, 1982.

Glaser, Barney G. *Theoretical Sensitivity: Advances in the Methodology of Grounded Theory.* Mill Valley, Calif.: Sociology Press, 1978.

Gliedman, John, and William Roth. *The Unexpected Minority: Handicapped Children in America.* New York: Harcourt Brace Jovanovich, 1980.

Goffman, Erving. *Stigma.* Englewood Cliffs, N.J.: Prentice-Hall, 1963.

Gold, Marc. *Like Normal People.* New York: McGraw Hill, 1978.

Golden, Marilyn. "A Good Place to Live." *Complete Elegance,* no. 6: 29.

———. "Physical Difference Workshop." *Complete Elegance,* no. 7: 28.

Goldenberg, Naomi R. *Returning Words to Flesh: Feminism, Psychoanalysis, and the Resurrection of the Body.* Boston: Beacon Press, 1990.

Goodman, Ellen. "The Right to Die" (syndicated column). *Oklahoma Observer,* Jan. 10, 1984, 16.

Gordon, Mary. "Baby M: New Questions About Biology and Destiny." *Conscience* 8, no. 3 (May/June 1987): 7.

Gordon, Rebecca. "In Defense of Big Words." *Lesbian Contradiction: A Journal of Irreverent Feminism,* no. 4 (Fall 1983): 20.

Graham, Jory. *In the Company of Others: Understanding the Needs of Cancer Patients.* New York: Harcourt Brace Jovanovich, 1982.

Grahn, Judy. *Another Mother Tongue: Gay Words, Gay Worlds.* Boston: Beacon Press, 1984.

Greenspan, Miriam. *A New Approach to Women and Therapy.* New York: McGraw-Hill, 1983.

Grier, Barbara. "The Garden Variety Lesbian." In *The Coming Out Stories,* edited by

Julia Penelope Stanley and Susan J. Wolfe. Watertown, Mass.: Persephone, 1980.

Griffin, Susan. *Woman and Nature: The Roaring Inside Her.* New York: Harper Colophon, 1978.

————. *Pornography and Silence: Culture's Revenge Against Nature.* New York: Harper & Row, 1981.

————. *Made from This Earth: An Anthology of Writings.* New York: Harper & Row, 1982.

————. "Split Culture." *Creative Woman* 8, no. 4 (Winter 1988): 4–7.

Grothaus, Rebecca S. "Abuse of Women with Disabilities." In *With the Power of Each Breath: A Disabled Women's Anthology,* edited by Susan Browne, Debra Connors, and Nanci Stern. San Francisco: Cleis, 1985.

Hackman, Margaret, and Monica Raymond. "Caring for Bobbi: An Incredible Gift." *Sojourner* 12, no. 4 (Dec. 1986): 22–23.

Hall, Edward T. *The Dance of Life.* New York: Doubleday, Anchor, 1973.

Hall, Jacquelyn H. "Stereotypes and Stigma: Barriers to Recovery." In *Women in Crisis,* edited by Penelope Russianoff. New York: Human Sciences Press, 1981.

Hancock, Emily. *The Girl Within.* New York: E. P. Dutton, 1989.

Harding, Sandra. "The Instability of the Analytical Categories of Feminist Theory." *Signs* 11, no. 4 (Summer 1986): 645–64.

Harris, Sandra L. "The Family and the Autistic Child: A Behavioral Perspective." *Family Relations* 33 (Jan. 1984): 127–34.

Hauch, Valerie C. "Depression in the Life of a Lesbian: My Struggle to Survive and Understand." *Common Lives/Lesbian Lives,* no. 22 (Spring 1987): 43–54.

Healey, Shevy. "Growing to Be an Old Woman: Aging and Ageism." *Calyx* 9, no. 2–3 (Winter 1986): 58–62.

Hearns, Kristin. "A Woman's Right to Cruise." In *Out the Other Side: Contemporary Lesbian Writing,* edited by Christian McEwan and Sue O'Sullivan. Freedom, Calif.: Crossing Press, 1989.

Henderson, George, and Willie V. Bryan. *Psychosocial Aspects of Disability.* Springfield, Ill.: Charles C Thomas, 1984.

Hendin, David. *Death as a Fact of Life.* New York: Norton, 1984.

Henley, Linda. "A Time to Dance." *Norman [Oklahoma] Transcript,* Feb. 28, 1986, 13.

Hevey, Jerome J. "We Have Come to Understand." *Journal of Current Social Issues* 16, no. 1 (Spring 1979): 9–13.

Hoagland, Sarah. "Dear Julie." *Lesbian Ethics* 1, no. 2 (Spring 1985): 73.

————. *Lesbian Ethics: Toward New Value.* Palo Alto, Calif.: Institute of Lesbian Studies, 1988.

Hollingsworth, Charles E., and Robert Pasnau. *The Family in Mourning: A Guide for Health Professionals.* New York: Grune & Stratton, 1977.

hooks, bell. *Feminist Theory: From Margin to Center.* Boston: South End Press, 1984.

————. "Telling the Story." *Catalyst* (Winter 1988): 63–66.

————. *Talking Back: Thinking Feminist, Thinking Black.* Boston: South End Press, 1989.

House, Seamoon. "A Radical Feminist Model of Psychological Disability." *Off Our Backs* 11, no. 5 (May 1981): 34–35.

Hubbard, Ruth. "Caring for Baby Doe, The Moral Issue of Our Time." *Ms.* 12, no. 11 (May 1984): 84–86, 165.

Humphrey, Mary Ann, ed. *My Country, My Right to Serve.* New York: Harper Collins, 1990.

Irvin, Nancy, John N. Kennell, and Marshall H. Klaus. "Caring for Parents of an Infant with a Congenital Malformation." In *Maternal-Infant Bonding: The Impact of Early Separation or Loss on Family Development,* edited by Marshall H. Klaus and John H. Kennell. St. Louis: C. V. Mosby Co., 1976.

Jacobs, Jerry. *The Search for Help: A Study of the Retarded Child in the Community.* New York: Brunner/Mazel, 1969.

Jelinek, Estelle C. *The Tradition of Women's Autobiography: From Antiquity to the Present.* Boston: Twayne, 1986.

Jennett, Bryan. "Disability After Head Injury." Third Annual James C. Hemphill Lecture, Rehabilitation Institute of Chicago, Sept. 12, 1984.

Johnson, Julie Tallard. *Hidden Victims: An Eight-Stage Healing Process for Families and Friends of the Mentally Ill.* New York: Doubleday, 1988.

Johnson, Sonia. *Wildfire: Igniting the She/volution.* Albuquerque: Wildfire Books, 1989.

Jones, Joanne. "Lights of My Life." *Journal of Current Social Issues* 16, no. 1 (Spring 1979): 65–67.

Junker, Karen S. *The Child in the Glass Ball.* New York: Abingdon, 1964.

Juul, Kristen D. "European Approaches and Innovations in Serving the Handicapped." *Exceptional Children* 44, no. 5 (Feb. 1978): 322–30.

Kaplan, David M. *The Ultimate Loss: Coping with the Death of a Child.* New York: Beaufort Books, 1982.

Kaplan, Helen, with Anne Marie Cunningham. "Fallacies of 'The Cinderella Complex.'" *Savvy* 2, no. 8 (Aug. 1981): 87–88.

Kaptchuk, Ted, and Michael Croucher. *The Healing Arts: Exploring the Medical Ways of the World.* New York: Summit Books, 1987.

Katz, Judy H. *No Fairy Godmothers, No Magic Wands: The Healing Process After Rape.* Saratoga, Calif.: R & E Publishers, 1984.

Katz, Stan J., and Aimee Liu. *The Codependency Conspiracy: How to Break the Recovery Habit and Take Charge of Your Life.* New York: Warner, 1991.

Kaufman, Caroline. "Disabled People and Enabling Technologies: Human Use of Ambulatory Devices." *Disability and Chronic Diseases Quarterly* 4, no. 4 (Oct. 1984): 8–9.

Kellogg, Polly. "Breaking Up." In *Our Right to Love: A Lesbian Resource Book,* edited by Ginny Vida. Englewood Cliffs, N.J.: Prentice Hall, 1978.

Kennedy, James R. "Maternal Reactions to the Birth of a Defective Baby." *Social Casework* 51 (1970): 410–16.

Kiley, Dan. *The Wendy Dilemma.* New York: Arbor House, 1984.

Killilea, Marie. *Karen.* Englewood Cliffs, N.J.: Prentice-Hall, 1952.

———. *With Love from Karen.* Englewood Cliffs, N.J.: Prentice-Hall, 1963.

Kirkpatrick, Jean. *Turnabout.* New York: Doubleday, 1978.

———. *A Fresh Start.* Quakertown, Penn.: Women for Sobriety, 1981.

Kirman, Brian H. *The Mentally Handicapped Child.* New York: Taplinger, 1973.

Klaich, Dolores. *Woman Plus Woman.* Tallahassee: Naiad, 1989.

Kleiman, Gary, and Sanford Dody. *No Time to Lose.* New York: William Morrow & Co., 1983.

Klepfisz, Irena. "Resisting and Surviving in America." In *Nice Jewish Girls,* edited by Evelyn Torton Beck. Watertown, Mass.: Persephone, 1982.

Klugman, Elana. "Meditations on Cancer." *Genesis 2: An Independent Voice for Jewish Renewal* 13, no. 2 (Nov. 1981): 10.

Kolb, Cynthia. "Assertiveness Training for Women with Visual Impairments." In *Women and Disability: The Double Handicap,* edited by Mary Jo Deegan and Nancy A. Brooks. New Brunswick, N.J.: Transaction Books, 1985.

Kolbenschlag, Madonna. *Kiss Sleeping Beauty Good-bye.* New York: Bantam, 1979.

Kolodny, Annette. *The Lay of the Land: Metaphor as Experience and History in American Life and Letters.* Chapel Hill: University of North Carolina Press, 1975.

――――. *The Land Before Her: Fantasy and Experience on the American Frontiers, 1630–1860.* Chapel Hill: University of North Carolina Press, 1984.

Konanc, Judy T., and Nancy J. Warren. "Graduation: Transitional Crisis for Mildly Developmentally Disabled Adolescents and Their Families." *Family Relations* 33 (Jan. 1984): 135–42.

Kopp, Sheldon. *An End to Innocence: Facing Life Without Illusions.* New York: Bantam, 1981.

Kornblatt, Susan. "Aging, Disability and Long-Term Care." *Aging Network News* 4, no. 6 (Oct. 1987): 9–11.

Kubie, Laurence S. "Chronic Illness and Hidden Neurotic Difficulties." In *Medical and Psychological Team Work in the Care of the Chronically Ill,* edited by Molly Harrower. Springfield, Ill.: Charles C Thomas, 1955.

Kus, Robert J., ed. *Keys to Caring: Assisting Your Gay and Lesbian Clients.* Boston: Alyson, 1990.

――――. "Coming Out: Its Nature, Stages, and Health Concerns." In *Keys to Caring: Assisting Your Gay and Lesbian Clients,* edited by Robert J. Kus. Boston: Alyson, 1990.

Kushner, Harold S. *When Bad Things Happen to Good People.* New York: Avon, 1983. (Originally published by Schocken, 1981.)

Kutner, Nancy G., and Heather L. Gray. "Women in Chronic Renal Failure." In *Women and Disability: The Double Handicap,* edited by Mary Jo Deegan and Nancy A. Brooks. New Brunswick, N.J.: Transaction Books, 1985.

Lambert, Sandra. "Disability and Intimacy." *Common Lives/Lesbian Lives,* no. 26 (Spring 1988): 5–15.

Lanser, Susan S. "Who *Are* the 'We'? The Shifting Terms of Feminist Discourse." *Women's Studies Quarterly* 14, no. 3/4 (Fall/Winter 1986): 18–20.

Leach, Christopher. *Letter to a Younger Son.* New York: Harcourt Brace Jovanovich, 1981.

Lerner, Gerda. *A Death of One's Own.* New York: Simon & Schuster, 1978.

Lerner, Harriet Goldhor. *Women in Therapy.* New York: Harper & Row, 1988.

――――. *The Dance of Intimacy: A Woman's Guide to Courageous Acts of Change in Key Relationships.* New York: Harper & Row, 1989.

Lessing, Jill. "Denial and Disability." *Off Our Backs* 11, no. 5, (May 1981): 21.

Levine, Robert, with Ellen Wolff. "Social Time: The Heartbeat of Culture." *Psychology Today* 19, no. 3 (Mar. 1985): 29–35.

Levy, Emily. "How the Rhino Got Its Flaky Skin." In *With the Power of Each Breath: A Disabled Women's Anthology,* edited by Susan Browne, Debra Connors, and Nanci Stern. San Francisco: Cleis, 1985.

Lewis, C. S. *A Grief Observed.* New York: Seabury, 1961.

Lewis, J. David, and Andrew J. Weigert. "The Structures and Meanings of Social Time." *Social Forces* 60, no. 2 (Dec. 1981): 432–59.

Lewis, Myrna. "Older Women and Health: An Overview." *Women and Health* 10, nos. 2/3 (Summer/Fall 1985): 1–16.

Lewis, Sasha Gregory. *Sunday's Women: A Report on Lesbian Life Today.* Boston: Beacon, 1979.

Lifchez, Raymond, and Cheryl Davis. "Living Upstairs, Leaving Home and at the Moscow Circus." In *With Wings: An Anthology of Literature by and About Women with Disabilities,* edited by Marsha Saxton and Florence Howe. New York: Feminist Press, 1987.

Lorde, Audre. *The Cancer Journals.* New York: Spinsters Ink, 1980.

_____. *Sister Outsider.* Trumansburg, New York: Crossing Press, 1984.

_____. *A Burst of Light.* Ithaca: Firebrand, 1988.

Lorenz, Sarah E. *Our Son, Ken.* New York: Dell, 1969.

Loulan, JoAnn. "It's a Wonder We Have Sex at All." In *Out from Under: Sober Dykes and Our Friends,* edited by Jean Swallow. San Francisco: Spinsters/Aunt Lute, 1983.

Luepnitz, Deborah Anna. *The Family Interpreted: Feminist Theory in Clinical Practice.* New York: Basic Books, 1988.

Lugones, Maria. "Playfulness, 'World'-Travelling, and Loving Perception." In *Lesbian Philosophies and Cultures,* edited by Jeffner Allen. Albany: State University of New York Press, 1990.

Lund, Doris. *Eric.* New York: Dell, 1974.

Luterman, David D. *Counseling Parents of Hearing-Impaired Children.* Boston: Little, Brown, 1979.

Lyon, Jeff. *Playing God in the Nursery.* New York: Norton, 1985.

MacDonald, Barbara. "Old Lesbians." *Lesbian Ethics* 1, no. 1 (Fall 1984): 58–59.

_____. "Ageism in the Women's Movement." *Broomstick* 8, no. 2 (March–April 1986): 6–9.

MacDonald, Barbara, with Cynthia Rich. *Look Me in the Eye: Old Women, Aging and Ageism.* San Francisco: Spinsters Ink, 1983.

Mace, Nancy L., and Peter V. Rabins. *The 36-Hour Day: A Family Guide to Caring for Persons with Alzheimer's Disease, Related Dementing Illnesses, and Memory Loss in Later Life.* Baltimore, Md.: Johns Hopkins University Press, 1981.

Mairs, Nancy. "On Being a Cripple." In *With Wings: An Anthology of Literature by and About Women with Disabilities,* edited by Marsha Saxton and Florence Howe. New York: Feminist Press, 1987.

_____. *Plaintext: Deciphering a Woman's Life.* New York: Harper & Row, 1987.

_____. "I'm Afraid. I'm Afraid. I'm Afraid." *American Voice,* no. 17 (Winter 1989): 81–87.

Malcolm, Andrew H. *This Far and No More.* New York: Random House, 1987.

Mannoni, Maud. *The Retarded Child and the Mother: A Psychoanalytic Study.* London: Tavistock, 1973.

Mantle, Margaret. "A Truly Formidable Challenge." *Ways* 1, no. 2 (Mar. 1986): 14–18.

Margolies, Liz, Martha Becker, and Karla Jackson-Brewer. "Internalized Homophobia: Identifying and Treating the Oppressor Within." In *Lesbian Psychologies,* edited by Boston Lesbian Psychologies Collective. Urbana: University of Illinois Press, 1987.

Marsh, Frank H. *The Emerging Rights of Children in Treatment for Mental and Catastrophic Illnesses.* Lanham, Md.: University Press of America, 1980.

Mason, Micheline. "Dear Harvey." *Complete Elegance,* no. 7: 21.

Massarani, Jared, and Alice Massarani. *Our Life with Caleb.* Philadelphia: Fortress Press, 1976.

Massie, Robert, and Suzanne Massie. *Journey.* New York: Alfred A. Knopf, 1973.

Matthews, Gwyneth. *Voices from the Shadows: Women with Disabilities Speak Out.* Toronto: Women's Educational Press, 1983.

McBridge, Leslie G. "The Slender Imbalance: Women and Body Image." *Journal of NAWDAC* 49, no. 1 (Fall 1985): 16–22.

McCoy, Kathleen. *Coping with Teenage Depression: A Parent's Guide.* New York: NAL Books, 1982.

McDonnell, Kathleen. *Not an Easy Choice: A Feminist Re-examines Abortion.* Boston: South End Press, 1984.

McGriff, Sylvia E. *Learning to Live with Neuromuscular Disease.* New York: Rawson, Wade, 1978.

McKay, Nellie. "Black Women's Autobiographies: Literature, History and the Politics of Self." *Hurricane Alice* 3, no. 4 (Fall 1986): 8–9.

Meadow, Mary Jo. " 'True Womanhood' and Women's Victimization." *Counseling Values* 26, no. 2 (Feb. 1982): 121–22.

Melton, David. *When Children Need Help: An Up-to-Date Handbook of Guidance for Parents of Children Who Have Been Diagnosed as Brain-Injured, Mentally Retarded, Cerebral Palsied, Learning Disabled, or Slow Learners.* New York: Crowell, 1972.

Menolascino, Frank J. "Psychiatric Aspects of Retardation in Young Children." In *The Mentally Retarded Child and His Family,* edited by Richard Koch and James C. Dobson. New York: Bruner/Mazel, 1976.

Meryman, Richard. *Hope: A Loss Survived.* Boston: Little, Brown, 1980.

Meyerdine, Jane. "Visual Impairment Politics" (letter). *Broomstick* 8, no. 4 (July–Aug. 1986): 16.

Meyerowitz, Beth E. "The Impact of Mastectomy on the Lives of Women." *Professional Psychology* 12, no. 1 (Feb. 1981): 118–27.

Meyers, Robert. *Like Normal People.* New York: McGraw-Hill, 1978.

Miller, Alice. *For Your Own Good: Hidden Cruelty in Child-Rearing Practices and the Roots of Violence.* New York: Farrar, Straus & Giroux, 1983.

Miller, Jean Baker. *Toward a New Psychology of Women.* Boston: Beacon, 1976.

Millman, Marcia. *Such a Pretty Face: Being Fat in America.* New York: Norton, 1980.

Mills, Patricia J. "Memory and Myth: Women's Time Reconceived." In *Taking Our Time: Feminist Perspectives on Temporality,* edited by Frieda Johles Forman and Caoran Sowton. New York: Pergamon, 1989.

Minnich, Elizabeth Kamarck. "Friendship Between Women: The Act of Feminist Biography." *Feminist Studies* 11, no. 2 (Summer 1985): 287–305.

Mitchell, Joyce Slayton. *See Me More Clearly: Career and Life Planning for Teens with Physical Disabilities.* New York: Harcourt Brace Jovanovich, 1980.

Monette, Paul. *Borrowed Time: An AIDS Memoir.* San Diego: Harcourt Brace Jovanovich, 1988.

Mushroom, Merril. "The Weight of Words" (letter). *Off Our Backs* 15, no. 8 (Aug.–Sept. 1985): 35.

Myrdal, Gunnar. *An American Dilemma: The Negro Problem and Modern Democracy.* New York: Harper & Row, 1962.

Nelson, Marjory. "Flowersong." In *Long Time Passing,* edited by Marcy Adelman. Boston: Alyson, 1986.

Nestle, Joan. "N.Y. Lesbian Illness Support Group: What Being a Lesbian Means in the Deepest Sense." *Off Our Backs,* 11 (5): 8.

Nighswonder, Carl A. "The Vectors and Vital Signs in Grief Synchronization." In *Anticipatory Grief,* edited by Bernard Schoenberg, Arthur C. Carr, Austin H. Kutscher, David Peretz, and Evan K. Goldberg. New York: Columbia University Press, 1974.

Noddings, Nel. *Caring: A Feminine Approach to Ethics and Moral Education.* Berkeley: University of California Press, 1984.

Norwood, Robin. *Women Who Love Too Much.* New York: St. Martin's, 1985.

————. *Letters from Women Who Love Too Much.* New York: Pocket Books, 1989.

O'Donnell, Mary. "Alcoholism and Co-Alcoholism: There Is a Solution." *Women: A Journal of Liberation* 7, no. 3 (1981): 64–69.

Oliver, Margot. "Killing Us Softly." In *Out from Under: Sober Dykes and Our Friends,* edited by Jean Swallow. San Francisco: Spinsters/Aunt Lute, 1983.

Olshansky, Simon. "Chronic Sorrow: A Response to Having a Mentally Defective Child." In *Counseling Parents of the Mentally Retarded: A Sourcebook,* edited by Robert L. Noland, Springfield, Ill.: Charles C Thomas, 1970.

Ortner, Sherry. "Is Female to Male as Nature Is to Culture?" In *Women, Culture, and Society,* edited by Michelle Zimbalist Rosaldo and Louise Lamphere. Palo Alto, Calif.: Stanford University Press, 1974.

Osmond, Humphry, Violet Franks, and Vasanti Burtle. "Changing Views of Women and Therapeutic Approaches: Some Historical Considerations." In *Women in Therapy,* edited by Violet Franks and Vasanti Burtle. New York: Bruner/Mazel, 1974.

Ottenberg, Miriam. *Pursuit of Hope.* New York: Rawson, Wade, 1978.

Park, Clara Clairborne, and Leon N. Shapiro. *You Are Not Alone: Understanding and Dealing with Mental Illness.* Boston: Little, Brown, 1976.

Parker, John. "Infant 'Death Row' Image at HSC Denied." *Oklahoma Daily,* Feb. 11, 1985, 1–2.

Parkes, Colin Murray. *Bereavement: Studies in Grief in Adult Life.* New York: International Universities Press, 1972.

Patterson, Joan M. "Chronic Illness in Children and the Impact on Families." In *Chronic Illness and Disability,* edited by Fred Cox. Beverly Hills: Sage, 1988.

Patton, Cindy. *Inventing AIDS.* New York: Routledge, 1990.

Pearson, Carol. *The Hero Within: Six Archetypes We Live By.* San Francisco: Harper & Row, 1986.

Penelope, Julia. *Speaking Freely: Unlearning the Lies of the Fathers' Tongues.* New York: Pergamon, 1990.

Perls, Fritz. *Gestalt Therapy Verbatim.* New York: Bantam, 1971.

Perrone, Bobette, H. Henrietta Stockel, and Victoria Krueger. *Medicine Women, Curanderas and Women Doctors.* Norman: University of Oklahoma Press, 1989.

Petchesky, Rosalind Pollack. "Fetal Images: The Power of Visual Culture in the Politics of Reproduction." *Feminist Studies* 13, no. 2 (Summer 1987): 263–92.

Pettigrew, Thomas F. *A Profile of the Negro American.* Princeton, N.J.: D. Van Nostrand, 1964.

Pharr, Suzanne. *Homophobia: A Weapon of Sexism.* Inverness, Calif.: Chardon Press, 1988.

Phillips, Marilynn. "Disability and Ethnicity in Conflict: A Study in Transformation." In *Women with Disabilities,* edited by Michelle Fine and Adrienne Asch. Philadelphia: Temple University Press, 1989.

Piasecki, Patricia. "The Day After Tomorrow Show." In *Out from Under: Sober Dykes and Our Friends,* edited by Jean Swallow. San Francisco: Spinsters/Aunt Lute, 1983.

Pitzele, Sefra Kobrin. *One More Day: Daily Meditations for People with Chronic Illnesses.* New York: Harper/Hazelden, 1988.

Plummer, Kenneth, ed. *The Making of the Modern Homosexual.* Totowa, N.J.: Barnes & Noble, 1981.

Ponse, Barbara. *Identities in the Lesbian World: The Social Construction of Self.* Westport, Conn.: Greenwood Press, 1978.

Poston, Carol. "Childbirth in Literature." *Feminist Studies* 4, no. 2 (June 1978): 18–31.

Powell, Lenore S. "Alzheimer's Disease: A Practical, Psychological Approach." *Women and Health* 10, no. 2/3 (Summer/Fall 1985): 53–62.

Pratt, Marty. "The Fallacy in the Concept of Deinstitutionalization." *Voice of the Retarded,* May 24 1990, 1–3.

Prince, Elizabeth. "Women and Love Ideology: Personal Conflicts, Political Implications." *New Women's Times* 9, no. 2 (Feb. 1983): 8–11.

Rabin, Roni. *Six Parts Love: A Family's Battle with Lou Gehrig's Disease (ALS).* New York: Charles Scribner's Sons, 1985.

Rafkin, Louise. *Different Daughters.* Pittsburgh: Cleis Press, 1987.

Rapp, Rayna. "A Womb of One's Own." *Women's Review of Books* 5, no. 7 (April 1988): 10.

Raven. "Reaching Across the Void." *Common Lives/Lesbian Lives,* no. 24 (Fall 1987): 117–19.

Raymond, Barbara Bisantz. "We're a Family Now." *McCall's* 113, no. 5 (Feb. 1986): 33–34, 39, 152–54.

Raymond, Janice G. "Medicine as Patriarchal Religion." *Journal of Medicine and Philosophy* 7, no. 2 (1982): 196–216.

———. *A Passion for Friends: Toward a Philosophy of Female Affection.* Boston: Beacon, 1986.

Reed, Allan W. "Anticipatory Grief Work." In *Anticipatory Grief,* edited by Bernard Schoenberg, Arthur C. Carr, Austin H. Kutscher, David Peretz, and Evan K. Goldberg. New York: Columbia University Press, 1974.

Register, Cheri. "Letting the Angel Die." *Hurricane Alice* 3, no. 1 (1986): 1–4.

Reinharz, Shulamit. "Friends or Foes: Gerontological and Feminist Theory." *Women's Studies International Forum* 9, no. 5–6: 503–14.

Remington, Judy. "Particles of Silence." *Hurricane Alice* 1, no. 1 (Spring 1983): 1, 3–5.

Rich, Adrienne. *Of Woman Born: Motherhood as Experience and Institution.* New York: Norton, 1976.

———. *On Lies, Secrets and Silence.* New York: Norton, 1979.

Rifkin, Jeremy. *Time Wars: The Primary Conflict in Human History.* New York: Henry Holt & Co., 1987.

Robbins, Dana. "Stroke: A Personal Perspective." *Women and Health* 10, no. 4 (Winter 1985/86): 9–32.

Robinault, Isabel P. *Sex, Society and the Disabled: A Developmental Inquiry into Roles, Reactions and Responsibilities.* New York: Harper & Row, 1978.

Rollin, Betty. *First, You Cry.* Philadelphia: J. B. Lippincott, 1976.

Rooney, Frances. "The Issue Is Ability." *RFR/DRF* 14, no. 1 (Mar. 1985): 64–68.

Rose, Keta. "Psychiatric Torture—The Struggle Feminists Ignore." *Off Our Backs* 12, no. 3 (Mar. 1982): 27.

Rosenblatt, Paul C. *Bitter, Bitter Tears: Nineteenth-Century Diarists and Twentieth-Century Grief Theories.* Minneapolis: University of Minnesota Press, 1983.

Rosenfeld, Stephen S. *The Time of Their Dying.* New York: Norton, 1977.

Roskies, Ethel. *Abnormality and Normality: The Mothering of Thalidomide Children.* Ithaca: Cornell University Press, 1972.

Rossi, Nancy. *From This Day Forward.* New York: New York Times Book Co., 1983.

Rousso, Harilyn. *Disabled, Female, and Proud! Stories of Ten Women with Disabilities.* Boston: Exceptional Parent Press, 1988.

Rubin, Diane. *Caring: A Daughter's Story.* New York: Holt, Rinehart & Winston, 1982.

Ruddick, Sara. "Maternal Thinking." In *Mothering,* edited by Joyce Trebilcot. Totowa, N.J.: Rowman & Allanheld, 1984.

————. "Preservative Love and Military Destruction: Some Reflections on Mothering and Peace." In *Mothering,* edited by Joyce Trebilcot. Totowa, N.J.: Rowman & Allanheld, 1984.

Rule, Jane. *Lesbian Images.* Freedom, Calif.: Crossing Press, 1975.

Russ, Joanna. "Power and Helplessness in the Women's Movement." *Sinister Wisdom* 18 (1981) 49–56.

Russell, Mark. "Letter from the Editor." *Ways* 1, no. 2 (Mar. 1986): 5.

Russianoff, Penelope. *Why Do I Think I Am Nothing Without a Man?* New York: Bantam, 1981.

————. *Women in Crisis.* New York: Human Sciences Press, 1981.

Ryan, Cornelius, and Kathryn Morgan Ryan. *A Private Battle.* New York: Simon & Schuster, 1979.

Sacks, Oliver W. *The Man Who Mistook His Wife for a Hat and Other Clinical Tales.* New York: Summit, 1985.

Sager, Jill. "Just Stories." In *With the Power of Each Breath: A Disabled Women's Anthology,* edited by Susan Browne, Debra Connors, and Nanci Stern. San Francisco: Cleis, 1985.

Samuelson, Deborah. "A Letter to My Daughter/Myself on Facing the Collective Fear of Being Different." *Feminist Studies* 12, no. 1 (Spring 1986): 155–67.

Sanford, Linda Tschirhart, and Mary Ellen Donovan. *Women and Self-Esteem.* New York: Penguin, 1985.

Sarton, May. *A World of Light: Portraits and Celebrations.* New York: Norton, 1976.

————. *The House by the Sea: A Journal.* New York: Norton, 1977.

————. *Recovering.* New York: Norton, 1980.

————. *After the Stroke.* New York: Norton, 1988.

Saviola, Marilyn E. "Personal Reflections on Physically Disabled Women and Dependency." *Professional Psychology* 12, no. 1 (Feb. 1981): 112–17.

Saxton, Marsha, and Florence Howe, eds. *With Wings: An Anthology of Literature by and About Women with Disabilities.* New York: Feminist Press, 1987.

Schaef, Anne Wilson. *Co-Dependence: Misunderstood-Mistreated.* San Francisco: Harper & Row, 1986.

————. *When Society Becomes an Addict.* San Francisco: Harper & Row, 1987.

Schaef, Anne Wilson, and Diane Fassel. *The Addictive Organization.* San Francisco: Harper & Row, 1988.

Schiff, Susan. "Learning the Lessons of Survival." *Genesis 2: An Independent Voice for Jewish Renewal* 13, no. 2 (Nov. 1981): 10.

Schild, Sylvia. "Social Work Services." In *The Mentally Retarded Child and His Family,* edited by Richard Koch and James C. Dobson. New York: Bruner/Mazel, 1976.

Schmidt, Carol. "Do Something About Your Weight." In *With the Power of Each Breath: A Disabled Women's Anthology,* edited by Susan Browne, Debra Connors, and Nanci Stern. San Francisco: Cleis, 1985.

Schoenfielder, Lisa, and Barb Wieser, eds. *Shadow on a Tightrope: Writings by Women on Fat Oppression.* Iowa City: Aunt Lute, 1983.

Scott, Kesho Yvonne. *The Habit of Surviving: Black Women's Strategies for Life.* New Brunswick, N.J.: Rutgers University Press, 1991.

Seidenberg, Robert, and Karen DeCrow. *Women Who Marry Houses: Panic and Protest in Agoraphobia.* New York: McGraw-Hill, 1983.

Seligman, Milton, and Rosalyn Benjamin Darling. *Ordinary Families, Special Children: A Systems Approach to Childhood Disability.* New York: Guilford, 1989.

Share, Jack. "Educational Services." In *The Mentally Retarded Child and His Family,* edited by Richard Koch and James C. Dobson. New York: Bruner/Mazel, 1976.

Shields, Laurie. "Who Will Need Me . . . Who Will Feed Me . . . When I'm Sixty-Four?" *New Directions for Women* 27, no. 1 (Jan.–Feb. 1988): 12–13.

Shilts, Randy. *And the Band Played On.* New York: St. Martin's, 1987.

Siegel, Bernie S. *Peace, Love and Healing.* New York: Harper & Row, 1989.

Silverman, Phyllis R. *Helping Women Cope with Grief.* Beverly Hills: Sage, 1981.

Simon, Barbara Levy. "Never-Married Women as Caregivers to Elderly Parents: Some Costs and Benefits." *Affilia: Journal of Women and Social Work* 1, no. 3 (Fall 1986): 29–41.

Simonton, O. Carl, Stephanie Matthews Simonton, and James L. Creighton. *Getting Well Again.* New York: Bantam, 1978.

Simonton, Stephanie Matthews. *The Healing Family: The Simonton Approach for Families Facing Illness.* New York: Bantam, 1984.

Smith, Janet Farrell. "Parenting and Property." In *Mothering,* edited by Joyce Trebilcot. Totowa, N.J.: Rowman & Allanheld, 1984.

Smith, JoAnn Kelley. *Free Fall.* Valley Forge, Penn: Judson Press, 1975.

Smith, Nina Jo. "Alcoholism: Violence Against Lesbians." In *Out from Under: Sober Dykes and Our Friends,* edited by Jean Swallow. San Francisco: Spinsters/Aunt Lute, 1983.

Snow, Judy. "Living at Home." *RFR/DRF* 14, no. 1 (Mar. 1985): 23–27.

Snowden, Shane. "The Education of a Blind Woman" (interview with JoAnn Giudicessi). *Sojourner* 9, no. 1 (Sept. 1983): 7.

Solnit, Albert J., and Mary H. Stark. "Mourning and the Birth of a Defective Child." *Psychological Studies of Children* 16 (1961): 523–37.

Sommers, Tish, and Laurie Shields. *Women Take Care: The Consequences of Caregiving in Today's Society.* Gainesville: Triad, 1987.

Sontag, Susan. *AIDS and Its Metaphors.* New York: Farrar, Straus & Giroux, 1989.

Sourkes, Barbara M. *The Deepening Shade: Psychological Aspects of Life-Threatening Illness.* Pittsburgh: University of Pittsburgh Press, 1982.

Spencer, Mickey. "The Politics of Disability." *Broomstick* 7, no. 3–4 (May–July 1985): 4–10.

Spender, Dale. *Man Made Language.* London: Routledge & Kegan Paul, 1980.

Spingarn, Natalie Davis. *Hanging in There.* New York: Stein & Day, 1982.

Squire, Susan. *The Slender Balance: Causes and Cures for Bulimia, Anorexia and the Weight-Loss/Weight-Gain Seesaw.* New York: G. P. Putnam's Sons, 1983.

Starhawk. *The Spiral Dance.* New York: Harper & Row, 1979.

———. *Dreaming the Dark: Magic, Sex and Politics.* Boston: Beacon, 1982.

Stearns, Ann Kaiser. *Living Through Personal Crisis.* New York: Ballantine, 1984.

Stewart, Jack C. *Counseling Parents of Exceptional Children.* Columbus, Ohio: Charles E. Merrill, 1978.

Stinson, Peggy and Robert Stinson. *The Long Dying of Baby Andrew.* New York: Atlantic Monthly Press, 1983.

Stonekey, Sharon. "Reminders." In *Out from Under: Sober Dykes and Our Friends,* edited by Jean Swallow. San Francisco: Spinters/Aunt Lute, 1983.

Strauss, Anselm L. *Chronic Illness and the Quality of Life.* St. Louis: C. V. Mosby, 1975.

Strong, Maggie. *Mainstay: For the Well Spouse of the Chronically Ill.* Boston: Little, Brown, 1988.

Sturdivant, Susan. *Therapy with Women: A Feminist Philosophy of Treatment.* New York: Springer, 1980.

Sturgis, Susanna. "Is This the New Thing We're Going to Have to Be Politically Correct About?" *Sinister Wisdom* 28 (Winter 1985): 16–27.

Sturgis, Susanna. "New Age Fills a Need" (letter). *Off Our Backs* 19, no. 2 (Feb. 1989): 17.

Subby, Robert. *Lost in the Shuffle: The Co-Dependent Reality.* Pompano Beach, Fla.: Health Communications, 1987.

Sugars, Stephanie. "Journal Piece." In *With the Power of Each Breath: A Disabled Women's Anthology,* edited by Susan Browne, Debra Connors, and Nanci Stern. San Francisco: Cleis, 1985.

Swallow, Jean, ed. *Out from Under: Sober Dykes and Our Friends.* San Francisco: Spinsters/Aunt Lute, 1983.

————. "Both Feet in Life: Interviews with Barbara MacDonald and Cynthia Rich." *Calyx* 9, nos. 2/3 (Winter 1986): 202.

Swan, Bonita L. *Thirteen Steps: An Empowerment Process for Women.* San Francisco: Spinsters/Aunt Lute, 1989.

Swartz, Leslie. "Is Thin a Feminist Issue?" *Women's Studies International Forum* 8, no. 5 (1985): 429–37.

Tallen, Bette S. "Twelve Step Programs: A Lesbian Feminist Critique." *NWSA Journal* 2, no. 3 (Summer 1990): 390–407.

Taves, Isabella. *The Widow's Guide.* New York: Schocken, 1982.

Tavris, Carol. "How Psychology Shortchanges Mothers." *Psychology Today* 23, no. 9 (Sept. 1989): 74–75.

Taylor, Shelley E. "Adjustment to Threatening Events: A Theory of Cognitive Adaptation." *American Psychologist* 38, no. 11 (1983): 1161–73.

Thompson, Dai R. "Anger." In *With the Power of Each Breath: A Disabled Women's Anthology,* edited by Susan Browne, Debra Connors, and Nanci Stern. San Francisco: Cleis, 1985.

Thompson, Karen, and Julie Andrzejewski. *Why Can't Sharon Kowalski Come Home?* San Francisco: Spinsters/Aunt Lute, 1988.

Thompson, Martha E. "Comment on Rich's 'Compulsory Heterosexuality and Lesbian Existence,'" *Signs* 6, no. 4 (Summer 1981): 790–94.

"Three Cheers for Work Center" (editorial), *Daily Oklahoman,* July 15, 1983.

Toder, Nancy. "Sexual Problems of Lesbians." In *Our Right to Love: A Lesbian Resource Book,* edited by Ginny Vida. Englewood Cliffs, N.J.: Prentice Hall, 1978.

Torrey, E. Fuller. *Witchdoctors and Psychiatrists: The Common Roots of Psychotherapy and Its Future.* Northvale, N.J.: Jason Arondale, 1986.

Trask, Huanani-Kay. *Eros and Power: The Promise of Feminist Theory.* Philadelphia: University of Pennsylvania Press, 1986.

Trautmann, Mary Winfrey. *The Absence of the Dead Is Their Way of Appearing*. San Francisco: Cleis, 1984.

Treadway, David. "Codependency: Disease, Metaphor, or Fad?" *Family Therapy Networker* 14, no. 1 (Jan.–Feb. 1990): 39–42.

Trimpey, Jack. *Rational Recovery from Alcoholism: The Small Book*. 3d ed. Lotus, Calif.: Lotus Press, 1989.

Ungerecht, Rene. "Age and Image." In *With the Power of Each Breath: A Disabled Women's Anthology*, edited by Susan Browne, Debra Connors, and Nanci Stern. San Francisco: Cleis, 1985.

VanGelder, Lindsy. "Elaine Brody." *Ms.* 14, no. 7 (Jan. 1986): 100–101.

Versluys, Hilda P. "Physical Rehabilitation and Family Dynamics." *Rehabilitation Literature* 40, no. 3–4 (Mar.–Apr. 1980): 58–65.

Voysey, Margaret. *A Constant Burden: The Reconstitution of Family Life*. Boston: Routledge & Kegan Paul, 1975.

Wagner, Marjorie. "A Four-Wheeled Journey." In *With the Power of Each Breath: A Disabled Women's Anthology*, edited by Susan Browne, Debra Connors, and Nanci Stern. San Francisco: Cleis, 1985.

Wainwright, Sonny. *Stage V: A Journal Through Illness*. Berkeley: Acacia Books, 1984.

Wallis, Claudia. "Diabetes' New Gospel of Control," *Time* 122, no. 25 (Dec. 12, 1983): 75.

Walsh, Maryellen. *Schizophrenia: Straight Talk for Families and Friends*. New York: William Morrow, 1985.

Wegscheider, Sharon. *Another Chance: Hope and Health for the Alcoholic Family*. Palo Alto, Calif.: Science and Behavior Books, 1981.

Weil, Jane. "Learning in a Partnership." *Journal of Current Social Issues* 16, no. 1 (Spring 1979): 63–64.

Weinberg, Joanna. "Autonomy as a Different Voice." In *Women with Disabilities*, edited by Michelle Fine and Adrienne Asch. Philadelphia: Temple University Press, 1989.

Weisman, Avery D. "Is Mourning Necessary?" In *Anticipatory Grief*, edited by Bernard Schoenberg, Arthur C. Carr, Austin H. Kutscher, David Peretz, and Evan K. Goldberg. New York: Columbia University Press, 1974.

Weisman, Mary-Lou. *Intensive Care*. New York: Random House, 1982.

Weiss, Jill. "Disabled Women." *RFR/DRF* 14, no. 1 (March 1985): 4–6.

Weisskopf, Susan. "Maternal Guilt and Mental Health Professionals: A Reconfirming Interaction." Michigan Occasional Paper no. 5 (Fall 1978).

Whillans, Penny. "Adjusting to Chronic Pain Through Imagery." *RFR/DRF* 14, no. 1 (Mar. 1985): 51–53.

Whitfield, Charles L. *Healing the Child Within*. Pompano Beach, Fla.: Health Communications, 1987.

Wikler, Lynn, Mona Wasow, and Elaine Hatfield. "Chronic Sorrow Revisited: Parent vs. Professional Depiction of the Adjustment of Parents of Mentally Retarded Children." *American Journal of Orthopsychiatry* 51, no. 1 (1981): 63–70.

Wilke, Harold. "The Wholeness of the Family of God." *Journal of Current Social Issues* 16, no. 1 (Spring 1979): 55–59.

Williams, Eddie. "Special Concerns in Counseling the Intellectually Limited." In *The Disabled and Their Parents*, by Leo Buscaglia. New York: Holt, Rinehart & Winston, 1983.

Wilson, Elizabeth, with Angela Weir. *Hidden Agendas: Theory, Politics and Experience in the Women's Movement*. New York: Tavistock, 1986.

Wilson, Louise. *This Stranger, My Son*. New York: G. P. Putnam & Sons, 1968.

Witherow, Judith K. "Hello Walls: Working Around the Limitations of Multiple Sclerosis." *Off Our Backs* 11, no. 5 (May 1981): 2–3.

Witkin-Lanoil, Georgia. *The Female Stress Syndrome: How to Recognize and Live with It.* New York: Newmarket Press, 1984.

Wolf, Naomi. *The Beauty Myth: How Images of Beauty Are Used Against Women.* New York: William Morrow, 1991.

Wolfe, Jane. "Surviving Your Children." *Dallas Morning News* June 10, 1982, 1c–2c, 5c.

Women and Disability Awareness Project. *Building Community: A Manual Exploring Issues of Women and Disability.* New York: Educational Equity Concepts, Inc., 1984.

Women for Sobriety, "Are You a Woman Who Drinks to Cope?" (pamphlet). Quakertown, Penn.: N.d.

Wood, John. "Labors of Love." *Modern Maturity* (Aug.–Sept. 1981): 28–34, 90, 92.

Wooley, Susan C. "Consuming Emotion." *Women's Review of Books* 3, no. 7 (Apr. 1986): 1–3.

Woronov, Naomi, "A See-by-Logic Life." In *With the Power of Each Breath: A Disabled Women's Anthology,* edited by Susan Browne, Debra Connors, and Nanci Stern. San Francisco: Cleis, 1985.

Wright, Beatrice A. "Devaluation in Chronic Illness." In *Medical and Psychological Team Work in the Care of the Chronically Ill,* edited by Molly Harrower. Springfield, Ill.: Charles C Thomas, 1955.

————. *Physical Disability—A Psychological Approach.* New York: Harper & Row, 1960.

Wright, M. Erik. "The Period of Mourning in Chronic Illness." In *Medical and Psychological Team Work in the Care of the Chronically Ill,* edited by Molly Harrower. Springfield, Ill.: Charles C Thomas, 1955.

Yalom, Irvin D. *Love's Executioner and Other Tales of Psychotherapy.* New York: Harper & Row, 1989.

Yates, Jenny. "Tools for Change." *Off Our Backs* 19, no. 2 (Feb. 1989): 17–19.

Zaiger, Nancy. "Women and Bereavement." *Women and Therapy* 4, no. 4 (Winter 1985–86): 33–43.

Zevy, Lee, and Sahli A. Cavallero. "Invisibility, Fantasy, and Intimacy: Prince Charming Is Not a Prince." In *Lesbian Psychologies,* edited by Boston Lesbian Psychologies Collective. Urbana: University of Illinois Press, 1987.

Zimmerman, Bonnie. "The Politics of Transliteration: Lesbian Personal Narratives." *Signs* 9, no. 4 (Summer 1984): 663–82.

Zitter, Sherry. "Coming Out to Mom: Theoretical Aspects of the Mother-Daughter Process." In *Lesbian Psychologies,* edited by Boston Lesbian Psychologies Collective. Urbana: University of Illinois Press, 1987.

Zola, Irving Kenneth. "Does It Matter What You Call Us?" *SWS Network News* 1, no. 1 (Jan. 1985).

————. "Depictions of Disability—Metaphor, Message and Medium in the Media: A Research and Political Agenda." *Social Science Journal* 22, no. 4 (Oct. 1985): 5–17.

# INDEX